In the Name of God

Of God

Violence and Destruction in the World's Religions

MICHAEL JORDAN

SUTTON PUBLISHING

First published in the United Kingdom in 2006 by
Sutton Publishing Limited · Phoenix Mill
Thrupp · Stroud · Gloucestershire · GL5 2BU

British Library Cataloguing in Publication Data
A catalogue record for this book is available from the British Library.

ISBN 0-7509-4194-4

Typeset in 11/14.5pt Sabon.
Typesetting and origination by
Sutton Publishing Limited.
Printed and bound in England by
J.H. Haynes & Co. Ltd, Sparkford.

Contents

Introduction

When the Cold War between the Soviet Union and the Western alliance effectively came to an end with Mikhail Gorbachev's election as Soviet leader in the mid-1980s, to be replaced by an easing of tension for which the new buzz word of détente was coined, most of us who were alive at the time probably breathed a large sigh of relief, believing that the prospect of major, if not global, conflagration was at last at an end. The previous generation had witnessed two world wars of cataclysmic proportions and the inhabitants of Planet Earth had now come to their senses, or so we thought. At the time the prospect of fresh conflict erupting, based on religious differences, would probably have seemed far-fetched to most of us, and yet the ending of the Cold War seems to have been the signal for a new, and also very old, style of aggression: violence in the name of God.

Now, at the outset of the twenty-first century, many of those fears for our security, at the whim of large-scale influences beyond our control, have returned, and this time the emphasis is very much on religious differences. At first, in the West, we may have lulled ourselves into viewing these new conflicts based on religious ideology as 'other people's wars', local fights taking place a long way off, generally in the Middle East. Israelis fought their neighbours, Iranian Shi'ites fought Sunni Iraqis, Afghan Talibans blew up giant Buddhist statues. In Britain we had the problems of Northern Ireland, yet those sectarian differences seemed less to do with religion, more social and economic in nature. The events of 9/11, however, brought violence in the name of God to the heart of the United States, and the wreckage of the Twin Towers became the most potent symbol of a new kind of vulnerability. In Britain the same reality hit us on a smaller scale in 2005 with the bombings of the London Underground.

Religious violence in all its many facets is a vast subject, its scope too wide to be covered in a single volume without skating over the surface so thinly as to make any analysis facile. This book is intended as a factual and comparative history of religious war and religious violence focused on the three great monotheisms: Judaism, Christianity and Islam. Its scope occasionally includes mention of other faiths, but only in passing. I have not attempted to address the psychology of violence, a subject about which I am in no way qualified to write, but I have examined the anthropology of religious violence, I hope, with an objective and impartial approach. It is all too easy to fall into the trap, in the present climate, of labelling Islam as the aggressive party while conveniently forgetting that Judaism and Christianity have been made the excuse for as much if not more violence and bloodletting in the past.

Readers may find what they consider to be notable omissions in the ensuing chapters. There is, for example, no mention of the Holocaust. This, however, was not violence carried out in the name of God. Adolf Hitler was interested in singling out the Jews as scapegoats for social and economic problems in Germany, not specifically because of their religious beliefs. Nor was Hitler particularly motivated by personal religious convictions. He had no desire to restore unadulterated Christianity to a new Holy Roman Empire, although there is some evidence that he envisaged his Third Reich as the custodian of a kind of Wagnerian, romanticised neo-Odinism. In other instances the appearance of a religious connection may actually be illusory, as in the case, for example, of the American Ku Klux Klan sect. Its members burnt flaming crosses and dressed in grotesquely monkish outfits more as a gimmick than as a religious statement; it actually originated in Tennessee after the American Civil War with the intention of discouraging newly enfranchised black African Americans from voting, and came to renewed prominence in 1915 when its members embarked on a fresh round of intimidation specifically to support Protestant homespun American businessmen against the commercial challenge of immigrant entrepreneurs.

Introduction

In a letter to his friend the Comte de Limoges in 1667, the Comte de Bussy-Rabutin made the dry observation, 'As you know, God is usually on the side of the big squadrons against the small.' His comment amounts to a passing but important mistranslation of the first-century Roman writer Tacitus, who actually wrote, 'the gods favour the braver'. What has changed in modern religious violence from that which took place in previous centuries is that fanatical elements on the fringes of religious movements have become 'the braver', taking on the established powers out of a conviction that they are fighting for a righteous moral cause. This impulse becomes so strong that they are prepared to kill and be killed for it, and will continue with their endeavours even when it is clear that the odds are stacked impossibly high against them.

If there is an observation to be made here about the psychology of violence in the name of God, it is that religion, much of which formalises our belief in a transcendental state, not only mollifies our fear of dying but also gives divine authority to our basic instinct for inflicting suffering and death on our fellow creatures. Lying at the core of religion, death and the darker aspects of our experience jostle for space with the spreading of light and goodwill. It is this deep internal contradiction that permits, as we shall discover, the paradox suggesting that our gods are merciful, compassionate, vengeful and bloody-minded at the same time. They are, after all, only reflections of our own complex patterns of behaviour.

ONE

Weapons of the Gods

Violence conducted in the name of god – and the identity of that
god is almost of secondary importance – has been going on
across the span of human history, during which both our basic
reasoning and modi operandi have not changed a great deal, and in
fact have proved remarkably constant. So let us travel back at least
to the known beginnings of religiously inspired bloodshed in the so-
called cradle of civilisation in the ancient Near East, Mesopotamia.
The name Assur-nasir-apli II does not slip easily off the tongue, yet
the conduct of this exceptionally aggressive man, who lived almost
3,000 years ago, makes an ideal starting point. In 884 BCE, after the
death of his father Tukulti-Ninurta II, he inherited the throne of
Assyria, the fertile northern part of Mesopotamia lying between the
rivers Tigris and Euphrates and now largely occupied by modern
Iraq. He reigned as its absolute ruler for twenty-six turbulent years,
overseeing the very zenith of Assyria's military and political
dominance of what was then the known world.

Assyrian history was already fairly well stained with blood before
Assur-nasir-apli inherited his throne, but from his stronghold in the
city of Kalakh, the Calah that in company with Nineveh and
Rehoboth is listed in the Book of Genesis,[1] he directed operations
that put the brutality and tyranny of his forebears firmly in the
shade. Even by Assyrian standards of punishment, the wars he
undertook against neighbours were singularly harsh in the treatment
of those he defeated. When he overran the rebellious and well-
fortified town of Kinabu in northern Mesopotamia, its precise
location now lost beneath the shifting soil of the desert, he delivered
a victory speech that happens by chance to have been preserved for
posterity by a scribe who incised his words in clay. 'I slew

1

six hundred with the sword, three thousand prisoners I burned alive in the fire. I kept no one alive as hostage. I piled their corpses as high as towers. The city king fell into my hands alive. The king I flayed and [I] hung his skin on the wall of Damdammusa.'[2]

The words give a fair indication of the personality and methods of Assur-nasir-apli, whose despotic regime eventually extended over the whole of Mesopotamia as far south as Babylon. If his name sounds unfamiliar beside those of Sennacherib or Esarhaddon, it is because he is not mentioned in the biblical texts of the Old Testament, but he probably ranks alongside such legendary figures as Genghis Khan and Alexander the Great in terms of the military kudos that he acquired during his lifetime. Details of his reign only surfaced as recently as 1846 when an English explorer, Austen Henry Layard, made a remarkable discovery near the modern Iraqi city of Mosul. Layard's lifelong obsession had been to find the lost city of Nineveh, a dream that he would not realise until a further three years of personal exploration had passed. But in 1846 a large tell, a mound of windblown earth covering an uncharted archaeological site, caught his interest near the village of Nimrud some 20 miles south of Mosul. He had stumbled, inadvertently, upon Kalakh, a much older city built by a distant predecessor of Assur-nasir-apli, Salmaneser I. Much of what is known about Assur-nasir-apli is thus attributable to the diligence of Layard, who brought large sections of Kalakh's urban artwork before the gaze of curious Londoners in 1849.[3]

At the heart of Kalakh, Layard excavated a royal residence, the so-called Northwest Palace that Assur-nasir-apli had rebuilt to his individual taste after it had fallen into long-term disrepair. This was no run-of-the-mill place but an immense architectural complex that once sprawled over 10,000 square metres. Records found at the site suggest that he was a pragmatist, a leader of some political shrewdness, but above all that he was a practical military man who bothered little with philosophy or letters, collected no library of scholarship and, when he was not letting the blood of his fellow man, spent much of his leisure time in the field letting that of lions and other game. Yet this portrait appears to include a contradiction.

The paradox comes into sharp focus when you examine the surviving art of the Northwest Palace, much of which, an assortment of bas-relief carvings, is housed in the British Museum in London. These were once fixed to the walls of the palace yard and they would have greeted a visitor to the royal court with reminders of the sack of Kinabu in all its gruesome detail. But in the art of the staterooms the mood was strongly at odds with the rest. The images portrayed there reveal the king and his courtiers paying homage to a small, curiously distorted tree.[4]

Opinion among archaeologists is that the object of attention amounts to a stylised and symbolic image of the paramount mother goddess of Assyria and Babylonia, Istar. So why did two contrasting and seemingly conflicting elements, death and motherhood, arise in such close proximity? The bond between war and the Queen of Heaven is one that we shall explore fully in a later chapter but, for the moment, let it suffice that the meeting of two unlikely bedfellows, slaughter and religious interest, forms a central plank in the earliest recognisable blueprint of society. It involves an ideal that was to prove remarkably tenacious: my god against your god! In the ancient Near East tribes regularly went to war under the pretext of one tutelary deity battling it out with another. This was invariably the explanation for combat in the Mesopotamian city states of Sumer, the oldest known civilised communities to leave a written history of their affairs. It was also an argument copied and widely adopted by the dynasties that arose in the wake of Sumerian culture: Akkadian, Old Babylonian, Assyrian and neo-Babylonian.

To appreciate the origin of such a strange bond between religion and slaughter we must travel to a still more distant era, stepping back in time to the age of the hunter-gatherers who roamed a sparsely populated earth, foraging and skirmishing long before settled communities arose. There is practically no conclusive evidence from prehistoric art and artefacts that such nomadic clans were especially interested in attacking each other. The painted caverns in south-west France, amounting to some of the world's oldest art galleries, reveal a relationship only between man and animal. Hunting tribes were separated too thinly in the landscape to have any great interest in butchering one another. Their principal interests lay in following the wild herds, in foraging freely and, at least in Europe, in surviving the atrocious climate of the Ice Age. The quarry of these ever-migrating clans was strictly four-legged, and any orchestrated hostile behaviour was restricted to chasing down and slaying bison, antelope and mammoth. Just occasionally the prehistoric art reveals the consequence of man's fatal assault upon man, but generally speaking it displays far more concern about the successful hunt for food.

The hunt had, nonetheless, already acquired a deeply spiritual allure. Consider the detail in one of the more dramatic canvases at the heart of the famous cavern system of Lascaux in the Dordogne region of south-west France. Halfway down a near-inaccessible 8-metre deep vertical shaft is preserved an extraordinary rock painting, a drama of death in which a prehistoric artist has depicted a bison standing mortally wounded with a lance thrust into its body. Beside it lies a man with the head of a bird and with his penis erect, the significance of which is not clear, but which one guesses must have been of profound, if esoteric, importance. This is no casual daubing for the benefit of passers-by. It reposes in pitch darkness and is deliberately executed in a part of the cavern system that can only be reached with extreme difficulty. There has arisen a conscious awareness that death, violent or otherwise, human or animal, amounts to a portal between our temporal world and another more mysterious plane. The Lascaux shaft painting lies at what may have been the very core of a prehistoric sanctuary, and even from this early time in human consciousness it hints at a probable linkage between slaughter and spirituality.[5]

Archaeologists will always argue about the precise nature of such links, but the intertwining of the two is revealed more clearly if one turns to comparatively modern nomadic tribes eking out a basic existence at a stage of development not unlike that of the prehistoric hunters. In the south-east of Siberia at the close of the nineteenth century, a number of clans, such as the Koryak and Chukchee, hunted reindeer for a living and in doing so placed a deep reverence on the act of animal slaughter. They would never speak of creatures that they had *killed*, but rather those whom they had *met*. Early ethnologists like Waldemar Jochelson recorded the extraordinary way in which the Koryak hunters behaved towards their dead quarry. A slain beast was treated as a dear and honoured friend. Its face was covered and the hunter did everything to disguise premeditated murder.[6] Jochelson was among the first Europeans to take a first-hand look at the rites of nomadic tribes with a lifestyle that must have been close to that of the prehistoric hunters. The form of belief that they followed became known as animism, though to call it a religion is to invite serious criticism from scholars who would argue that it was more a case of superstitious dabbling in otherworldly magic. If consistency or conformity of faith is proof that a religious framework exists, if it includes an organised pantheon of gods and goddesses, then scholarly dismissal is probably correct, because animism functions very much 'on the hoof'. But if religion can be said to amount to recognising the presence of higher and unseen controlling powers, then the nomadic hunters could indeed be said to have invented and practised it in a primitive form.

Animism involves a special awareness of the world among people who live hand in glove with nature. It is a world in which every natural object – from an animal, to a rock in the landscape, to a cloud in the sky – possesses and is possessed by a spiritual counterpart or guardian. This spiritual entity, never clearly defined but always present, is powerful and capricious, capable of such trickery as shape-shifting so that nothing is necessarily what it seems through the physical senses. To kill an animal is also to risk offending the spirit under whose control it has performed during its life. The inanimate can become reanimated, because that same hidden entity possesses the means to restore the dead animal to a future existence in which it may take revenge against its slayer. So there is always a sense that the killing has been carried out after formal agreement between the hunter and the animal's guardian spirit.[7]

Animism may have little or no formal structure, but it is nevertheless controlled by a kind of hierarchy. At whatever moment it emerged in history or prehistory, spiritual leadership and direction rested in the hands of shamans, the earliest recognisable priests and wizards. These are men, and occasionally women, who direct the sentient life of the tribe. They are generally also individuals of singular strength and self-will, looked up to and feared by their peers. The shaman alone is able to communicate with the unseen world and even to commute from one dimension to the other with a degree of impunity. This sets him or her apart with a special kind of authority. In nomadic societies the shaman is treated as a person of enormous influence and spiritual power, and becomes a kind of embryonic demigod. Stories develop and enter the vernacular about how shamans have triumphed over great dangers and obstacles in order to bring sustenance and prosperity to the tribe. They have wrested pledges of security against the elements from spiritual guardians of tempest, ice and flood, negotiated contracts of protection from revenge attack by those of wild animals. They have interceded with and sometimes tackled head-on a capricious and spiteful spirit world on behalf of humankind.

The business of shamanism has always involved the premise that if a spirit is offended it must be placated; if it is likely to be irritated by some future action or inaction, insurance must be paid to guard against its wrath. If any activity in day-to-day life incurs the risk of annoying the non-temporal world, it is important to do whatever is necessary to render that action acceptable. The human activity must be legitimate in the eyes of the guardians and thus insure against possible supernatural reaction. Legitimising the hunt has generally meant 'passing the buck' onto the spirit concerned, because unless appeased over the slaughter of its protégé it may bring illness, failure in the chase or accidental death. The agency to provide release from impending misfortune, or illness, is the intercession of the shaman. Therein lies the power base of the oldest forms of priesthood.

When communities evolve and language develops, those people tend to gain a more sophisticated awareness of the wider world, and so many of the ideas inherent in animism and shamanism become outmoded. Nonetheless, with the passing of the era of the nomadic hunting clans, some vestiges of old spiritual associations remained. When the last Ice Age eventually receded, the prehistoric hunters either chose to stay put or began to range further afield. Of those who journeyed some followed the sun south and founded the first city states in Mesopotamia; others migrated northwards after the receding ice. Among the latter were clans that eventually became known as the Celts. At first they had settled along the upper reaches of the Danube, but from about 500 BCE they pushed westwards out of their heartland to dominate much of Europe before the arrival of the Romans. These herdsmen probably represented a halfway house between nomadic and truly settled life. They retained traces of animism, including strong superstitions about the killing of animals. One of the more important of their pastoral festivals was Samhain (today known as Hallowe'en), celebrated at the end of October and marking the close of one year and the dawning of the next. The objective of Samhain was twofold: to invoke the gods to restore the power of the waning sun at the end of winter, but also to witness the slaughter of livestock in the correct manner. It represented a rite at which the barriers between temporal and spiritual worlds were at their weakest and communication with the dead was at its most feasible.[8]

Samhain was not the only ritual to preserve the echoes of animism. The Celtic fashion of carrying off the severed heads of enemies slung around the necks of their horses after a fight did not equate with mindless butchery. The Celtic warriors believed that the brain was immortal, the place of the soul. They attached great religious significance to human skulls, convinced that forces contained within a severed head would protect its new owner and deter evil from striking. Decapitation seems to have been carried out to a precise ritual, and the heads were sometimes decorated, embalmed or even used as talismanic drinking cups. This suggests that an early link was also forged between violent death and the acquisition of wisdom. Collections of skulls ceremonially deposited in shrines have turned up in many archaeological sites in Gaul known to have served as religious sanctuaries. Walls at Roquepertuse in Bouches-du-Rhône are peppered with small niches that can only have contained human heads, and at Entremont this was confirmed by the discovery of a carved pillar containing fifteen human skulls set in recesses, some still holding iron nails that may once have been used to impale them on a doorway or a tree trunk.[9]

The Celtic warrior and his forebears viewed their weaponry with much the same spiritual esteem. In the early European Bronze Age at locations such as Val Camonica in the Italian Alps artists created rock carvings, apparently of religious significance, and these regularly feature weapons such as halberds and daggers.[10] Other evidence emerges from funerary sites, since graves are frequently stocked with the equipment needed to fight battles in the next world. Hoards of weapons dating from at least the Middle Bronze Age have been found buried in what are believed to have been mass offerings to the gods of war. The archaeology of these and Celtic war graves is still the main source of information on the armaments of the time.[11]

There are also many examples of inscriptions and dedications to gods of war dating from the later Romano-Celtic period, particularly in the British Isles. In a stone carving discovered at Maryport in Cumbria the artist has depicted a horned and naked warrior god carrying a shield and spear. In the chronicles of the Roman legions they often encounter local tribal war gods such as Teutates who eventually become merged with the Roman god Mars, so that at Barkway in Hertfordshire a dedication was unearthed invoking 'Mars Toutatis'. At Kelvedon in Essex a pot from the late Iron Age depicting warriors mentions the name Teutates. Among the most famous pieces of Celtic art linking gods and war is the silver Gundestrup Bowl found in 1891 in a bog near Borremøse in Denmark. Probably made in the Danube heartland, it may have come to Denmark as a peace offering. On its moulded plates the artist has drawn armed horsemen and marching foot soldiers, but one of the sections also pictures a horned deity pushing a man's body head first into a cauldron.[12]

The evidence from the earlier Celts is useful because not only were they involved in the transition from nomadic to settled existence, but also the combination of warfare and religion loomed large. Generally speaking when societies coalesce and their surroundings become fixed, their religious beliefs undergo a degree of change to reflect the new lifestyle, but in spite of this the bonds between war, god and priesthood remain surprisingly strong.

The role of the shaman is modified and his title changes, but he is still the overlord of the community whose word is absolute and whose demands may not be questioned. The essence of his legitimacy remains that of an agent of the gods carrying out their bidding among men, but he now also becomes a king. He, and the aura in which he is clothed, is the new common factor linking the various elements of war and religion, god, battle and death. The king chooses whether or not he fancies going to war with his neighbour and he also governs the religious life of the community; because his rule is absolute and he is divine. Only as the first settled communities evolved further over the passage of time did the king or emperor become the mere agent of the gods.

Perceptions about where the interests of the spirit world lie have also changed. When clans ceased their perennial wanderings in search of the wild herds on which they once depended and became societies with roots and domestic stocks and agricultural fields, so the focus shifted from the intensely intimate relationship between man and animal to one between man and man. Settled communities needed territory on which to graze their domesticated herds and grow their crops. Sooner or later it was inevitable that they would start to encroach upon one another for bigger slices of the available real estate. The needs of the temporal world were seen to reflect those of the spiritual realm, and the gods were thought to have become more interested in matters of land acquisition than in observing correct protocol over the hunt for food. Animals were now largely bereft of spirituality, placed on earth by the celestial forces to provide sustenance, weaponry and clothing. However, if the animals had been reduced to a function as animate but useful 'lumps of meat', so also had the great mass of humanity! Many of these societies narrowed their view of who or what possessed a spiritual counterpart and thus benefited from unseen guardianship. In ancient Egypt only the king was automatically eligible for transport beyond the mortal coil, blessed with the prospect of an afterlife beyond death; without his direct intercession the remainder

9

could look forward to utter oblivion. In Mesopotamia the common man and woman were even less fortunate, destined only for oblivion. This took on new significance in a competitive world wherein the drive for survival sometimes necessitated predating one's next-door neighbour rather than a wild beast. If the neighbour did not benefit from protective interest in the spirit world, he might be dispatched with impunity to the clay whence he came. Less reverential treatment was therefore accorded to the fallen but this may also have made the rank and file 'battle fodder' troops less willing to fight to the death.

The newly settled communities that gave up the nomadic habit and put down roots in Mesopotamia, the birthplace of civilisation, brought with them a pantheon of spirits that gradually became less ethereal and assumed more distinct personalities. In their style of government most nations quickly became theocracies in which gods were regarded as sovereigns, or vice versa, and in which the laws of the realm were divine commands rather than human ordinances. When his time in the temporal world was finished, the king as a living divinity returned to the gods whence he had come. In the meantime he governed by divine right, living in the aura of his personal guardian deity, the tutelary god that protected his city.

It matters little whether we turn to the dynasties of the Assyrians, Babylonians, Egyptians, that of Alexander the Great in Macedonia, or the emperors of Rome. Rulers robustly proclaimed themselves as gods in human dress and were venerated accordingly by their subjects. Every quirk of the king's behaviour was a mark of the god of whom he was the tangible manifestation, and thus beyond criticism. If a king went to war it was a battle between his god and the god of his enemy. This notion of god-kings persisted in Mesopotamia until as late as the mid-1600s BCE. By the Assyrian period they were no longer deified in their lifetimes, but as the high priests of the national god Assur they were still considered indispensable. The idea seems to have been prevalent that, if they were usurped or vanquished, the god went with them. In reality, of course, the margins between being a deity-made-flesh and the exclusively privileged agent of a deity often became blurred.

I do not believe that these immensely powerful and privileged individuals harboured any qualms about the morality of making war and killing either for the sake of land acquisition or defence of territory. They were, by and large, of the firm opinion, until they discovered otherwise, that being a deity incarnate amounted to a kind of immortality. On the other hand the death of their subjects and those of the enemy was not worthy of consideration. The famous Stele of the Vultures erected by Eanatum of Lagas during the Early Dynastic Period (before 2350 BCE) to mark victory over his neighbour at Umma – it is one of the earliest records of Mesopotamian conflict – is so-called because it depicts vultures preying on the flesh of the fallen enemy. Other imagery, such as the Royal Standard of Ur, reveals the practice of the victorious general of driving his chariot over the bodies, trampling them into the dust as mere lumps of detritus bereft of dignity.[13]

The new preoccupation of humankind with seeing off their fellows was sanctified because it was believed, through the agency of the king, to be a reflection of heavenly intentions. In the mind of an autocrat such as Assur-nasir-apli, ruling over his empire in the ninth century BCE, and probably in the minds of his subjects too, his actions in war added to his nation's breadbasket and provided a stock of captive slaves to work it, but no less vitally it fulfilled an obligation to the deities he represented in his earthly guise. It met what our distant ancestors firmly believed to be the demands of the gods and so warfare and religion became the same inseparable companions that hunting and animistic spirituality had once been. Like hunting, war required the approval and sanction of heaven in order to stand a reasonable chance of success. Beneath almost all of the carvings depicting the king and his much-altered goddess is a standard inscription that Layard found repeated on carvings and sculptures from end to end of the city.

> Palace of Assur-nasir-apli, the priest of Assur,
> Favourite of Enlil and Ninurta, beloved of Anu and Dagan,
> The weapon of the great gods, the mighty king
> King of the world, King of Assyria . . .[14]

Assur-nasir-apli would have claimed that he was not acting out of personal compulsion when he embarked on his interminable military campaigns, but was carrying out the indisputable wishes of the gods he served. The armies that he went out to slaughter with such vigour were not merely the adversaries of Assyria; they fought as instruments of Assyria's celestial enemies. As the high priest of Assur, the king was bound to prosecute a war of 'my god against your god'. If he failed to do so he would surely stand to lose the support of those heavenly forces that had placed him and his country in the ascendancy. The other names mentioned in his inscription are no less heavy with significance. Enlil had once been the tutelary deity of Sumer, the loose amalgamation of city states in Mesopotamia until about 1750 BCE, and was the god of the air, but he also manifested himself in destructive violence. Ninurta, the son of Enlil, was a hero of the pantheon and linked closely with confrontation battles between the forces of good and evil. He stood as the patron deity of Kalakh. The name of the modern village Nimrud is thought to be a corruption of Nimrod, probably a Biblical corruption of Ninurta. Anu was the Mesopotamian creator god, while Dagan, essentially a deity associated with cereal crops and fertility, became associated with Anu in giving added status to cities including Kalakh.[15] As the urban centres grew in population density and division of labour they became heavily dependent on their agricultural bases in the surrounding lands. Not only was it imperative to guard the produce of these areas against the predations of neighbours but also there was a constant pressure to acquire new territories. Through artwork and inscriptions Assur-nasir-apli went to considerable lengths to identify himself as the tangible 'weapon' of the deities, his arm, his sword and his strategic prowess guided exclusively by their will.

In the oral traditions of the early cultures, campfire romance about past deeds blended secular and non-secular into a seamless whole; myths arose about the adventures of gods and heroes; great epics of conflict, part imaginary, part historical, often took pride of place. These sagas drew portraits of an idealised, heroic society wherein forces of righteousness and light constantly pitted

12

themselves against those of darkness and evil. While ritual permits the formalisation of a faith, myth constitutes much of its building material. It also serves to constrain the powers of the spirit world to a selective beneficence. Hence that which is taken to be an immutable truth by one culture another cynically regards as little more than 'fairy story'. People come to rely on the precedent of epic mythical events in order not only to sanction and justify warfare but also to boost the fighting morale of troops. The gods are on their side, have battled against adversity in the celestial realms and have triumphed! Much as with the oral traditions of the hunters wherein myth established a precedent and therefore a reassurance that the spirit world was forgiving of the chase, so such campfire stories also came to play a critical role in justifying warfare and giving confidence that the fight could be won. When myth involved confrontation and conflict set in a 'once upon a time' age, it implied to the listener that here was a just example, enacted by the guardian deities, to any earthly strife in which they might be obliged to fight, kill and perhaps be killed, even if sometimes in the mythology store cupboard the rights and wrongs of opposing forces were vaguely drawn or even ambivalent. This was not especially characteristic of Mesopotamian traditions, but in others such as Hindu mythology the two sides often merged and even replaced one another, each taking on the characteristics of the opposing protagonist.

One of the mightiest battle tales in Mesopotamian armoury is that between the god Ninurta and a demon named Anzu who paraded in the guise of an eagle with the head of a lion. It took place between the forces of good and evil over control of the Tablet of Destinies, one of those miraculous devices that allows its possessor to rule the world, which, needless to say, has been the driving ambition of many an earthly despot. The myth of Anzu dates from early in the second millennium BCE and copies have been found at a number of sites, the most significant being the royal library of Assurbanipal at Nineveh. But it was also chosen by Assur-nasir-apli at Kalakh as a suitable theme of cosmic combat with which to decorate the Temple of Ninurta. Having triumphed over Anzu and having wrested the Tablet of Destinies from his adversary, Ninurta returned it to its rightful cult centre in the old Sumerian city state of Nippur, along with an assortment of booty that had been brought back strapped to chariots and enslaved captives.[16] In earthly combat the spoils of war were taken de facto and tokens were often deposited as votive offerings in the shrines of guardian deities; but booty tended not to include the cult statues of vanquished city states, and for a long time during Mesopotamian history the temples were respected because their deities were commonly invoked throughout the region. But matters were to change as cults developed along separate paths, so that when, for example, the Hittites captured Babylon they did not hesitate to cart away the statue of the Babylonian god Marduk because he was not a member of the Hittite pantheon.

Tellers of mythical tales have often pitched the problems experienced by the gods on similar lines to those of their earthly audience. Among the legatees of Sumerian tradition were the Canaanites, whose culture extended in biblical times down the eastern seaboard of the Mediterranean from Syria to Lebanon and whose national god was Baal. In Canaan the greatest threat to national integrity came from the 'sea peoples', probably Phoenicians, and in the largest and most significant of the Baal myths discovered among the ruins of the ancient capital, Ugarit, on the north Syrian coast near modern Ras Samra, the prologue of the story reveals a world menaced by the increasing power of the demonic sea and river tyrannies. This closely reflects the temporal situation during the mid-second millennium BCE when the Baal cycle was at the height of its popularity. The authority of Baal was challenged when the emissaries of the sea people entered the assembly of the gods, demanding control over the lands ruled by Baal. Not to be outdone, he elected to take the fight directly to the authorities of sea and river and, using magic weapons, he slew the forces of tyranny.[17]

The purpose of invoking gods and goddesses in their more aggressive pursuits was to obtain divine endorsement for these activities in order to enhance their chances of success. If the god of your own power base was generally held in greater reverence than that of your neighbour, it boded well for the outcome of conflict and this led to the more powerful cities and states claiming as their guardian deities those considered best equipped for the job. That Assur-nasir-apli identified himself as 'the weapon of the great gods' probably made him seem more intimidating and invincible that he might otherwise have been. It amounted to a form of jingoistic propaganda. He was the personification of the war god who would lead his people to victory.

That such rulers thought in this manner is revealed pithily in a critical letter from Yarim-Lim, the king of Aleppo, to the ruler of a city state named Der that lay east of the Tigris on the route to Susa.

Say to Yasub-Yahad, Yarim-Lim your brother says: May Samas (god of justice) investigate my conduct and yours, and render judgement. I behave to you like a father and brother and you behave to me like an ill-wisher and enemy. What requital is this for the fact that the weapons of Adad (god of storms) and Yarim-Lim rescued the city of Babylon and gave life to your land and yourself? Had it not been for Adad and Yarim-Lim, the city of Der would have been blown away like chaff fifteen years ago so that one would be unable to find it.[18]

The incumbents of the ancient heavens were seen to possess traits imitated by their earthly subjects. Conversely, the gods considered humankind, in some respects, akin to themselves, because although the body was fashioned from clay a divine spark animated it. The gods were the fathers and the men were the sons. So gods and goddesses walked, talked, ate, slept, went to the lavatory, fornicated and regularly scrapped with one another for supremacy. The cast list included its heroes and villains, much as in the world of men and women. Generally speaking the outcome of these spirit battles was a win for the good guys. The losers were identified as devils, demons and fallen angels. It did not always work out this way and many of the myths of battle carried a form of moral message. Gods may be seen to be the harbingers of their own misfortunes against demons or other adversaries. Perhaps defeat had resulted from unreasonable covetousness, greed or some other form of weakness.

15

In Norse mythology, Loki, the hybrid progeny of the gods and their arch-enemies the giants, is courted by the gods when they have need of his cunning, but is otherwise spurned and generally given a hard time by the rest of the pantheon, with the result that he harbours a grudge against them. This animosity eventually resolves itself in the day of doom, Ragnarok, when Loki's demonic offspring rise up to defeat the pantheon of gods and bring about the end of the world. But defeat in war was never attributable to the sin of killing one's fellow creature, because when it came to state-sanctioned aggression such a crime did not exist. Moral law encompassed many aspects of life, including truthfulness, family honour and adultery. One man could be held liable for the murder of another in a civil disturbance and prosecuted accordingly. There was no such thing as repentance unless it was towards a deity for failing to meet his or her demands. But if a king went to war against another king it was regularly justifiable provided that he ended the day leading the winning side. The forces of your enemy were seen to be the forces of disorder, so that to keep order at home it was entirely acceptable to fight abroad. It is this philosophy that accounts for much of the triumphalist propaganda with which the royal palaces were decorated. One good victorious battle could be relied on to supplant the image of an otherwise disastrous reign.

As long as the gods of righteousness and justice were on your side, the likelihood was increased that victory would be swift and decisive. One of the oldest oral traditions in Classical Greek, recorded by Plato in the *Timaeus* and the *Critias*, is that relating the battle supposedly waged by the Athenians in about 9000 BCE over the island of Atlantis, lying somewhere in the Atlantic Ocean west of the Pillars of Herakles. The rulers of the island are said to have become progressively more ambitious and tyrannical until they attempted world domination. The outcome of the war was a rout of the forces of Atlantis, with the island and all its inhabitants becoming engulfed by the sea as the Athenian god, Poseidon, took final retribution against the arrogance of the Atlantaeans. Once more we have here a story in which it is a god that actually guides the destiny of battle.

The ideology of god-kings leading their subjects into battle by divine right, serving god against god, has not been limited to the ancient Near East. The same principles have cropped up the world over at different times in history as cultures pass through identifiable stages of their evolution. To call this a 'grand design' would be a euphemism. There was no carbon copy of religious activities and experiences, but there have been astonishing similarities. These may be explained in part by the obscure channels of communication forged through cultural exchange, trade and force of arms, yet other bonds seem inexplicable and about these we can do no more than wonder.

Irish Celtic traditions provide what seems on first inspection a strong echo of the influence of the ancient Near Eastern cultures, yet there are notable differences. In one clear respect the Celtic realm did not conform to the pattern of belief seen through much of the ancient world, most notably the kingdoms of the Near East and Egypt, where god-kings and their immediate families earned an exclusive right to life beyond death. There can be very little doubt that the Celts forged a strong sentient association between war and death, but the prospect of a journey into the afterlife was common to all their peoples, probably because the Celtic star arose that much later in history and the view was coloured by the rationale that had developed in other cultures of their time. Julius Caesar in his annals of the Gallic Wars was perhaps the first writer in history to put his finger on an important causative factor stimulating the direction of interest: 'The Druids attach particular importance to the belief that the soul does not perish but passes after death from one body to another; they think that this belief is the most effective way to encourage bravery because it removes the fear of death.'[19]

In this respect of belief in the afterlife, it's worth drawing comparison with at least one other contemporary cultural experience, that of Hasmonaean Judaism. For much of Israelite history there was no recognition of life after death, at least none of any account. They imagined a place of the dead, Sheol, a nothingness, a total limbo. It is not until the comparatively modern Book of Daniel in the Old Testament, and in the experience of the

Jewish Maccabean revolt that took place in the second century BCE, that the idea of a life beyond the grave was anticipated. 'Many of them that sleep in the dust of the earth shall awake, some to everlasting life . . .'[20] The rebellion claimed large numbers of victims and it is likely that an afterlife, hitherto well established for divine kings, managed to extend its franchise to the common man under circumstances of great bereavement.

In Celtic Ireland, that remote island that Greek travellers knew as Ierne, kings may not have been alone in obtaining the prospect of an afterlife, but they took on certain unique trappings of godliness. On the sacred hill of Tara sovereign rulers wed not one but two consorts. The first gave earthly comfort and companionship; the other was a priestess who assumed the mantle of a fertility goddess, the beautiful and mythical queen of Connaght – Medb or Maeve. By repute the king was descended from the tribal god, and in his prosperity, his health and strength, lay that of his people. So strong was the belief in his divine status that if any wrinkles and blemishes appeared, or if he received battle scars, these tangible signals of mortality became the auguries of doom. No king of Ireland was allowed to slide into infirmity or live as a scarred veteran and also preside over the temporal earth. As physical human decay made its first unwelcomed appearance, or if the land became barren, the goddess-queen was replaced by a hag, the signal for the man to begin his lonely march towards abdication or slaughter. There survives a bizarre Irish tale underlining the kingly necessity of maintaining a perfect physical appearance, that of Nuadu Argatlam, 'Nuadu of the Silver Hand'. This legendary god-king of Ireland reputedly lost his right hand in a famous battle staged on a ground referred to as Moytura. In a desperate attempt to retain his sovereignty Nuadu begged the physician god, Dian Cecht, to fashion a perfect prosthesis made of silver. But, when it was gifted to the king, even with this device it was impossible to hide Nuadu's mortality and thus the disfavour of the Other World, so he was forced to abdicate.[21]

While alive and whole, the kings of Connaght led their warriors into repeated skirmishes and wars against those of rival clans, most notably from Ulster, for the acquisition of territory and livestock. Yet again precedent for warfare is to be discovered in the great epic sagas of Irish mythology. The best known of these is the so-called *Tain bo Cuailgne* (the Cattle Raid of Cuailgne). Derived from an oral tradition whose antiquity is unknown, it seems to have been first recorded by Snechan Torpeist, the chief bard of Ireland, in the eighth century CE. The original written version has been lost, but incomplete later copies survive from the eleventh and twelfth centuries, compiled by Christian monks. The myth narrates an attempt by Medb, queen of Connaght (Connaught) in the south, to wrest the Brown Bull of Cuailgne from the Ulster-based clan of Ulaid, who once lived in the Armagh region and whose mythical hero was a warrior named Cu Chulainn. The saga provides a good illustration of how in the minds of early societies the interests of the spirit world and those of temporal society mirrored one another. The logic that humankind was fashioned in the image of the gods meant that the aspirations of each paralleled the other. What was appropriate for the gods was also good for men, but also vice versa. When a clan needed to vanquish a neighbour to achieve material gain, it stood to reason that the gods of that tribe also had a need to overcome the gods of its rivals.

Mythical warriors are always unparalleled in strength, intellect and bravery, but they are also vulnerable, which gives them human qualities. Like earthly recruits they have studied the use of arms, although generally at an earlier age and with more sensational capabilities. At the tender age of 5 Cu Chulainn had shed his parental protection and travelled alone to the stronghold of Emain Macha, the old religious centre of Ulster just west of the modern town of Armagh, in order to learn the use of weapons. On arrival he had been set upon by no less than 150 other trainees but had thrown them off. Within three years he was fully versed in the arts of war and been promoted as leader and guardian of the rest. He had also developed certain unusual physical attributes to boost an already intimidating appearance. Before battle his red hair stood on end and seemed to catch fire, and while one eye almost disappeared in his head the other expanded and rolled around menacingly in its socket. Most earthly recruits may have found it difficult to emulate all of Cu Chulainn's abilities, but such sanguine campfire anecdotes provided strong jingoistic encouragement to young warriors who were generally both deeply superstitious and illiterate.

A fascinating contrast can be discovered in the traditions of dynastic China where, over time, an actual historical event became rewritten in a wholly mythical context to the extent that the mortal conflict was envisaged as a celestial battle fought between opposing forces of immortal beings. Chinese spiritual beliefs seem to have originated in prehistoric times in much the same fashion as those elsewhere in the world at a comparable stage of social development. The ancient religion of Wu was essentially shamanistic. But out of this developed Daoisim (Taoism), which, unlike transcendental beliefs, recognises that all deities were once mortals who went through a process of apotheosis after their death to become immortals. The significance in this instance was not so much to give heavenly sanction to bloodshed as to explain, in an exemplary fashion, how many of the deified figures representing an old order became ousted by new names and personalities. The historically verifiable Battle of Mu was fought in 1122 BCE between two rival dynasties, the Shang and the Zhou. The conflict gains its provenance both from the official Shi Zhi records and from the independent writings of the historian Su-Ma Zhien, who lived during the second and first centuries BCE. In reality the forces of the Zhou defeated those of the Shang, and its leading family assumed the imperial control of the country. As is not infrequently the case, one then threw out the gods of the other in favour of its own pantheon.[22]

The epic myth that developed became known as the Battle of the Ten Thousand Spirits, detailed in Daoist religious texts including the *Book on the Making of Immortals* and the *Catalogue of Spirits and Immortals*. The principal characters include Zhou Wang, who actually lived from 1154 to 1121 BCE as the tyrannical head of the outgoing Shang dynasty, but underwent transfiguration into the evil god of sodomy; and Wu Wang, known in his earthly existence as Fa, who took over as first ruler of the incoming radical Zhou dynasty.

In mythological tradition the founder of the dynasty was actually Fa's father, Xi Beh, who also underwent apotheosis to emerge as the god Wen Wang. In short there appears in such myths a confused blurring between flesh-and-blood historical personalities on the one hand and deities on the other. In the popular mind the imagery of battle between mortal combatants slowly evaporates and is replaced by one placed in a wholly celestial context. The expansion of events into mythical proportions tends, however, to provide licence for romance! The spirit heroes of the new dynasty were said to include Li No-Cha, a remarkable warrior who had grown to a height of 60 feet and sprouted three heads each with as many eyes, as well as eight arms bearing an assortment of formidable weapons. More remarkable still, when one of Zhou Wang's more prominent generals was slain, his three immortal sisters became determined to avenge his death. Not having more conventional weapons at their disposal they relied on their well-charged lavatory bucket, the Golden Bushel of Troubled Origins, which was dispatched repeatedly as a lethal projectile until Li No-Cha rendered it impotent with his Wind and Fire weapon. Generally, the most compelling reason for a victorious army to make the deities of the defeated forces redundant is precisely because they are seen to have fought on the side of the vanquished and thus to be inferior to those sponsoring the victors.

Superhuman physical attributes are more or less de rigueur for any fighting deity worth his or her salt, and even junior officers may be remarkably well equipped. In the epic of Ten Thousand Spirits, and not to be outdone by Zhou Wang's vengeful sorority with their lavatory bucket, one of his senior ministers cultivates three eyes (one of which emits a deathly ray) and rides upon a black unicorn that travels at the speed of light.

Generally speaking, a multiplicity of heads, eyes and arms represents a favoured option for artists; it amounts to a considerable added potency if the celestial warrior happens to be supporting your forces, but is, of course, equally intimidating if not! Opposing storytellers and artists have thus been encouraged to outdo their counterparts with ever-greater levels of inventiveness. Some of the most bizarrely equipped characters are to be found in Hindu mythology. Vaisnavites in southern India, devotees of the god Visnu, envisage him to have grown at least four heads and four pairs of arms, each holding a wide assortment of weaponry, including most typically a discus, bow, arrow, club, sword and shield. Not to be outdone, the Saivite followers of Siva in the region of Bengal depict his formidable and malignant consort Kali with fanglike teeth, claws, bloody lips and as many as eighteen arms carrying swords and severed heads.[23]

By and large theocratic beliefs were set to erode and eventually die out as nations and cultures progressed during history. In the ancient Near East it was not until the advent of Judaism, with its radical ideas of a single transcendental god, that god-kings started to wane in popularity. The Old Testament Book of Daniel makes much of the tale of Nebuchadnezzar, the Babylonian despot who set up his own image, cast in gold, in the plain of Dura near Babylon and demanded that all the various provinces under his command paid homage to it. The name Nebuchadnezzar means literally 'may the god Nabu protect the succession', although from the strictly historical perspective this was probably a man named Nabonidus, the last king of the neo-Babylon empire, whose career had apparently begun in the service of Nebuchadnezzar and who, having assumed power in 556 BCE, had himself deified in a last-ditch attempt to unify the disparate religions of his empire. From the Israelite perspective, his downfall as a blasphemer was more or less guaranteed. Nebuchadnezzar (Nabonidus) is said to have lost his mind after the miraculous salvation of Shadrach, Meshach and Abednego from the fiery furnace, which also persuaded him to proclaim allegiance to the one true God. He probably died in 539 BCE when Babylon fell to Cyrus, king of the Persians, but the story of madness brought on by way of divine retribution against the sin of self-deification has better survived the passage of time in popular Christian and Jewish tradition.

But vestiges of theocracies remain. In twenty-first century Britain we still retain an amalgam of secular and non-secular authority in the shape of the monarch who is not only titular head of state but is also head of the Church of England. One notable exception to the decline of theocracies among modern industrialised states has been that of Japan, where many other archaic elements have persisted into modern times, particularly in social and family life. Festivals and rites are still observed that, to a Western mind, may seem quaint and anachronistic. Significantly, until Japan's defeat at the end of the Second World War, her emperor, Hirohito, was regarded as a living deity.

The ancient prehistoric beliefs and religious traditions that would evolve into the imperial Japanese religion of Shintoism after the nomadic tribes had begun to gather into settled communities were probably little different from those of countless other primitive societies around the globe. They involved a strong and influential role for shamans and shamanesses, who were regarded as priests and magicians. Shinto, literally 'the way of the gods', is focused on the worship and invocation of the Japanese celestial pantheon at the head of which stands Amaterasu, the supreme Sun Goddess from whom the national flag takes its inspiration in the form of the red sun disc, or more precisely the magical mirror that reflected Amaterasu's rays. The paramount goddess is also the ancestral mother of the royal lineage of Japanese emperors. According to mythological tradition it was her grandson, Prince Ninigi-no-mikoto, who descended to earth and founded the imperial Nippon dynasty. While in the heavens he stood as the deification of the rising sun, but he was sent to earth to bring order to the world after a succession of lesser envoys had failed. To achieve this goal, however, Ninigi with his celestial cohorts was obliged to fight his way from the southerly point where he touched down on terra firma towards the Yamato plain on Honshu island, where he established himself as the head of the Yamato tribe and thus became the first earthly emperor. In the minds of countless Japanese faithful, stability and order had been achieved only by the shedding of blood.

Shintoism thus recognises that in mythical times there occurred a transition from godly to earthly rule and that the transformed individual, representing the head of the Japanese imperial dynasty, was bestowed with the divine right to govern. From the eighth century CE onwards, chroniclers employed by the Yamato imperial court had effectively 'confirmed' the divine status of the emperor and given his absolute rule its legitimacy through spiritual precedent. The emperor was, literally, the divine presence on earth and became known as *arami-kami*, meaning 'visible god'. From the moment of his birth he was treated as a divinity incarnate in a politicisation of religion that became known as Kokutai Shinto.

For a long period, roughly from the eleventh to nineteenth centuries during the feudal rule of the Tokugawa shoguns, this overarching influence of the imperial dynasty was set to decline, but the emperors bounced back to prominence in 1868 at the time of the Meiji restoration, which ended the shogunate. Once more they were granted not only divine but also secular administrative power, and as little as three years later Shinto was declared the state religion. This rediscovered imperial muscle was further enlarged by the rising popularity of Confucianism in Japan, which placed considerable emphasis on unswerving loyalty to the emperor, and the aura in which the emperor was held contributed strongly to the more extreme demonstrations of Japanese imperialism and militaristic adventuring that erupted in the 1940s. It was not until 1945, when Hirohito broadcast to the Japanese people with his message of surrender, that Shinto lost its status as the official state religion and the emperor was obliged to renounce all claims to divinity. The perils of blending religious and militaristic fanaticism were not hard to see, and for this reason the 1947 postwar constitution of Japan included an absolute ban on any involvement by the state in religious matters. This, however, may not represent a final chapter, since there are now rumblings of disquiet about the rising level of aggressive religious sectarianism that has gripped the country in recent years.

If Japan represents one notable example of theocratic rule that has penetrated into the modern era, another must surely be that of militant Islamic fundamentalism, a subject to be explored in depth in a later chapter.

TWO

The Word of God

The *raison d'être* for killing in the name of God was set to change with the arrival in Western Asia of monotheism, or, in the case of the Hebrew patriarch Abraham, monolatry, because according to Biblical tradition he recognised not a solitary God but one that is universal and superior to the rest. The manner in which divine militancy was perceived also took on a new slant, and thus we arrive at the chicken-and-egg dilemma: which came first, God's word or man's deed? Did God rattle the sabre expecting his earthly legions obediently to follow him into holy war, as many fundamentalists will, I am sure, insist or, as objective reasoning must go, did those engaged in the battle carry out their strategic aims and then invent divine bidding to suit? It is of course impossible to prove in a forensic sense that God ever uttered belligerent words to humankind. In reality the two possibilities almost certainly arose side by side, each encouraging the other. But, because in the minds of the faithful Holy Scripture is the driving force, and those who hear the word act upon it in the genuine belief that it carries divine authority, we should logically deal with aggressive commands from heaven before considering the events on the ground.

In polytheistic religions where a god or goddess generally enjoys tangible presence in the form of a statue or cult image, his or her aggressive nature can be demonstrated to the wider world through art. So the warrior divine is depicted bristling with weapons to indicate a fighting disposition. But with the new all-powerful God of Abraham conveying his wish to remain out of sight, any interpretation of his likeness being strictly forbidden, problems of communication had to be overcome. In this situation natural signs and portents may still offer some indication of what is going on in

25

the heavenly mind, but the word of God conveyed through the mouths of visionaries and prophets becomes just about the only means of allowing the public an ear to divine will. For the Israelite tribes the cult image was replaced by the Covenant, God's message to the earthbound, and this, rather than an inarticulate statue, was to become their most treasured and fiercely protected religious symbol.

For Judaism and then for the cults of Christianity and Islam that arose in its wake, the received word would have been limited at first to brief utterances, those direct quotes that become preserved in the memory of the faithful and which are no doubt judiciously edited from time to time. But as compilations of text were developed and assembled, so the resulting biblical and qur'ānic scriptures became sanctified in their entirety as 'the word of God'. Whole chapters of Old Testament books, including that of the prophet Jeremiah, were elaborated as divinely inspired narratives prefaced by suitable qualifications: 'The Lord put forth his hand and touched my mouth.'[1] In Islam the first *surah* proper (after the Exordium) of the Qur'ān opens in similar manner: 'This book is not to be doubted. It is a guide for the righteous, who believe in the unseen and are steadfast in prayer; who give in alms from what We [Allah] gave them; who believe in what has been revealed to you [Muhammad] and what was revealed before you, and have absolute faith in the life to come. These are rightly guided by their Lord; these shall surely triumph.'[2]

In trawling the sacred texts today, however, there are a number of caveats to keep in mind. The Hebrew Bible, assembled piecemeal over a considerable period of time, is far from being a single work of one author, and its scope and remit are also far broader than divine revelation and the provision of a law code. It is intended as an account – in fact our only existing near-contemporary account – of the long and complex biblical history of Israel. The Qur'ān, in contrast, is strictly a series of divine messages obtained over a twenty-two-year period of Muhammad's life from the age of 40 when he received the first of the revelations until his death in 632 CE. These messages include the bedrock of Islamic law and are provided for the faithful to observe and follow. They are, however, without a historical component.

A literary trap for the unwary lies in that divine pronouncements both to the early Israelite leaders, to the Christian fathers and to the founder of Islam, Muhammad, each obtained circulation and survived for lengthy periods by word of mouth before ever being written down. In its earliest form each set of scriptures probably constituted an independent collection of laws, sayings and other pieces of narrative that was then reworked, perhaps more than once, into an editorial framework. We may safely assume that Moses did not descend from Mount Horeb clutching a stack of neatly etched tablets confirming God's wishes, and we know that transmission of the Qur'ān, a word that translates literally as 'recitation', was strictly an oral tradition for decades after the time of Muhammad, having been memorised by his early followers. It is well established that the earliest books of the Christian New Testament were not committed to writing until decades after the events they describe. Islamic fundamentalists may reject any suggestion that the material of the Qur'ān is anything other than original and unedited, but research carried out from the late 1970s reveals that manuscripts do not actually exist from the seventh century, when the first copies were allegedly compiled. In fact no qur'ānic manuscript has materialised from anywhere in the Islamic realms that can be reliably dated to the period within a century of the Prophet's birth.[3]

The Hebrew Bible that became known to the Western world as the Old Testament is particularly suspect in the amount of editing it received *after* its individual components were first written down. Two 'early' instructions permeating the texts – conquest and religious solidarity – are largely retrospective, because, although the period covered extends from the turn of the second millennium to the end of the second century BCE, none of the manuscripts of the Old Testament as we know it today was finalised until after the composition of the book of Daniel in about 170 BCE. Some parts of the original material may have been committed to writing as early as the end of the first millennium BCE, but most was penned after the Israelites were exiled to Babylon in 587 BCE, and, significantly, none of the original manuscripts or tablets exists. We only possess generations of copies that have been through many changes and translations. What this means is that we have first an exclusively Israelite viewpoint, then one with a partisan slant favouring the southern state of Judah, from among whose scribes virtually all the texts emanated. Beside such a subjective approach there is very little independent literature with which to judge objectivity and accuracy.[4]

It is probably the case that few of the word-of-mouth traditions remained in their original form even after being written down, and many were adapted to changing circumstances and norms. There is a good argument that scripture only finds meaning through a history of interpretation, and thus cannot be read independently of its interpretation. Scripture as the word of God is constantly shaped and moulded in the very attempt to understand its meaning, and, inevitably, original traditions become adapted to reflect a consensus of political interests at the time when each version is produced. Much of the raw material contained, for example, in the pages of Deuteronomy must have been in word-of-mouth circulation from close to the time of events described, but the book was only compiled as a self-contained text late in the Monarchic period ending in the sixth century BCE. There is broad agreement that one or more 'theological schools' edited together a bundle of strongly militant, pro-Yahwist material with the purpose of boosting an anti-pagan purge demanded by the Judahite king Josiah.[5]

Given these caveats, Jewish, Christian and Islamic scriptures discuss violent aggression and its morality fairly extensively. There is a commonly held but erroneous notion that the more influential of the world's holy scriptures do not advocate the shedding of blood in anger. But closer inspection reveals that the idea of transcendentally sanctified war, both defensive and otherwise, is a much-repeated theme in the pages of the Holy Bible and the Qur'ān. These two great religious canons that still influence much of the modern world are bespattered with gore, though not in equal measure, since the Bible emerges bathed in a distinctly more sanguine light when it comes to flexing muscles. The so-called Old Covenant, or Old Testament, consisting of thirty-nine orthodox texts from Genesis to Zechariah, is neither for the squeamish nor the peaceably minded, and judging by appearances its assorted writers would have found little sympathy for the Geneva Convention had it existed in their day. A rough calculation indicates that variation on the words 'destroy' and 'destruction' is included not less than 500 times within its pages.[6] In comparison the word 'mercy' and its variants find mention only 240 times. Divine interest in violent behaviour is apparent almost from the outset and, as in the Qur'ān, much is framed in a context of retribution against others that have first caused offence by abrogating the rules of heaven. Moreover, this retribution is almost unparalleled in the sheer ferocity with which it is conducted. It amounts to an awesome manifestation of divine justice to a fallen world, and the manner in which the justice is apportioned seems unimportant so long as it is done with sufficient overkill to communicate effectively the extent of God's rage.[7]

In the Hebrew Bible the Book of Deuteronomy is by no means isolated in its tone of belligerence, but it takes the most aggressive line of any of the orthodox texts. In the books of the Qur'ān, notoriously haphazard and lacking any logical sequence, the references to war are scattered throughout. The Christian canon, by comparison, has little to say on the subject other than generally to eschew violence, so that most of the Christian inspiration for warmongering relies on aggressive trumpeting of the Old Testament.

Biblical justification for mass slaughter is something over which religious historians, particularly those in the West, tend to be a little squeamish. In his Introduction to the *History of the Jewish People*, Ben Sasson manages to gloss over the issue of Israelite savagery when he writes, 'the liberation and upsurge of the peoples in order to establish themselves as new national entities . . . the Israelites now played a major role, eventually emerging victorious and bringing about a major change in the fortunes of the country . . . the people of Israel was unique among the nations in that it bestowed upon the land of Canaan, the classic land of transit, a relatively lengthy period of political sovereignty and national autonomy . . . it was this struggle for selfhood that gave the emerging culture of Israel its unique character as a nation'.[8] The *Eerdmans Bible Dictionary* includes the bland and faintly ludicrous assertion that 'in the Old Testament love for other people is part of the broader duty for keeping God's commandments, God's people are to love their fellow Israelites as well as sojourners or resident aliens'. But other writers are less confident, pointing out that simply putting aside those texts that now seem unattractive or problematic in the modern context is no way to solve the moral questions they raise.[9] In 1992 the Jewish historian Michael Walzer declared that 'the religious doctrine of holy war does not seem to have any intrinsic connection to Israel's covenantal faith'. He describes the conquest of Canaan as 'the most problematic moment in the history of ancient Israel', a polite way of saying that its conduct defied any reasonable norms of a civilised people.[10]

During the nineteenth and early twentieth centuries it was fashionable to complain that Islam 'converted by the sword' and amounted to little more than a warrior cult lacking spiritual and ethical depth. Modern Muslim scholars are understandably touchy, since they are saddled not only with the at-times unsavoury history of jihad but also with the incessant media publicity surrounding its worst current excesses. The Muslim writer Abdullah Schleifer concedes that the subject of jihad is one of great sensitivity for a modern Islamic community stung by accusations.[11]

The 'Word of God' was to become pivotal when prosecuting wars in the name of God, but in order to achieve this it needed to secure a major advance in communication techniques. The Sumerians, the first civilised people of the ancient Near East, developed a method of recording known as cuneiform, pictorial images that evolved into simple representative characters pressed into soft clay surfaces using a wedge-shaped tool. The Akkadians, Babylonians and Assyrians then largely copied their innovation. But in time a more flexible style of linear script developed using ink and a fine stylus to transfer characters onto substances like papyrus, and this allowed for more complex transmission of information. With an ability to exploit script, societies gained new levels of awareness not only concerning material affairs but also in their understanding of the non-secular, or spiritual, world.

With the advent of more sophisticated writing techniques, relating the whimsy of the unseen world was not limited to campfire storytelling and what little could be recorded in cuneiform inscriptions. The wishes and actions of the gods could be described in detail on as many scrolls and codices as was convenient to turn out. In the hands of a new breed of shamans and priests and with acceptable provenance – in other words, providing that the right people had drawn them up – scriptures could provide a far more thorough and permanent insight into the will of heaven. Nevertheless, for a long time the communities in the ancient Near East remained deeply superstitious in almost all that they did and understood concerning the world around them, believing implacably that events unfolded only through the intentions of supernatural beings and supernatural forces. In today's world there are still many individuals and communities for whom superstition remains a major driving force in their faith.

The advent of religious scripture coincided with, and inevitably contributed to, the spread of differing ideologies. The transition from a simple 'my god against your god' argument to one of 'my god is being wronged and will bring retribution upon those who wrong him' is a subtle but significant one. Although the despots of the ancient Near East, both great and small, claimed to be carrying out the wishes of heaven under grandiose titles like 'weapon of the great gods', it was always difficult to take the logic too far because the pantheon was more or less universally recognised across the entire region. Since most people worshipped members of the same 'cast list' of deities, it was difficult to justify aggression on the grounds of preserving religious integrity. The gods of one city state or political regime largely mirrored those revered by its next-door neighbours, and so the position tended to be that one ruler served a tutelary deity better and with more muscle than his rival.

The paramount goddess Istar was universally recognised whether she went under the title of Inana, Asherah, Astarte, Artemis, Ashtoreth, Kybele or Isis, and so there were few ideological differences among the beliefs of the Canaanites, Assyrians, Hittites, Babylonians and even the Egyptians other than those dictated by environment. Canaanites were concerned about flood and foreign invasion from the sea; Hittites about the destruction wrought by

31

sudden storm and tempest in the mountains of Anatolia; Assyrians, Babylonians and Egyptians by the life-threatening effects of drought on the plains of Mesopotamia and in the Nile Valley. Even when Aten was brought to prominence as a supreme deity in Egypt, through an experimental cult of monotheism under Amenhotep IV, he was not a distinctly new and separate creator deity but a sublimation of the personalities of all the gods in the Egyptian pantheon.[12]

In the old polytheistic religions members of the pantheon got on reasonably well with one another and only mortal despots had them engaging in the occasional contest of strength, but all of this would change with the shift of popular interest towards monolatry, the worship of a dominant deity, better and more powerful than the rest. It's worth reiterating that monotheism, recognition of a single universal God, did not arise straight away. The nomadic tribes who would consolidate into the Children of Israel were persuaded by their elders into the exclusive worship of one deity known to the southern tribes as Yahweh and to those of the north as El. While not alone in the heavens, this deity was definitely unwilling to brook any form of challenge to his supremacy and from the outset was portrayed as demonstrating a human attribute hitherto uncommon among deities, that of jealousy. The most oft-quoted reference to this effect comes from Exodus 20, 'Thou shalt not bow down thyself to them, nor serve them: for I the Lord thy God am a jealous God',[13] but among the writers of the Pentateuch books, the oldest part of the Hebrew canon, the author of Exodus emphasises the possessiveness of the Israelite God on two separate occasions. In Deuteronomy it is remarked on no less than three times.

The specific phrase 'holy war' appears very infrequently in the biblical texts. Among the rare examples, the Book of Numbers refers to 'the wars of the Lord'[14] and the same phrase is reiterated twice in the first book of Samuel. Nevertheless, several books of the Old Testament, in particular Deuteronomy, make clear that battle firstly for the purpose of defence and then divinely encouraged and even divinely implemented to meet offensive objectives is entirely justified. Furthermore, when war is divinely sanctioned, it is recognised that the violent actions of the participants become sanctified and free from restraint. Those who end their lives fighting in holy war can anticipate the ultimate goal of everlasting life in a transcendent world. War can thus be seen not only to be just but also justifying.[15]

Deuteronomy provides an unequivocal reflection of God's intentions for the Israelites, namely to conquer the land that he had promised to them and to rid it of idolatry. It is the adamant rejection of this particular aspect of the old polytheistic religions that chiefly separates and sets the Israelites apart from the peoples living around them. The Deuteronomist explicitly calls for the destruction of idolators and warns that God's chosen people will themselves be destroyed if they forsake the covenant and backslide into practising 'abominations'. The reader is left in no doubt about the consequences of straying into religious infidelity. 'They provoked him to jealousy with strange gods, with abominations provoked they him to anger . . . and he said, I will hide my face from them, I will see what their end shall be . . . for a fire is kindled in mine anger, and shall burn unto the lowest hell, and shall consume the earth with her increase, and set on fire the foundations of the mountains'.[16] The later prophetic books of the Old Testament also refer to God's intolerance of straying, but probably more in a literal, less a canonical, sense. Nonetheless, throughout the Old Testament there is a sense that he is jealous of his own and positively encourages violent behaviour in order to see off potential opposition.

The men responsible for passing on the word of God at various times in Jewish history were first the patriarchs, followed by the judges and then the priestly kings and prophets, superseded eventually by the rabbinical clergy. Whatever messages they conveyed from the ether, including the wishes of heaven on such matters as warfare, these became accepted as orthodox, literally the 'right way'. In order to justify armed aggression during the earlier periods of Israelite history the religious leaders and their scribes were destined to work overtime in letting the tribes know just how angry their God was with the defenders and how keen he was to see them punished.

From the outset the singular God revered by Abraham and his descendants was willing to obliterate any and all that displeased him, at home or abroad and by whatever means of annihilation were at his disposal. In the Book of Genesis a catastrophic flood was the first demolition weapon that he turned to: 'And the Lord said I will destroy man whom I have created from the face of the earth; both man, and beast, and the creeping thing, and the fowls of the air; for it repenteth me that I have made them.'[17] It was not long before the citizens of Sodom and Gomorrah came in for aggressive attention on account of their unholy behaviour, and among their number the wife of Lot was turned into a pillar of salt for showing signs of 'backsliding'. A number of other minor kingdoms also suffered similar experience to the extent that, while entertaining Abraham to dinner, the king of Salem was prompted to comment, 'Blessed be the most high God, which hath delivered thine enemies into thy hand'.[18] The biblical writers generally described such cosmic punishments as the rewards of 'sin', and the word of God was used effectively to keep the Hebrew flock under tight discipline by example. The message was that if the ungodly erred then God would know and God would punish. 'And the Lord said, Because the cry of Sodom and Gomorrah is great and because their sin is very grievous: I will go down now and see whether they have done altogether according to the cry of it, which is come unto me; and if not I will know.'[19]

Defining the wickedness of the opposition was not straightforward, and it had to be couched in vague terms. The usual recourse, however, was to denounce the spiritual conduct of those resisting the Hebrews, on the grounds that this allegedly caused offence to God, who would then wreak bloody retribution. The dire example of Sodom and Gomorrah was called upon on more than one occasion as a warning about the way things could turn out. Moses delivered a timely reminder to the troops in a singularly forthright lecture just as they were about to set foot in the land of Canaan. 'Their vine is of the vine of Sodom, and of the fields of Gomorrah: their grapes are grapes of gall, their clusters are bitter: their wine is the poison of dragons, and the cruel venom of asps . . . to me belongeth vengeance, and recompence; their foot shall slide in due time; for the day of their calamity is at hand, and the things that shall come upon them make haste . . . I will render vengeance to mine enemies, and will reward them that hate me. I will make mine arrows drunk with blood, and my sword shall devour flesh; and that with the blood of the slain and of the captives from the beginning of revenges upon the enemy.'[20] When it came to categorising and sorting out the enemy, God tended not to mince his words.

It is not entirely surprising, given the uncompromising preface laid out in the Book of Genesis, that by the next book in the Old Testament collection, Exodus, God has begun employing humankind to carry out much of his wrecking activities. At this stage the emphasis is on conquest. When an enemy of God is encountered the jingoism goes into high gear, with the biblical writers hurrying to convey the message that he is the one 'pointing the sword'.

The notion of divinely inspired war developed in parallel with Israel's evolution out of a mêlée of ethnically related nomadic tribes and into a unified people occupying its own, albeit plundered, land. The first 'enemy' of note to suffer at God's hand were the Egyptians, when a variety of lethal misfortunes came upon them as they attempted to stop the Hebrews from fleeing north across the Red Sea. The next clearly defined targets of assault by the migrating Hebrews on the orders of their God were the indigenous inhabitants of Syrio-Palestine, the armed gangs that occasionally marauded from the East, and the so-called Sea Peoples who are assumed to have invaded the region from somewhere in the Mediterranean Basin. Having survived the impositions of forced labour placed on them in Egypt, the Hebrews were eventually encouraged by their leader Moses to trek through the Negev Desert in order to settle a land that had somehow been promised to them as a divinely ordained gift. When the message endorsing violent assault was delivered from aloft it came in uncompromising terms: 'I will send my fear before thee and will destroy all the people to whom thou shalt come, and I will make all thine enemies turn their backs unto thee. By little and little I will drive them out from before thee until thou be increased and inherit the land . . . I will deliver the inhabitants of the land into your hand, and thou shalt drive them out before thee.'[21]

The scriptural justification for 'delivering the inhabitants' is a polite euphemism for mass slaughter. This style of overkill began in the context of defence but then changed into divinely commanded offensive tactics. The opening words of Joshua, the first of the Old Testament's historical books, convey a precise message that conquest of the region is being carried out under the authority of heaven. God, we are told, has spoken to Joshua, the successor to Moses, urging him on to victory. 'Every place that the sole of your foot shall tread upon, that have I given unto you . . . there shall not any man be able to stand before thee all the days of thy life.'[22]

The Promised Land, the sovereign territory of Canaan, was not going to be presented to the Hebrews as a gift; it would have to be wrested from its existing inhabitants by force of arms and through a substantial measure of bloodletting. But it was consistently emphasised that God was responsible for the strategy, showering divine potency on his chosen people in order to achieve the desired end. For the ordinary fighting man footslogging through hostile territory this ideal was not always easy to accept, not least because the Israelite God did not appear at the head of his troops either as a divine king or even as a militant statue. The leaders quickly appreciated that their God's invisibility amounted to a potential problem when it came to keeping up morale. So, when the Israelite army was about to cross the River Jordan into foreign territory, Joshua made an eve-of-battle rallying cry to his troops, urging them to believe that the supernatural fighting spirit was contained in, and emanated from the Ark of the Covenant. 'Hereby ye shall know that the living God is among you . . . behold the Ark of the Covenant of the Lord passeth over before you into Jordan.'[23] Coincidentally, the extraordinary power of the Ark and its Covenant, the tangible presence of a heavenly arm administering vengeance on the side of righteousness, was strikingly retold in a modern setting through the popular Harrison Ford film of the 1980s, *Raiders of the Lost Ark*.

Tactics in divinely propelled war have rarely equated with restraint. The employment of minimum appropriate force is not advocated in the biblical military manual, and in the five books of the Pentateuch mass destruction tends to be the order of the day. When the various indigenous kingdoms of the region came together in a last-ditch effort to defend their homelands from the invading tribes, even this was attributed to the will of the Israelite God in order that his armies might find the enemy in one place and defeat them all the more thoroughly. 'For it was of the Lord to harden their hearts, that they should come against Israel in battle, that he might destroy them utterly.'[24]

The theme of utter destruction, known as herem, or anathema, becomes a familiar one in the Old Testament. The Mesopotamian god-kings sometimes issued similar instruction. Secular inscriptions suggest that Assur-nasir-apli II demanded total obliteration when his forces conquered a number of neighbouring city states, but among the world's holy scriptures it is unique. It effectively involves consecrating the opposition and then delivering it to God through being totally consumed, as if in a sacrificial fire. Not even the Hindu *Mahabharata*, an unusually belligerent saga of religious conflict, goes to the extreme and terrifying command that is disclosed by the Deuteronomist: 'Of the cities of these people, which the Lord thy God doth give thee for an inheritance, thou shalt save alive nothing that breatheth: but thou shalt utterly destroy them; namely the Hittites, and the Amorites, the Canaanites, and the Perizzites, the Hivites, and the Jebusites; as the Lord thy God hath commanded thee.'[25]

If assaults in Israel's war of conquest were generally explained in terms of God requiring his armed forces to take massive retribution, military setbacks were attributed to defaulting on precisely this extreme violence and the terms of anathema laid down by God. After the fall of Jericho, a man named Achan of the tribe of Judah is said to have failed in this obligation by stealing a quantity of enemy plunder including gold and silver. Described as 'the accursed thing' there is a hint that this horde may have been of ritualistic significance for the inhabitants of Jericho. Although it was destined for the confederate treasury as the loot of war, officially it had been labelled as belonging 'to the Lord' because God had commanded

Israel to destroy everything in Jericho. When the Israelite forces
were ambushed in the process of mopping up in the nearby town of
Ai, the setback was rapidly attributed to the 'sin' of Achan who, the
scripture stresses, had brought down divine retribution on the whole
nation through his conduct. God's displeasure was made clear.
'Israel hath sinned and they have also transgressed my covenant
which I commanded them: for they have even taken of the accursed
thing, and have also stolen, and dissembled also, and they have put
it even among their own stuff.'[26] For this crime, and in order to
bring atonement, Achan and his entire family were stoned to death.
God, we are told, then instructed Joshua to attack a second time, on
this occasion with a guarantee of success. A similar situation arose
when Saul failed to obey God's command to 'utterly destroy' the
Amalekite population, including all of its possessions. Saul chose to
spare the life of the Amalekite king, Agag, and to preserve much of
the captured livestock, for which transgression against the command
of total obliteration he was allegedly punished by his own
destruction at the hands of David.

It is possible to discern a clear change of mood in God's
pronouncements to his chosen people as Israelite history progresses
through expansion and comparative stability to decline and
disintegration. Unlike the message of the Qur'ān, which is fairly
consistent on the subject of religious violence, that of the Old
Testament ends less in a spirit of jingoism than with a whimper of
contrition. When the Babylonians vanquished Judah, the biblical
writers interpreted the destruction wrought upon Jerusalem as an
act of divine punishment for the sins of the strongly pagan Judahite
ruler Manasseh, who had taken over the reins of power from his
father, the reformist and Yahwist king Hezekiah, in 687 BCE. 'Surely
at the commandment of the Lord came this upon Judah, to remove
them out of his sight, for the sins of Manasseh.'[27]

The prophet Jeremiah made the point even more forcibly in the
context of a message allegedly delivered to Zedekiah, prior to the
Exile, by a thoroughly incandescent God. 'Behold I will turn back
the weapons of war that are in your hands, wherewith ye fight
against the kings of Babylon, and against the Chaldeans, which

besiege you without the walls, and I will assemble them into the midst of this city. And I myself will fight against you with an outstretched hand and with a strong arm, even in anger and in fury, and in great wrath. And I will smite the inhabitants of this city, both man and beast; they shall die of a great pestilence.'[28]

Later Jewish rabbinical literature begins to dwell less on the sober view that the wrath of God has been visited on the Israelites on account of their own failings, and its tone changes to one of new hope for divine intervention on behalf of the Jewish people at sometime in the future. There is now a profound anticipation of a day of final judgement when the God of Israel will intercede and vanquish those who have oppressed his people, whether deservedly or not. The message, allegedly delivered through the apocalyptic dreams of visionaries such as Enoch, is that divine strength will eventually empower Israel once more to victory. Although attributed to Enoch, the son of Jared, the work is probably a compilation of the writings of various authors during the second and first centuries BCE at a time when Greater Judaea had come under the yoke of the Roman occupation forces and when the Jewish people were looking somewhat desperately for redemption. 'In those days the angels will assemble and thrust themselves to the east at the Parthians and Medes. They will shake up the kings. A spirit of unrest shall come upon them, and stir them up from their thrones; and they will break forth from their beds like lions and like hungry hyenas among their own flocks, and they will go up and trample upon the land of my elect ones, and the land of my elect ones shall be like a threshing floor or a highway. But the city of my righteous ones will become an obstacle to their horses. And they shall begin to fight among themselves and by their own right hands they shall prevail against themselves.'[29]

So much for the sanguinary Old Testament and its pseudepigrapha; a more controversial issue, and one that has never been satisfactorily resolved, is whether the New Testament contains divine pronouncements that sanction violence. Did Jesus support violent overthrow of the Roman occupation? We have to remember that he was tried and convicted on charges brought by the colonial

Roman government, which executed him for the specific crime of sedition, albeit egged on by the Jewish community.[30] More than one statement contained in the orthodox New Testament supports the claim of violent intent. When the twelve disciples were given their instructions prior to being sent out into the wider world, Jesus warned them that he was willing to wield the sword, and the term 'sword' is often used in the Bible as a euphemism for war: 'Whosoever shall deny me before men, him will I also deny before my father which is in heaven. Think not that I am come to send peace on earth: I came not to send peace but a sword. For I am come to set a man at variance against his father, and daughter against her mother, and the daughter-in-law against her mother-in-law.'[31] A similar prophetic utterance is recorded in the Gospel according to Luke: 'Suppose ye that I come to give peace on earth? I tell you, Nay, but rather division.'[32] This warning is repeated, in stronger terms, in the apocryphal Gospel of Thomas: 'Jesus said, Men might think that it is peace that I have come to impose on the world but they do not know that it is dissension I have come to cast on the earth: fire, sword, war.'[33] That Jesus was occasionally willing to condone aggressive behaviour is also evident from the incident recorded in Matthew 21:12 when he forcibly overturned tables and drove the moneychangers from the Temple in Jerusalem. Those who object to the argument that Jesus supported violence point to another key statement in Matthew: 'I say unto you, Love your enemies, bless them that curse you, and do good to them that hate you.'[34]

The Qur'ān generally echoes Old Testament attitudes towards violent defence and attack, though not in the same degree. During the early development of Islam, the delivery of the message of Allah and his prophet Muhammad was taken on by the various religious leaders, the ulemas in the Sunni sect and the ayatollahs among the Shi'ites. A familiar message emerges that allies and foes, saints and sinners, are to be judged according to their religious persuasion. 'Believers take neither the Jews nor the Christians for your friends. They are friends with one another. Whoever of you seeks their friendship shall become one of their number. Allah does not guide the wrongdoers.'[35] The Qur'ān makes plain that Jews and Christians have disobeyed the commandments of a universal God. Jews are singled out for corrupting the scriptures and Christians for worshipping Jesus as the Son of God contrary to divine commandments. All who have gone astray must therefore be brought back to the true religion.[36] For the unrepentant infidel there is only one justifiable consequence, no less severe than that ordained by Yahweh. 'Those that make war against Allah and his apostle (Muhammad) and spread disorder in the land shall be slain or crucified or have their hands and feet cut off on alternate sides, or be banished from the land.'[37]

The scattered sections of the Qur'ān that touch on violence are known as the War Verses, and they often appear markedly contradictory so that one demands restraint and the next total war. The second book, or Sura, of the Qur'ān, entitled Al-Baqarah (The Cow), instructs Muslims ambiguously in this way. It does not echo the recurrent message in the Bible that pre-emptive strikes are the favoured option, but still suggests that any and all who do not respond to the call of Islam may be regarded as aggressors against Allah and open to violent retaliation. Slaughtering idolators is all right! 'Fight for the sake of God those that fight against you, but do not attack them first. God does not love aggressors. Slay them wherever you find them. Drive them out of the places from which they drove you. Idolatry is more grievous than bloodshed. But do not fight them within the precincts of the Holy Mosque unless they attack you there; if they attack you put them to the sword. Thus shall unbelievers be rewarded; but if they mend their ways, know that God is forgiving and merciful. Fight against them until idolatry is no more and God's religion reigns supreme. But if they desist, fight none except the evil doers.'[38]

Similar sentiment is expressed elsewhere in the qur'ānic scriptures. 'Make peace between them [the protagonists], but if one persists in aggression against the other, fight the aggressors until they revert to God's commandment.'[39] A similar theme is taken up in the chapter entitled The Prophets, namely that mercy is somewhat dependent on religious persuasion. 'If only the unbelievers knew the day when they shall strive in vain to shield their faces and backs from the fire of Hell; the day when none shall help them! Indeed it will overtake them unawares and stupefy them . . . Have they other gods to defend them? Their idols shall be powerless over their own salvation, nor shall they be protected from our scourge.'[40]

The Qur'ān differs markedly in tone from the later texts of the Old Testament because of the different historical experiences of the two cultures. Biblical Judaism ended in a succession of defeats and finally disintegration, whereas Islam at the time of Muhammad's death was set on a programme of vigorous expansion. Nonetheless, Islamic scholars tend to agree that the qur'ānic attitude to conflict can be traced through a number of stages indicating that God delivered instructions to Muhammad responding to the changing situations confronting him. The first of these instructions probably reflects the period when the followers of Muhammad were living in the once-hostile surroundings of Mecca. It is thoroughly muted in tone and implies that any violence towards infidels or breakaway sects remains a matter for the future. 'We will surely punish the schismatics, who have broken up the scriptures into separate parts, believing in some and denying others. By the Lord we will question them all about their doings. Proclaim, then, what you are bidden and let the idolators be. We will ourselves sustain you against those that mock you and serve other deities besides God. They shall learn.'[41]

By the time that Muhammad's followers had escaped from Mecca and completed the Hegira, or journey, to the more congenial setting of Medina, the message becomes more forthright and God sanctions fighting as a means of defence. 'Permission to take up arms is hereby given to those who are attacked, because they have been wronged. God has the power to grant them victory: those who have been unjustly driven from their homes, only because they said: "Our Lord is God".'[42]

As Muslim power increased, the tone was destined to turn more aggressive, and eventually it becomes all-encompassing. 'Proclaim a woeful punishment to the unbelievers, except to those idolators who have honoured their treaties with you in every detail and aided none against you. With these keep faith, until their treaties have run their term. When the sacred months are over slay the idolators wherever you find them. Arrest them, besiege them and lie in ambush everywhere for them.'[43] These words are said to have been the most frequently cited among the War Verses, and are claimed by some fundamentalist Muslims to abrogate not less than 124 other qur'ānic verses of more forgiving disposition.[44]

Jewish, Christian and Islamic scriptures probably contain the bulk of godly utterances justifying war, but they are not alone. Similar sentiments are to be found in sacred Hindu literature, but this is a religion wherein the cult image is still central to devotion, and so the word of the god assumes a far less prominent position. Divine opinion on the subject of violence emerges most notably in the *Bhagavadgita*. This remarkable text is inserted in the narrative of the epic and exceptionally bloody story of *Mahabharata* just before the outbreak of a decisive battle at Kurukshetra between two clans fighting for control of a kingdom. But an exhortation to fight is interposed not so much as a divine command, rather a brief lecture delivered for the benefit of those questioning the morality of aggression. The *Bhagavadgita* is a brilliantly constructed address to Arjuna, the hero of the story, by Krishna, the mortal incarnation of the creator god Vishnu in his guise as a charioteer. Faced with the prospect of killing his fellow man, Arjuna throws away his weapons, but Krishna urges him to battle, telling him that it is unmanly not to fight here and now. It is only when Arjuna continues to delay that Krishna responds as a guru who would instruct his disciple. Wisdom, he tells Arjuna, consists in realisation that the atman, the soul of man, the divine core of his personality, is permanent, while the body is doomed to die and there is therefore no reason to grieve for the living or dead. 'One man believes he is the slayer, another believes he is the slain. Both are ignorant; there is neither slayer nor slain. You were never born; you will never die. You have never changed, you can never change. Unborn, eternal, immutable, immemorial, you do not die when the body dies. Realising that which is indestructible, eternal, unborn and unchanging, how can you slay or cause another to slay?'[45]

In a brilliant survey of Hinduism, Klaus Klostermaier points out that this rationale assists us in getting rid of guilt feelings about fighting a war by suggesting the violent killing of another remains on the periphery of reality, in the sphere of change and death that is inevitable.[46] The underlying logic found in the Bible and the Qur'ān is nonetheless also present. Krishna tells Arjuna that for a Kshatriya, a military leader, there is no greater good than engaging in a just war following the rules of dharma, the law that expresses and sustains the unity of creation. For the warrior to fight for what is right against what is wrong opens the door to heaven. But to abrogate one's duty to engage in such essential conflict is shameful and cowardly. Risk in war, Krishna tells his disciple, is preferable to abstention from war. 'Death means the attainment of heaven; victory means the enjoyment of the earth. Therefore rise up, Arjuna, resolved to fight! Having made yourself alike in pain and pleasure, profit and loss, victory and defeat, engage in this great battle and you will be freed from sin.'[47]

There is a good argument that any notion we may have of receiving instruction about our actions from God amounts to a kind of predestiny. It is all out of our hands; we are merely obeying a higher authority. This takes away any sense of moral discipline. At a trivial level it is one of the objections to fortune-telling. But it is also one of the greatest problems in dealing with the current spate of religious terrorism. Religious fanatics become indoctrinated with the certainty that predatory and violent behaviour in this world is directed, not by their own will, but by a higher presence. God-given orders to fight included in scriptures many centuries past and in wholly different circumstances might appear to bear little relevance to a modern context, but they are known to have triggered terrorist attacks and more structured forms of aggression. Many of the most brutal slayings, in and out of war, have been carried out on the strength of being told by God to go out and kill someone. Persons and social movements engaged in religious conflict have gained a sense that their destinies are governed by the will of God and that warfare on behalf of God is an expression of godly power. Violence renders divine judgement, and this is one of the elements that make religious ideology so potent in the world, not only yesterday but also today.

The influence of scripture on fundamentalist Muslims is self-evident, but perhaps less so its impact on the Christian militants of yesterday and today. The so-called Song of Moses claims that the Yahwist divinity is a war god: 'The Lord is a man of war: the Lord is his name.'[48] This brief passage has been seized on as justification for violence in the name of religion down the centuries. Whether or not blood actually flowed to the degree claimed in the Old Testament books of Deuteronomy and Joshua is slightly irrelevant. Of more profound importance to humanity, some of those who believe the Bible stands as the absolute and irrefutable word of God have taken the commandment of anathema, or herem, total destruction, to be binding upon themselves. It drove them to the vicious extremes of the Christian Crusades, and little has changed since. During the 1980s era of militant sectarianism in the Bible Belt of the United States the Arkansas-based Christian Identity leader Kerry Noble relayed the message to his followers congregated in the compound of the so-called Covenant, the Sword, and the Arm of the Lord situated near Branson, Missouri. Noble relied on the Old Testament to justify his actions by arguing that because God was a 'man of war' who took vengeance on his enemies, and the Bible, the immutable word of God said so, the followers of the Christian Army of God were entitled to do the same.[49]

The Christian Identity compound was broken up during an FBI raid that began on 19 April 1985, but one of Noble's followers, Richard Snell, continued to take the battle cry literally as a mandate for violence. Snell was subsequently implicated in the slaying of a Texacarna, Arkansas, pawnshop owner in the mistaken belief that he was Jewish. Earlier Snell had also killed a black Arkansas state trooper who had stopped him for a traffic violation. On conviction he was executed by lethal injection.[50] Another of Noble's former colleagues, Bob Matthews, implicated in the slaying of a Jewish radio talk-show host, issued a statement from his hideout that he and his religious associates were in 'a full and unremitting state of war' against the US Government. At about the same time a spokesman for Christian Identity emphasised that its authority for aggressive action rested in holy scripture. He declared the Bible to be 'a book of war, a book of hate'.[51]

Today the official Internet website of Christian Identity reveals that it is an ultranationalist right-wing sectarian movement active in several countries. In the UK its home-page opening rant declares: 'Immigration is a race hate weapon of mass destruction – our government is destroying us for the new world satanic order.' Turning to the section headed 'What we believe', the Christian Identity website provides the inquirer with the uncompromising message that,

It's all in the Bible that the Jews are the children of the devil (John 8:44). We are dedicated to saving our white race and our nation from the evils of multi-racialism, and the promotion of interbreeding, which destroys our God-given Identity and hands control of our people to the evil of globalism . . . God tells us that eventually Satan and his globalists will become dominant but their triumph will be short-lived; then those of us who have resisted will be rescued from multi-racial hell – but only those who have not mixed their race.

THREE

Persecution

The violent behaviour taking place at the turn of the third millennium in the Middle East in demonstration of Islamic fundamentalism, and in the United States among militant born-again Christians, is only the most recent turn in a process that can be traced from the beginning of Christian history, and exhibits a marked similarity to that seen in various other world belief systems. Aggression of the kind that affects religious movements tends to follow a pattern, passing through a predictable series of stages by way of interaction with the wider world and within the movements themselves. These stages can be labelled, albeit simplistically, as inspiration, formalisation, expansion, consolidation, stagnation and decline. And they may occur more than once. The religion of Judaism has arisen again from the ashes and Israel has regained a national identity. Christian fundamentalism is re-emergent in Bible Belt America. We may consider that old-style pantheism is dead and buried aside from the romantic ideals of neo-pagans, but it is worth remembering that Adolf Hitler dreamed of a 1,000-year Third Reich modelled on the old Aryan religious purity of Odin and the gods of Asgard, to the extent that his guardian storm troopers were depicted on the walls of the Berlin bunker carrying the weapons of the ancient Valkyrie.

Inspiration and formalisation of a religion rarely includes displays of violent behaviour stemming from within. If aggression occurs it is generally levelled by a third party at those defending the new religious movement. The violence amounts to a knee-jerk reaction from the conservative establishment in which the new pioneering faith has begun to make its presence felt. Secular or otherwise, the one takes umbrage at the other. In early Jewish history it was the

47

indigenous clans of Palestine that took the umbrage and instigated the persecution of the pioneering Hebrews, but Jewish history then became a roller coaster of conquest and subjection. It is probably fair to say that little is known of biblical Israel at peace, and the historical books of the Old Testament read as a more or less unremitting military campaign. The prophet Samuel set the terms of the Israelite kingship very clearly, when he decreed of future rulers: 'This will be the manner of the king that shall reign over you: He will take your sons, and appoint them for himself, for his chariots and to be his horsemen; and some shall run before his chariots. And he will appoint his captains over thousands, and captains over fifties, and will set them to ear his ground and to reap his harvest, and to make his instruments of war, and instruments of his chariots', 1 Samuel 8: 11–12. From the moment of Saul's accession, Israel was a nation at war, first against the Ammonites, then the Philistines and many others who stood in its path.

But in the early period of the nation's history the wandering Hebrews who eventually merged into a federation of twelve Israelite tribes had, in fact, gone through a long and comparatively peaceable formative period. It is easy to miss the extended time element in the earliest prehistorical period of the country. Abraham's clansmen first entered Palestine from the north-east towards the start of the third millennium, and then, slowly developing an allegiance to their universal God, they wandered extensively as the many place names to be found in Genesis reveal.

In order to gain any impression of the sequence of Israelite migration and conquest we are heavily reliant on the Hebrew Bible. But we risk falling into a trap if we take much of what it contains at anything approaching face value or as an objective history. As we have already established, the first five books, the Pentateuch, purport to be a narrative of events that took place before anyone chose to commit them to writing, certainly long before the date of the earliest compilations that we have before us today. The text is a transmission of earlier but now lost material, and, as the original manuscripts were copied and recopied, they will have been subject to adaptation and reformulation, not to mention unforced error, by strings of redactors and compilers. We should not assume that the account of an event or a biographical detail is bona fide simply because it claims to come from a relatively early but no longer surviving literary source. Even if we accept that a narration is reasonably accurate, some scholars maintain the principle that all narrative amounts to a literary artefact because it imposes a structure, coherence and meaning on events that those events do not possess when related as a mere sequence.[1]

We know with reasonable certainty that the events portrayed in the Pentateuch are not chronologically accurate and that various later editors assembled chapters and books made up of disparate 'windows'. More often than not the intention appears to have been to promote a politically convenient story rather than an accurate history. It is generally accepted today, for example, that in the south more than one exodus took place from Egypt and that it was only after the final northbound migration through the Negev Desert, mainly involving the tribe of Levi, that the 'religion of Moses' became consolidated. The chain of events cannot have taken place as described in Exodus because the fall of Jericho took place much earlier than the Exodus, at sometime close to 1400 BCE, when nomadic Hebrew tribes from the eastern frontiers were making ever-deeper incursions into the arable regions of Transjordan. It must have been these tribal groups that staged the assault on Jericho, but a politically slanted Judahite version of events has come down to us by way of the Old Testament, and this tends to be loaded in favour of the southern view of history. Exodus narrates that the famous trek headed by Moses opened the way into the 'Promised Land', but it actually took place perhaps as late as 1194 BCE and did not enter Canaan directly – Egypt maintained strong defences along the southern borders – but instead adopted a flanking approach via Transjordan.[2]

During a drawn-out period prior to the mid-second century BCE the Hebrews were probably subjected to comparatively little persecution and any assaults that did take place were not on account of their religious beliefs. Even the Egyptian hosts with whom the southern tribes had initially sought refuge did not treat them unusually badly other than to make them work under conditions of forced labour on state building projects. The trigger that launched the nomadic Hebrews in a bid to change their lifestyles and discover a permanent homeland in Syrio-Palestine was the collapse of the existing political order in Western Asia during the thirteenth century BCE. Hitherto the power-brokers sparring for control had been the Egyptians in the south-west and the Hittites (Hattusas) in the north. But when the Pharaoh Amenhotep IV (1369–1353 BCE) quarrelled with the powerful Amon priesthood in favour of the sun god Aten, changing his name to Akhenaten as a mark of his conviction, the Egyptian 18th Dynasty fell into disarray and with it pharaonic colonial power evaporated for a time, a state of affairs that was set to continue into the 19th Dynasty. In the north the influence of the Hittite hegemony was also on the wane prior to its total collapse in about 1200 BCE. The struggle between Egypt and Hattusas had reached a climax during the reign of Ramesses II (1290–1224 BCE) with the battle for Kadesh, the ancient city south of Emesa on the Orontes. Although Ramesses II claimed victory of sorts, another sixteen years of costly skirmishing took place before a peace treaty could be negotiated with the Hittites in 1269 BCE, and in reality the conflict had been a near disaster for the Egyptian forces. Palestine thus descended into a state of lawless anarchy. Travellers in the region were obliged for their own safety to keep to obscure secondary routes, and caravans faced mortal dangers from marauding gangs. It was during this time that the Hebrews chose their moment and escaped from Egypt via the Red Sea, although there is scholarly argument over whether the Exodus took place during the reign of Ramesses II, Seti II or Ramesses III, the last of the imperial pharaohs. The Israelite trek was, however, merely one facet of the more general upheavals going on.[3]

It was during this long period of transition that those fermenting ideas about loyalty to a single deity took root among the tribes and became a cohesive influence, strengthened especially by the experience of those who had emigrated from Egypt. There remains fierce argument over whether the universal deity announced by

Akhenaten, earning such opprobrium from his people, influenced the tribes, but Hebrews were in Egypt at the time and Aten preceded Yahweh.

The Exodus of some of the Hebrews from Egypt northwards, probably during the reign of Ramesses II early in the thirteenth century, was merely one movement in what amounted to a wholesale migration of peoples in various directions. Their first real adversaries were the Philistines, who had arrived in the Palestine region along with a mêlée of other migrants in the thirteenth or early twelfth century BCE, most of whom were making an opportunist drive south towards the Egyptian frontier. The Philistines settled the area of the Canaanite coast probably shortly after the Exodus. But at that time the Israelites were scarcely in a position to fight on behalf of God or anyone else. Reminiscing on Israel's nomadic past the Song of Deborah and Barak reminds its listeners of a time when 'They [the people of Israel] chose new gods; then was war in the gates: was there a shield or spear seen among forty thousand in Israel?'[4] Because they were largely unarmed their encounters with the Philistines (from whose name 'Palestine' comes) and with other raiders from the north and east involved the Hebrews in hit-and-run tactics. They could not attack any of the larger conurbations because they had no siege weapons and had to rely on tricks and subterfuge. Philistine forces on the other hand possessed iron weapons, chariots and heavy armour, and so were easily able to repel assaults. Matters reached a crisis point when the Israelites were defeated at Aphek and lost the Ark of the Covenant to the enemy. 'And the Philistines fought, and Israel was smitten, and they fled every man into his tent: and there was a very great slaughter; for there fell of Israel thirty thousand footmen. And the ark of God was taken.'[5]

The Ark of the Covenant was a portable chest made of acacia wood, the precise construction of which is said to have been to God's specific instruction. It contained various cultic articles and is believed to have served as the meeting place between God and Israel. According to the description in Exodus the chest was decorated with two guardian cherubim facing one another with spread wings.

The symbolic space between them became known as the 'mercy seat', from which an unseen God administered judgement. The unmitigated disaster of losing its most sacred national object became the principal catalyst for the rise of Israel's monarchy.[6]

From that point on the strategy changed from defensive to offensive, although there is, at face value, a slightly topsy-turvy sequence of behaviour in that aggression mounted against the Israelites recurred after their period of expansion and has continued in a manner not seen in the histories of the other two faiths, Christianity and Islam. This is explained in part, however, by the fact that the military history of Syria and Palestine represents a continuous chain of conquests and oppression directed by various powers against the local populations. Until recently these wars were not fought on religious grounds but fed the secular ambitions of would-be conquerors, each wanting to enhance their personal status.[7]

The founding fathers of the Christian movement trod a similar early path in relations with the broader swathe of society, which in the Christian context meant Rome. Christianity did not arise in an incandescent blaze of glory and a clash of arms. By the end of its first century of life it is probably fair to say that most of the inhabitants of the Roman Empire neither knew nor cared a great deal about what was only the latest among a hotchpotch of sects in various stages of life, from the wholly untested to the time-honoured. Two of the more prolific social writers of the time, Martial and Juvenal, make no clearly defined reference to the new religion, though Martial in his *Epigrams* derides Jews and Judaism, while Juvenal adopts much the same tone in his *Satires*. The writings of the prominent theological author Plutarch contain many parallels with early Christian doctrine, yet he too ignores the Christians. Perhaps the most striking omission among near-contemporary writers is that of Cassius Dio. As late as the 230s CE he managed to complete a massive eighty-volume history of Rome without a single mention of the Christians, although the omission may have been contrived because he names a certain Gaius Cilnius Maecenas as recommending the persecution of 'religious innovators'.

The significance of bringing Maecenas into the discussion is that he lived immediately prior to the time of Christ, between about 63 and 8 BCE, serving as friend and adviser to the Emperor Augustus and in particular being entrusted with the maintenance of law and order in Rome. Clearly Maecenas cannot have given his advice to Augustus with an eye on the Christians, but it is difficult to see why Cassius Dio would have included this particular comment, albeit anachronistically, unless alluding to the sect, since few of the pagan cults at that time, old or new, could be described as innovative.[8]

Imperial Romans tended to view Christians as another eccentric sect in a city already heaving with cults of every description. For as long as they did not cause trouble Christians could technically be left alone, and prior to Nero's purge in 64 CE the chief opposition to them came from disaffected Jews. Nonetheless, for a welter of reasons the Christians were destined to become the future objects of suspicion in the eyes of the Roman authorities. This was not because the religious ideals they espoused were especially new, but because they were potentially threatening to the stability of Rome. The Christian founder had been tried and convicted on charges of sedition against the Empire, crucified under the title 'King of the Jews', a capital punishment reserved under Roman law for non-Roman citizens found guilty of insurrection against the state.[9] Christians refused to take up either military or civil-service positions, which did not go down well with the authorities and laid them open to accusations of disloyalty. They were also viewed by many Romans as being inextricably linked with the Jews, whose ability to cause trouble was already well known, and who, in Rome's eyes, amounted to a notoriously ill-behaved rabble, their obsessive and frequently fanatical Zealots bent on launching guerrilla strikes as and when the opportunity arose. It is often asked why the Romans persecuted the Jews far less for their faith (as distinct from their ability to make a nuisance of themselves) in the early Christian era, even though, unlike the Christians, they had been responsible for engaging Rome in three major wars, the last one ending in the destruction of Jerusalem in 135 CE. In short the reason lay with Rome's respect for most of the ancient forms of religion. That of the Jews conformed to 'statutory requirements'. Synagogues and the Jewish style of worship were familiar and fairly open, and thus did not pose any hidden threat to Rome's political stability, while the manner in which Christians came together in private houses and practised their strange new faith was mysterious and sinister. Thus Christians became objects of hostility because of their novel religious ideas, while Jews were generally tolerated as long as they remained peaceable.[10]

What really agitated the Roman authorities, however, was the persistent refusal of the Christians to perform pagan sacrifice to the gods of Rome, coupled with their impertinence in proclaiming a kingdom other than that of Caesar. It has sometimes been claimed that they were victimised because they refused to accept the Emperor as a divinity, but scholars of biblical history claim that Emperor-worship in itself was a factor of almost no importance in the persecution of Christians. Only occasionally were they arraigned when, as part of their refusal to participate in the cult act, they also declined to worship the 'Genius' of the Emperor.[11] Christian religious ideals in favour of monotheism, and therefore against the pantheon of divinities that protected Rome and maintained her greatness, amounted to a clear leaning towards political insurrection. The New Testament book of the Revelation of John, composed towards the end of the first century, confirmed some of the worst suspicions. Fulminating against Rome and its evil empire in barely disguised terms, the writer depicted Rome unflatteringly as the beast and the harlot. Although the author identified Babylon, Rome was palpably the object of vilification. 'And the woman was arrayed in purple and scarlet colour, and decked with gold and precious stones and pearls, having a golden cup in her hand full of abominations and filthiness of her fornication . . . and I saw the woman drunken with the blood of the saints, and with the blood of the martyrs of Jesus.'[12]

In some sections the work was seen to amount to such an out-and-out expression of hostility that it positively discouraged the Roman authorities from treating the Christians charitably.[13] In one sense or another Christian loyalty to Rome came to appear highly questionable, and between periods of comparative harmony the Christian community was destined to fall victim to a spate of violent persecutions.[14] This was a somewhat unusual reaction. By and large Rome was tolerant of religious sects, following the logic that the more gods it welcomed, the greater the divine protection.

The first definite assault on individual Christians came during the reign of the Emperor Nero. It is generally accepted that Nero was keen to exploit the Christians in Rome as convenient scapegoats to draw attention away from his own mounting unpopularity. According to the Roman historian Tacitus, compiling his *Annals* of the period between 14 and 68 CE, published several decades after the reign of Nero, the general populace of Rome by that time detested the new sectarians, whom they regarded as the immoral enemies of the entire human race. After the great fire of Rome was ignited in 64 CE Nero blamed Christians for arson, and this official version of culpability gained widespread acceptance. Tacitus himself, although not enamoured of the Christians, actually remained sceptical about their involvement,[15] and the fact that Christians rather than Jews were the selected target of accusation may, on this occasion, have been down to the intervention of the Empress Poppaea Sabina, who was openly sympathetic towards the city's Jewish community.[16] Nero mounted a vicious purge that resulted in the summary execution of Peter and Paul, two of the leading Christian figures. Paul was singled out, almost certainly by Jewish agitators, and labelled with conduct 'contrary to Caesar', which translated as activities rebellious against Rome's protecting gods. Although as a Roman citizen he fell back on a statutory right of appeal, the plea was rejected, and his sentencing marked the first occasion on which the death penalty was meted out to self-confessed Christians.[17]

Peter and Paul were not the first martyrs to their Christian convictions; that honour goes to Stephen. However, Stephen was tried for blasphemy and executed by stoning on the orders of the Jewish Sanhedrin because, as a staunch Hellenist, he had criticised the people of Israel for their failure to live up to God's expectations as his chosen flock. Christian martyrdom in the face of state oppression thus effectively began with Peter and Paul, and a general acceptance soon arose that violent death as an extreme demonstration of faith and atonement brought grace and assured a place in paradise. The most steadfast Christians in the early Church were thus neither the virgins nor the visionaries but those members whom pagans executed because they refused to honour pagan gods.[18]

Many people tend to assume that Islam was the first faith to practise martyrdom to any great extent, but in reality it had become an expression of extreme and fanatical devotion long before even the Christian era. In Rome generations of followers of the goddess Kybele, emulating the personal sacrifice of manhood made by the god Attis, had castrated themselves and often bled to death during the infamous Day of Blood celebrated each year on 22 March. It was, however, with the Jewish and Christian communities labouring under Roman domination that the concept of immortal martyrdom, and the heavenly rewards that ensued, first took root. It had developed comparatively late in Jewish history, but for Christians, with their strong interest in eschatology, or life beyond the grave, it was a driving element from the outset.

After Nero the next period of victimisation by the authorities on religious grounds came towards the end of the first century during the reign of Domitian (81–96), who styled himself 'Master and God', a choice of title that did not augur well for anyone other than pantheists. Anticipating that Jews and Christians were likely to resist a decree to venerate him as a divinity, members of Domitian's court instructed that Jews were to be hunted down and inspected physically for circumcision, the clearest outward sign of their faith. This also presented a risk for the many Christians who lived with telltale evidence of having once been Jews. Large numbers of both communities were slaughtered around 94 CE according to a source that was preserved by Christian chroniclers, the so-called History of Bruttius. This was a pagan work generally thought attributable to Bruttius Praesens, a friend of Pliny the Younger who served as a military commander in the eastern legions.

The crisis triggered indirectly by Domitian was short-lived, however, because his successor, Trajan, adopted a more tolerant attitude and, in response to a letter from Pliny the Younger in about 110 CE that Christians were to be found among people of 'every rank, age and sex', Trajan even issued a much-quoted instruction that 'The Christians are not to be hunted down.' Trajan had appointed Pliny as governor to the province of Bithynia Pontus, where he had the responsibility to sit in judgement on people accused of being Christians. His attitude was to punish those who admitted following Christian teachings on the reasoning that their obstinacy in rejecting the traditional gods of Rome deserved to be punished, but he was less certain about what to do with lapsed Christians, who could also be found guilty of a capital crime. Punishment was meted out not only to those confessing their faith, but also those who had publicly apostatised. Pliny the Younger described charges in the latter category as 'offences attached to the name'.[19] It was hence from 112 CE onwards that the Roman authorities punished Christians specifically for 'being Christian', a detail confirmed by second- and early third-century apologists including Justin, who was himself destined for martyrdom.[20] Trajan, however, affirmed that if a defendant arraigned for having once been Christian performed an offering to the pagan gods, there and then before witnesses in the court of law, he or she could be acquitted. For his part Pliny did a great service to the Christian community by investigating widespread rumours among pagan Romans that the sect's members practised a lurid range of immoral acts, and deciding that the allegations were without foundation.[21]

During the reign of Hadrian (117–38) the anti-Christian mood in the empire softened for a while and a number of Greek writers were even willing to come out publicly against pagan propaganda. The years between 161 and 190 CE, however, witnessed another spate of anti-Christian sentiment during the reign of Marcus Aurelius. Having been brought up in a strictly conservative Stoic pagan family and groomed into an abhorrence of Christianity by his tutor Fronto, he became Emperor at a time when the might of Rome was being harassed on all sides by barbarians, and, from his point of view, the

Christian sect was just another fringe rabble denying the gods that had ensured Rome's prosperity for generations. There is also strong circumstantial evidence that Fronto, acknowledged as an eminent writer in his day, was willing to embellish already lurid reports of secret Christian conduct. No copies of his literary polemic *Against Pelops* have survived, but it is believed to have contained details of alleged ritual murders by Christian groups.[22] The evidence comes from a Christian apologist named Athenagoras, who compiled a *Plea on Behalf of the Christians* specifically refuting the charges and presented it to Marcus Aurelius personally when he visited Athens in 176 CE.[23] During Marcus Aurelius' reign another influential writer, Apuleius, also did much to fuel anti-Christian passions among Romans. He set his famous novel *Metamorphoses*, better known as *The Golden Ass*, in Greece but drew one of its villains, the wife of the baker who purchased the hero, as a Christian described as 'the wickedest of women'.

In about 177 CE one of the most notorious early massacres of Christians took place at Lyons and Vienne, with at least fifty being executed. A rampaging mob dragged its victims into the forum, where a public interrogation took place before the city authorities, after which the Christians were incarcerated awaiting the arrival of the regional governor. On consultation with Marcus Aurelius it was agreed that those who recanted would be set free, but few did so and the punishment of the rest was truly horrific. Among those that survived the intense overcrowding in the prison, the deacon Sanctus of Vienne, plus Matturus, Attalus and a slave girl named Blandina are recorded in the *Acts of the Martyrs* as having been singled out for the most severe forms of torture. Having been put through a series of physical ordeals they were led into the arena, where they were exposed to wild beasts and then placed in a particularly unpleasant device known as the 'iron seat', which was heated to a temperature at which it was designed to roast the flesh of victims. Blandina was later crucified and finally placed in a net in which she was repeatedly gored by a bull. The bodies were put on display for six days before being incinerated and swept into the River Rhône so that no trace remained.

After these outrages the latter part of the second century was mostly uneventful for the Christians until another spate of persecutions took place between 193 and 211 CE during the reign of Septimius Severus. This coincided with a time when the empire was largely in the hands of non-Roman administrators and when the Church had become progressively stronger. Writing from Carthage in 197 the patriarch Tertullian insisted that the Christian community, now established in every corner of Roman society, should be treated as a respectable corporation conducting its business much as a Roman curia would do.[24] In about 202 CE, however, Septimius, worried that Christianity threatened to become an empire within an empire unless discouraged, issued an edict forbidding proselytism on the part of both Christians and Jews. With the exception of North Africa the ruling was largely observed, but in Alexandria in 203 CE seven prominent Christians suffered martyrdom, and later in the same year the church in Carthage was attacked. One of the victims there was a free and well-educated woman named Perpetua, who is believed to have been the author of the first part of the *Acts of the Martyrs*, much of which reads as an eyewitness account. Prior to execution, her personal slave Felicitas accompanied her to prison and would give birth during their mutual incarceration. In the second part of the *Acts*, probably compiled by the Bishop of Carthage, Tertullian, there is a graphic record of how the sight of Felicitas being led naked into the arena, to be attacked by wild animals before having her throat slit, briefly horrified the crowd when it realised that her breasts were dripping with milk. Tertullian was to maintain his theme of 'Christians in every stratum', and in 212 CE he penned a somewhat waspish letter to the proconsul Scapula, warning that if he continued to execute Christians he would decimate his own entourage. The persecutions under Septimius amounted to the first carried out by official edict, but they also heralded a generation of peace.[25]

The accounts of suffering by early Christian martyrs are undoubtedly graphic and gruesome. But their inclusion demonstrates that Christianity was conceived and went through its infancy in a framework of violence, and there are good arguments that in travelling to Jerusalem, where he knew that his fate would be sealed, Jesus Christ himself adopted the view that violent death was necessary as a supreme demonstration of faith. Many of the converts kept their faith to themselves, not prepared for this extreme measure, and during much of the first two Christian centuries it was risky openly to practise the faith. Early Christian thinking set the Church and the secular world apart, one from the other. The Church authorities distrusted and even hated most of what Imperial Rome stood for. Not surprisingly, therefore, the early bishops, established in the role of being spokesmen for the Christian community to the often-hostile authorities, came in for punishment and were not infrequently martyred along with their congregations, until, under the rule of Constantine, the sect gained imperial support and protection from persecution.

Although there were isolated exceptions, as in the reign of Septimius Severus, intolerance and outright violence towards Christians began to lessen from about 180 CE onwards. The writer Galen, who lived from about 133 to 200 CE, was critical of Jews and Christians alike, but he was also prepared to admire Christian steadfastness when faced by death. Their sense of justice appealed to him, as did the by-now acknowledged sexual restraint of their communities. In 250 CE there was, nevertheless, a renewed attempt to ring-fence Christian progress. The 1,000th anniversary of the founding of Rome had just been celebrated, though 'celebration' is a relative term because all the indications were that Rome was now facing a downhill slide in terms of moral corruption and the dilution of its former religious purity. Too many emperors of recent times had engaged in a love affair with Eastern wisdom and had tolerated increasing levels of syncretism. In an attempt to stop the rot, the newly crowned emperor Decius set out to compel all the inhabitants of the Roman Empire, with the notable exception of Jews, to sacrifice to the traditional pagan gods of Rome in order to safeguard the welfare of the state. Once more the climate hardly boded well for the health of Roman Christians. Decius was particularly concerned that Christians would foment disloyalty to the empire when it was threatened increasingly from beyond its borders.

His cause was also aided by a new visitation of the plague, which the pagan community could attribute to religious backsliding.

The outcome of Decius' policy was initially to weed out the Christian waverers but then to stiffen resistance. However, in some respects superstition worked in favour of the Christians and was to play its role in encouraging a final softening of attitude on the part of the state. When Decius was slain later in the same year during a fraught campaign against the Goths, he became the first Roman emperor to die in battle against a barbarian enemy on Roman soil. The news acted to swing public opinion around to the notion that the Christian God afforded better talismanic protection than did his traditional pagan counterparts. A few years later this regard was to be enhanced. Decius' successor Valerian also adopted a pro-pagan attitude, having become convinced that the Christians were shirking their responsibilities in defence of the empire. He confiscated more Christian property and in 258 CE had the Bishop of Rome, Sixtus II, decapitated along with four of his deacons as he sat in his episcopal chair. Their felony had been in refusing to obey an injunction against congregating in the catacombs to celebrate Christian worship. But in 260 Valerian was captured by the Persians and died in captivity. In the minds of the public the efficacy of the Christian deity was now in little doubt, and Valerian's successor, Gallienus, was prudent enough to halt the persecutions.

The young Church settled into another relatively untroubled niche as a minority religion, growing in strength but considered by most politicians to be incapable of disrupting the empire or of ruffling the feathers of Rome's gods to any significant degree.[26] It was a measure of tolerance that prevailed for some forty-three years in the hands of a succession of largely unmemorable and short-duration emperors. Matters changed with the coming of Diocletian, another strongly conservative authoritarian. In the opinion of Diocletian, a military general from Africa, management of the empire had become sloppy and reforms were not only desirable but were well overdue. Meanwhile, the only Christian figure of note who managed to cause something of a minor stir was Paul of Samosata, a decidedly risqué individual who took the post of

Bishop of Antioch between 260 and 270 CE and who also earned the unlikely job of chancellor to Zenobia, the Queen of Palmyra. His Christian teachings, while popular, hardly conformed to anything approaching orthodoxy. Paul of Samosata, however, came and went with barely more than a ripple.

Diocletian's outlook was not necessarily anti-Christian, but he had an eye to restoring the religious unanimity of the past by bringing the peoples of his empire together in common worship of the old traditional gods. His accession as emperor in 284 CE heralded an anti-Christian purge that became known in 303 CE as the Great Persecution. Most of the pressure, however, came not from Diocletian but from his son-in-law Caesar Galerius, who had gained considerable influence after a decisive victory over the Persians in 298 CE. According to Eusebius, whose *History of the Church* covers the first three hundred years of Christendom and is the only surviving account from a contemporary Christian pen, Galerius would make the first tentative moves when he obliged Christian officers in the Roman army either to sacrifice or to leave the service.[27]

The conflict began and for a while progressed as a propaganda war, with intellectuals firing off verbal ripostes from both pagan and Christian sides. The pagan protagonists drew heavily on the opinions that had been set out by the Greek-speaking Platonist Celsus in his great work *The True Word*, thought to have been penned in about 178 CE in Alexandria. This was the first large-scale written polemic against the Christians, and it carried a strong impact, so much so that subsequently all known copies of it appear to have been confiscated and destroyed by the Church. Our knowledge of Celsus' arguments stems more or less exclusively from the pen of the Christian writer Origen. He compiled a massive refutation, *Contra Celsum*, quoting extensively from the original material. Notwithstanding Origen's condemnation, it is clear that Celsus was widely respected in his arguments because he had a thorough knowledge of Jewish and Christian scriptures.[28] His work included the claim that the Christian God possessed most of the human characteristics of cruelty and ruthlessness.[29] Celsus also dished up the old arguments that Christians had abandoned the true religion of Judaism and were a danger to society and state because of their fanatical adherence to an illegal association bound together by oaths that were no less unlawful.

Under Diocletian power had shifted from the senators of Rome to the army generals, and in recognition of this change he moved his court from Rome to Nicomedia in the east, where he could oversee defence of the empire's threatened frontiers from closer to hand. Diocletian split his administration into two wings, east and west. In the west he appointed Maximianus as his inferior counterpart with Constantius as an assisting Caesar, while in the east he appointed Galerius as his own right-hand man. In the winter of 302 CE Diocletian and Galerius were thus both in Nicomedia where, according to the chronicler Lactantius, writing in Nicomedia late in the fourth century, it was Galerius who pressed for a draconian disciplining of the wayward Christians. After initially resisting Galerius' demands, Diocletian is said to have consulted with the oracle of the Milesian Apollo, who responded with the words 'ut divinae religionis inimicus'. As so often with oracular utterances, this one is slightly obscure, but it implies that the gods were hostile towards the Christians. Diocletian then agreed on condition that the proposed repression did not involve bloodshed. Although the text of his formal edict has been lost and is not cited in the *Acts of the Martyrs*, scholars believe that it included orders to destroy churches and private houses known to be gathering places for Christian worship. Christian assemblies were banned; orders were issued that scriptures and liturgical books be handed over and burnt in town squares. Christians with any kind of rank were stripped of privileges and the sectarian community as a whole suddenly found itself outside the law, thus losing the right to a defence in court or immunity from torture. On 23 February 203 CE the physical onslaught against what was seen as Christian heresy began when imperial agents entered the cathedral at Nicomedia and commenced a systematic round of destruction. Diocletian placed the empire under the patronage of Jupiter and Heracles (represented on earth by Diocletian and his colleague Maximianus) and minted vast numbers of a coin known as the follis, a kind of poor man's currency made of copper and then plated thinly with silver. Its significance lay in the imagery on the reverse depicting Jupiter holding a sacrificial dish and in the accompanying inscription, 'to the Genius of the Roman people'.[30]

Matters might have been limited to destruction of property and removal of benefits had it not been for the outbreak of two fires in the imperial palace. Galerius, frustrated that countermeasures against the Christians had been far too soft, took a leaf from Nero's book and indicted them as the arsonists. Christian clergy were promptly rounded up, incarcerated, and offered two options: to recant and undertake pagan sacrifice, in which case they would be liberated, or to stick to their principles and be tortured to death. In one final act of idiotic desperation Diocletian ordered that even those Christians who did recant were to suffer the same fate. Even the staunchest of pagans blanched at this prospect and the policy was withdrawn. In 305 CE Diocletian and Maximianus both abdicated. Civil war erupted in the west, and, although in the east Galerius pressed on for a while with his conservative policies, his position became progressively weakened and he died of a particularly revolting illness, probably gangrene, in 311 CE. But one man who was to change Roman policy forever was waiting on the sidelines – the son of Constantius, Constantine.

With Constantine, state violence against the Christian community ended. For almost three centuries they had been victimised in the name of religion. It happened to be a pagan religion staffed by pagan gods, but religious jealousy and the potential power of religious devotion to upset the political apple cart was the *raison d'être* nonetheless. The radical problem for the Christians in their relations with their Roman masters rested in their view of a single universal God, which clashed with the already somewhat antiquated ideology that the Roman Emperor was a living divinity. In this the Romans had followed the traditions of much of the ancient Near East, especially of Egypt, but with religious adherence and the politics of the secular state already inextricable bedfellows in Rome, criticism of religious dogma amounted to criticism of the state. Back in the 60s Paul had recognised the dangers inherent in broadcasting the kind of aggravation inherent in denying the divinity of the Emperor when he instructed Christians that they must obey the orders of the empire and that Nero was 'God's minister', whose authority prevailed for everyday purposes.[31] Others did not and paid the supreme price, their deaths promptly idealised as martyrdoms.

This was not the time in the evolution of Christianity for its own aggressive potential to be unleashed, and during the formative period Christians are not known to have attacked their pagan enemies. Martyrdom was the favoured option. In his *History of the Church*, Eusebius lists the deaths of 146 martyrs, and many of these devotees met appalling ends in defence of their faith. Those arrested on the charge of being Christians would generally obtain a reprieve if they were prepared, in court, to swear by 'the Genius of the Emperor' and to perform sacrifice to the pagan gods. Few were willing to comply, and much of the detail of their collective fate is preserved in the *Acts of the Martyrs*. The hostile treatment of those pioneering Christians was not a continuous affair, but erupted from time to time, generally for one of two reasons. Occasionally, a newly crowned emperor would look critically at the state of things and conclude that discipline within the empire (and this frequently included religious discipline) needed tightening up. Popular resentment was also fuelled by pagan orators whenever the opportunity arose, who were generally adept at raising mob passion that resulted in acts of anti-Christian violence.[32] Among the most notable of these was the burning of the 86-year-old Bishop Polycarp in the amphitheatre at Smyrna sometime between 156 and 159 CE on the orders of the Asiarch Philippus.

It is worth bearing in mind that the attitude of the Christians did not just upset emperors and their courts. It also tended to infuriate the populace, who were essentially conservative when it came to religious devotion. When it was announced that Bishop Polycarp had refused the pagan oblations needed to save his life, the crowd bayed, 'Here is the schoolmaster of Asia, the father of Christians, the destroyer of our gods.'[33] The crowds agitating for Polycarp's death wanted him ripped apart by a lion, but, on the grounds that this was now illegal under Roman law, Philippus adjudicated that he should be burnt alive. Polycarp's grim experience was a demonstration of the power of mob rule. During the reign of the Emperor Decius, proselytes including Papylus, Carpus and Agathonice in Pergamum, Asia Minor, were hung naked, 'scraped' with iron claws and then burnt alive. In the reign of Marcus Aurelius, Justin and his Christian colleagues were scourged and beheaded by the urban prefect Rusticus in Rome sometime between 164 and 168 CE, having refused the usual pagan sacrifices. At Carthage in the summer of 180 CE the so-called Scillitan martyrs, including Speratus, Nartzalus, Cittinus, Donata, Secunda and Vestia, were executed for similar offences on the orders of the proconsul Vigellus Saturninus. Torture was de rigueur for these miserable victims, though they did not see themselves as such. Many are reported to have gone joyfully to meet their end. When the Scillitan martyrs were condemned to be decapitated by the sword, Speratus reportedly cried, 'Thank God', and Nartzalus echoed, 'Today we are martyrs in heaven. Thanks be to God!'[34]

The martyrs' resilience rested in an absolute conviction that, through violent death in the profession of their faith, they would be fast-tracked to heaven. The Psalms of the Hebrew Bible told them this, or so they thought, even if the Psalmist had not necessarily had resurrection in mind. 'Precious in the sight of the Lord is the death of his holy ones.'[35] Those destined for slaughter in the arena saw themselves in a martial context as soldiers fighting a battle in which they would be the victors and their oppressors the vanquished. The resolve of these confessed Christians could be stiffened through letters of support from their bishops. Writing to those imprisoned on Carthage's 'death row' during the latter part of the third century, the Bishop of Carthage, Cyprian, named them 'my brothers most brave and most blessed'.

> The combat has increased and with it the glory of the combatants. You have not hung back from the battlefront from fear of the torturers, rather the tortures have themselves incited you on to join the battlefront. Courageous, steadfast, you have advanced

with generous self-sacrifice into the very heart of the fighting. Some of your number I hear have already received their crowns, others are very close to winning their crowns of victory . . . the course confers nobility and glory. By the one [way], the surer way [of steadfastness in the face of torture and death] you hasten to the Lord by the completion of your victory.[36]

In its formative years Islam was faced with not dissimilar experiences to those of early Judaism and Christianity, although the limited amount of available information is largely based on popular tradition with little corroboration from independent sources. Conservative forces, immediately jealous of a new vogue of spiritual popularity and political muscle, rained down persecution upon the pioneering Muslims of the sixth century CE. The Prophet Muhammad was born into the aristocratic Quraysh tribe in Mecca in about 570 CE. True to the thrust of revelations made to him by God and memorised, he began to urge loyalty to his new Islamic faith over that of tribal affiliations and in preference to the paganism that had held sway with his ancestors for hundreds of years; they had followed the old and more conventional style of polytheistic faith in a pantheon of celestial deities and household gods. Thus he began to attract hostility not only from the Meccan leaders but also from within his own clan, antagonism spearheaded most notably by his uncle 'Abu Lahab. He is said to have stood accused of coming under the influence of devils and of disseminating notions of an absolute deity to a world where polytheism dominated the religious scene. Members of his first following were singled out for harassment and the more affluent found themselves under forms of house arrest, while there is indication that others, particularly slaves attracted to his demands for social reform, were tortured and killed. Assault on the conservative social order in a city made affluent through its position as a key trading centre was not well received by the more powerful families. The first victim of persecution was allegedly a woman named Umm Ammar, and records indicate that in 615 CE Muhammad sent eighty-three families for their own safety into

Ethiopia, a country ruled by a Christian known for his tolerance. By 622 the situation had become sufficiently precarious that in September Muhammad himself was forced to leave the city after the Meccan authorities delivered an ultimatum to the Quraysh tribe to hand him over for execution. When they declined to do so, tradition suggests they were boycotted.

Muhammad's flight into exile with his followers became celebrated as the hijrah, or Hegira, and since then this event has signified the opening year of the Islamic calendar. The initial destination of the escaping Muslim faithful was the town of Ta'if some 90 kilometres south-east of Mecca, but the reception there was no less hostile so they opted for the city of Medina, then known as Yathrib, some 300 kilometres to the north of Mecca, where the civic leaders had expressed positive interest in the new vogue of ideals. They were also concerned about tribal feuding in the area and believed that, in return for a safe haven, Muhammad might be prepared to act as a competent arbitrator. Eventually, some sixty families were safely transferred to Medina, and from this point in time the Islamic position shifted from avoidance of persecution to an increasing interest in its own power of militancy.

Aggression stemming from within a religious movement and aimed outwards tends to characterise its expansion phase, and to see this in action one has to search no further than modern-day Islam. But Islam is not alone and, although aggression in the name of God has been going on since the beginnings of recorded history, during the last 3,500 years charges of religious violence could have been laid at the doors of all three major monotheistic faiths. What is unusual about the current spate of warlike conduct in parts of the Christian world, particularly in the USA, is its emergence out of what might otherwise appear to be the terminal stages of stagnation and decline.

We have already explored some of the root causes of warlike behaviour, but a more detailed look at the ways in which outward aggression was conducted among the trio of Judaism, Christianity and Islam is the main focus in the following chapters. Similarities and differences become apparent. Each of the three has developed a thoroughly uncompromising and belligerent attitude in defence of its own vision of monotheism, and none can readily accept any dilution of the singular ideal, not only of one God but of its own interpretation of that supreme being. Various theories have been advanced as to why these faiths have surpassed many others in their preoccupation with violence. The author James Aho, who has written on the relationship between religion, mythology and war, believes that reasons can be found in the nature of a male transcendent God who creates the material world by command rather than gestation and then becomes partly alienated from what he has manufactured. Humankind, part and parcel of the production line, turns out to be fallen by nature. Having been produced from the substance of the Earth (the word 'Adam' means 'of the soil') man is only fit to revert to earth. 'Dust thou art and unto dust shalt thou return.'[37]

It is clear that the Hebrew tribes became steeped in the belief that man is intrinsically sinful, having been so since the Fall of Adam, and that God is more than happy to vent his spleen on humankind in response. For the early Israelite there was no concept of a spiritual life beyond death, and in fact death was considered final until as recently as the time of the Maccabean revolt.[38] But humanity is also offered a way out, a means of redemption. Through the agency of Moses, God revealed a more merciful side to his nature in delivering a Covenant, and this loving 'deal' was to be supported through prophecy, sacrifice, word and writing. Holy war was thus envisaged by the Israelites as a means through which God's wrath could be delivered by the loyal to the disloyal, those who elected to ignore divine revelation, in order to establish a new sense of order in the world. The responsibility for prosecuting this conflict to punish the sinful and restore God's kingdom on Earth rested upon a specially chosen people, the Children of Israel. Much the same style of ideology was subsequently applied to early Christianity and Islam.

Holy war among the monotheistic trio has been waged as a response to injustice, fought on the principle that absolute good is collectively challenging absolute evil.[39] Embedded within respective dogmas is the unshakeable mantra that each brand of faith in the one God is the true conveyor of the word and wish of the Almighty, and, by implication, that its rivals are poor imitators who have simply got it wrong and thus are to be led, kicking, bleeding and squealing towards the truth or, if necessary, eliminated altogether. Of course, differences exist between the three religions in the manner and development of holy warfare, because each has experienced a peculiar set of social and historical conditions that in each case has moulded a distinctive character and style of violence.

FOUR

Destroy Them Utterly

How strictly did the faithful carry out the wishes of God? Aside from scriptural pronouncements, most religions (with the notable exception of Buddhism) until recent times appear to have recognised a divine mandate for destruction. In one of the first videotapes issued by Osama bin Laden after the destruction of the Twin Towers on 11 September 2001, he praised Allah, stating that 'it was by His will that the World Trade Center towers have collapsed'. It has been believed by almost all religious warriors that they are merely following the commands of God delivered through 'the Word'. Irrespective of their brand of belief, the faithful have consistently relied on this divine will as the justification for their own acts of religious violence.

All three of the great monotheistic movements suffered persecution in their infancy, but as they matured they inflicted retribution in measures that sometimes far outweighed the original tribulations of their pioneers. Each, however, began its offensive phase for different reasons and under different conditions. Judaism has never been a missionary religion. Even within its territorial frontiers during biblical times it was not interested in converting polytheists to Yahwism. Its core aim was to maintain religious purity within its own ranks and present an image of divine superiority to its neighbours. In truth, holy war beyond the borders of the Promised Land was never seriously considered until modern times, and then only on the premise that the state of Israel needed to adopt defensive measures. Judaism probably did work out a form of politico-religious policy, but it only evolved long after the biblical era.[1] So violence in Judaism has always been focused in and around Syrio-Palestine.

Christians were to display aggressive conduct in plenty but not for a considerable period after the foundation of the sect because initially it showed no interest in statehood or politics. It was also not especially interested in aggressive behaviour because for the first few centuries the members clung to the belief that the end of the world was imminent. With a universal scenario for cosmic war and destruction just around the corner there would have been no point in getting involved in local sparring even if they had possessed the political clout. Christianity began, if anything, as an anti-state religion, which its leader had made clear when he declared his kingdom to be not of this world. The Roman Emperors Constantine the Great and Theodosius I turned Christianity into the religion of the empire, but the Christian hierarchy was largely detached from politics and remained so until much later, when its own political machine came to the fore during the medieval period. It was only then that Christendom truly erupted into self-styled violence.

Islam, in contrast, began its passage in the spirit of a quest for statehood and imperial power. More or less from the outset the expansion of the Muslim state and the spread of the Islamic faith demanded a marriage of religion and politics. Islam declared war on unbelievers, and it mattered little, according to the qur'ānic scriptures, whether this was achieved by violent or peaceful means. The current level of atrocity perpetrated in the name of Islam is only the latest chapter in a long-running saga in which some of those fighting to preserve the integrity of a faith appear to have abandoned most of the rules of decency and humanity that canons of religion are often alleged to proclaim. The encouragement to commit atrocity, however, is generally to be discovered enshrined in the spiritual rulebooks, and in this respect Islam is far from being alone. The question arises, inevitably, as to whether aggressors in the name of God are misreading the scriptures. It is probably fair to say that the ancient Israelites were instructed by God as the pioneers of anathema, and can hardly have misread his edicts given that they were so consistently belligerent. In the Christian case, the very limited pronouncements of Jesus Christ on the subject are ambiguous, and his advice concerning the bringing of a sword was probably intended as a reference to a spiritual weapon. Islamic scriptures tend to be contradictory and therefore offer readers the opportunity to 'take their pick'. In this respect Islam comes closest to Hinduism, where there is understanding of a godhead that is both creator and destroyer. But actually this notion of a cosmic balance between destructive and creative forces, which worshippers often see as a puzzling contradiction, is enshrined in all three of the great monotheisms.

Israel's biblical history, encapsulated in the pages of the Old Testament, includes a narrative of strife at least until the post-exilic period. It adds up to the most extensively recorded and unquestionably one of the most brutal chronicles from the ancient world. It is also the history of a military rise and fall that, in one sense or another, consistently obeyed or disobeyed religious principles. The Old Testament therefore provides a neat picture of changing fortunes against which the more fragmented canvases of other religions can be compared and contrasted according to their different historical, environmental and cultural experiences. Furthermore, it provides an important background to the fundamental causes of a major area of strife in the world today, one of the most intractable and pivotal conflicts to have beset the modern world, which continues to threaten global stability. The Arab–Israeli problem is rooted in ideological and religious differences that go back over thousands of years and have proved almost impossible to resolve. Israel justifies its stance towards the Palestinians by asserting that it has, literally, a God-given right to the land and that its distant ancestors conquered Syrio-Palestine under the direction of God. The fact that the followers of Islam also shared this same God is the perverse twist that appears infrequently remembered by the belligerents on either side. Israel defends a vision of a venerable Jewish society residing in the 'Holy Land' with Jerusalem as its spiritual heart. The Palestinians, with equal ferocity, defend their historical, and more lately spiritual, entitlement to the same piece of real estate. Heritage and religion thus become bound together as political tools, and, as we shall discover, the heritage of the vanquished often becomes a pressing political concern of the victor.

The Hebrew coalition inspired, though not initiated, by Moses and consolidated, at least for a time, under the Israelite kings came up with new justifications for going to war. Even prior to consolidation the leaders of the independent tribes no longer found it satisfactory to explain the militant aspirations of heaven in the context of legendary battles that had taken place in a mythical past. The world had moved on and demand was growing for more specific and contemporary reasons.

It was not simply that old traditions had become passé. The Israelite leaders believed that they had to carve out a common cultural identity that was different from anything else around, for which reason, in part, they elected to dispense with the recognised pantheon of ancient Near Eastern deities and replace it with a single omnipotent God, a kind of celestial dictator who would brook no challenge to his authority. The concept was radically different from that of a close-knit community of deities who all got on with one another in convivial and occasionally lustful circumstances. In the emerging identity of the Israelites the excuses for military offensive amounted, more often than not, to a cry that the ideological wishes of their God had been thwarted or wronged by a congregation of different religious persuasion. The exhortations contained in the word of God had now to be acted out on the ground. The cry of 'my god against your god', implying equality of divine status and an imbalance only in putative muscle power, gradually became replaced by one of 'My god is offended by the behaviour of the followers of your foreign and strictly inferior deity.' In other words a notion of territorialism through ideological differences began to gain prominence over a simple hankering for more land or the need to defend a sovereign patch against the covetous aspirations of others.

The picture of Israelite solidarity in following their new-found God is, however, a romantic one that on close inspection proves palpably inaccurate. In reality the early Hebrew rank and file expended large amounts of energy and ingenuity on devising means of sloping away from the austerity demanded by Moses into the more pleasing arms of idolatry. Nevertheless, the illusion of ideological togetherness was to become increasingly important, never more so than when the descendants of the Hebrew tribes and their Promised Land found themselves under the domination of successive foreign regimes, ending with those of the Greeks and Romans. The Old Testament played a major part in bolstering the dream of unity and religious purity. It came to stand for much more than a chronicle of Jewish history and a book of social and moral law. It was held up as a rallying focus for Jewish nationalism and, through a succession of crises, Jewish identity was sustained by its very existence. So, in some respects the Old Testament books have to be read as an exercise in political jingoism rather than an objective chronicle of events. They promote the ideals of a strong and righteous faith to which the establishment aspired even if it did not always obtain the intended results 'on the ground'. Scriptural passages thus invariably describe either the 'other side' or an individual transgressor as being in the wrong, to be judged by a God preoccupied with punishing evildoers. The benchmark of who constitutes an 'evildoer' is, of course, subjective, but the scriptural writer generally means anyone who is not of suitable religious and, by implication, nationalistic persuasion.

A clearer view of ancient Israel's military expansion can only be gained by stripping away the cant from the Old Testament writings. When the first great leader of the Hebrew people, Moses, brought some of the tribes out of enslavement in Egypt, they amounted to a motley rabble with no clear focus other than their vision of a new homeland. In order to keep them together as one, Moses was prudent enough to recognise that they needed some additional and magical bonding essence. He and his successors therefore adopted a form of theocratic government in order to press home to a highly superstitious congregation the message that adherence to the will of Yahweh – literally 'I am who I am', the title given to an otherwise unseen and unnamed God – was of fundamental importance to their well-being.

It would be difficult to overestimate the power and influence held by the tribal leaders of the Israelites. In spite of a tendency to regress in favour of pagan abominations the common people still revered the patriarchs in a truly messianic light as the anointed of God and the bringers of salvation. The patriarch Joseph had once told the Hebrews suffering their enforced servitude in Egypt, 'God sent me before you to preserve you in a posterity in the earth and to save your lives by a great deliverance.'[2] His name means, literally, 'may God add posterity'. Those members of the tribes blessed with prophetic vision also gained immense status in the minds of a superstitious following. Joseph's ability to interpret dreams had a profound effect on his fate even as a slave in Egypt when, having correctly predicted various national misfortunes, he was elevated into royal circles and given the hand of Asenath, a princess in the pharaonic household.

Men of the calibre of Moses governed their people effectively as the high priests and successors of shamans. But strategically the tribes were far from being united under a common leadership, with each being essentially autonomous. Israel had no standing army, and the tribes only banded together occasionally in times of crisis. After Moses' death and before the era of the monarchy, the tribes continued to operate as a loose political confederation under the guidance of several charismatic leaders who, as 'judges', kept faith with his spiritual vision and were seen no less clearly as deliverers. When freed from the oppression of the Mesopotamian ruler Cushan-rishathaim at the turn of the fifteenth century BCE, the Hebrews believed that they had found salvation in the shape of the military leader Othniel, who also served as Israel's first judge. 'When the children of Israel cried unto the Lord, the Lord raised up a deliverer to the children of Israel.'[3] Empowered to administer control on behalf of Yahweh these influential clerics adjudicated on religious matters and continued to demand the common allegiance of the tribes to a singular God in order to develop a national identity. Israel means literally 'God fights' – from *sarah* (contends) and *el* (god) – and life in almost all aspects, officially at any rate, conformed to the presumed wishes of Yahweh. He, his people were assured through the dark pronouncements of such bellicose writers as the Deuteronomist, was committed to waging war through his chosen people in order to increase his influence in the less holy realms of Earth and to save his own from corruption. 'Oh Israel, ye approach this day unto battle against your enemies: let not your hearts faint, fear not and do not tremble, neither be ye terrified because of them. For the Lord your God is he that goeth with you, to fight for you against your enemies, to save you.'[4]

The behaviour of the Israelites became unremittingly aggressive from the moment when they found themselves militarily strong enough to fight back. Implementation of their programme of settlement and domination of Syrio-Palestine, the land which according to Moses had been promised to them by God, ultimately necessitated ousting or slaying large parts of the indigenous population. At the same time they were obliged to counter incursions from the Transjordanian kingdoms and to repel the Philistines striking out from cities in the south-west. Archaeology indicates that although the Israelite invasion was marked at first by a protracted campaign of intermittent skirmishes, some of which took place at the same time as fresh assaults by expeditionary Egyptian forces, the offensive was to intensify sharply in its extent and level of savagery. The Israelite God, so his forces were frequently informed, demanded a policy of 'scorched earth', which meant total obliteration or anathema.

The indigenous people of Canaan were among the first to suffer extreme sanction at the hands of the invaders. 'And the Lord harkened to the voice of Israel, and delivered up the Canaanites; and they utterly destroyed them and their cities.'[5] 'Destroy them utterly' came to be a favoured instruction, and the authors of the Book of Joshua, the sixth book of the Old Testament and the first of the 'former prophets', related how the Canaanite urban centres of Jericho, Ai and Hebron were subjected to this measure. According to the narrative the Israelites eventually slaughtered the entire population of the town of Ai, numbering 12,000 men, women and children. This included the capture and hanging of the local ruler, whereupon they burnt the town to ashes. Another notable passage reveals in jingoistic mood that Joshua 'smote all the country of the hills, and of the south, and of the vale, and of the springs, and all their kings: he left none remaining, but utterly destroyed all that breathed, as the Lord God of Israel commanded.'[6]

At least to a degree one can see that the style of narration has been politically inspired and is retrospective in much of its content. There has been intense argument about the origin and provenance of the Book of Joshua. It contains various types of material, including possible eyewitness accounts, historical records and legendary anecdotes, and in part it is peppered with the rhetoric of the Yahwist cult.[7] Evidence found in several places in the text has led biblical scholars to believe that the work was compiled at some distance in time from actual events and was intended to deliver a graphic political image of all twelve of the tribes participating as one in total conquest of the entire territory. 'And Joshua set up twelve stones in the midst of Jordan, in the place where the feet of the priests which bare the ark of the covenant stood: and they are there unto this day.'[8]

Incitement to mass destruction was not limited to the pens of earlier biblical writers. Books, including Samuel and Daniel, compiled in the post-exilic period are among several that not only advocate war in the name of religion but also positively encourage the indiscriminate slaughter of men, women, children and domestic animals. Sometimes it is possible to discover a progressive embellishment of events that actually took place in order to explain away aggressive behaviour as some kind of justifiable retribution. For a pithy example of the hand of propagandists at work one needs to look no further than the record of relations with the tribe of Amalekites. These were a nomadic desert people, one of a plethora of independent clans jostling for space in the region. Tradition has it that they were the descendants of Esau, the first-born son of Isaac and Rebekah, who came originally from somewhere near the city of Kadesh and then roamed the Negev Desert beyond Judah's southern borders. Skirmishes took place when the Amalekites encountered hostile bands of Israelites trekking north through the Wilderness of Sin and attempted to defend themselves against the invaders. The 'oldest' record of events comes in the second book of the Pentateuch, Exodus, which is regarded in both Jewish and Christian popular tradition as the work of Moses. According to the narrative the Israelites engaged with the defenders shortly after having miraculously discovered a much-needed supply of water in the region of Horeb. 'Then came Amalek and fought with Israel in Rephidim. And Moses said unto Joshua, Choose us out men, and go out, fight with Amalek . . . and Joshua discomfited Amalek with the edge of the sword.'[9] When this same event came to be recorded by the Deuteronomist and edited at a much later period, the circumstances had changed somewhat. The authors painted the Amalek defenders as slayers of the sick and weary. 'Remember what Amalek did unto thee by the way, when ye were come forth out of Egypt; how he met thee by the way, and smote the hindmost of thee, even all that were feeble behind thee, when thou wast faint and weary; and he feared not God.'[10] By the time of the completion of the Book of Samuel, again compiled it is thought over a period of time and in parts edited as late as the post-exilic period, recollection of the Amalekites and their attempts at defence of land had been embellished with even darker shades. 'I remember that which Amalek did to Israel, how he laid wait for him in the Way, when he came up from Egypt. Now go and smite Amalek, and utterly destroy all that they have, and spare them not; but slay both man and woman, infant and suckling, ox and sheep, camel and ass.'[11]

The loose federal arrangement of the Israelite tribes was to change with the crowning of Saul, the first king of a united Israel, whose accession took place in the mid to late eleventh century BCE. The meshing of politics and religion now became stronger than ever, and adherence to a particular spiritual ideology was viewed as an advertisement of one's political loyalties in a way that had not been obvious in earlier times. The catalyst for more thorough cohesion had been the expansionist ambitions of the Philistines in the southwest, and Saul had been placed at the head of the tribal confederacy with the intention of unseating them and driving them out of the region. Saul's time in office did not result in a satisfactory solution to the Philistine problem but it marked the advent of the kingship, and with it government of the loosely knit tribes by priestly leaders came to an end. Some writers have claimed that Judaism in company with the other monotheistic faiths at one time presided over a theocracy; but this is a misapplication of the term, and Jewish theocracy only existed in theory as part of a process of rationalising when the nation was in steep decline and when the leadership was trying to impress on the people that God had forsaken them because of their collective misbehaviour.[12] A true theocracy is one in which the ruler is divine, literally a god incarnate.[13] Hence the ancient Mesopotamian nations operated as theocracies, and in more recent times Tibet and imperial Japan were managed in a similar manner because the Tibetan Lama and, prior to 1945, the Japanese Emperor were revered as living gods. But Judaism, Christianity and Islam have never involved government directly by God, only by his appointed agents. The essential feature in governmental control has been the God-given law, a process technically known as divine nomocracy. God-kings in the mould of the rulers of Mesopotamia did not evolve in Israel, but the monarch standing at the head of his troops was nonetheless regarded as a leader selected and ordained by God, a Shiloh or Messiah. Messiah is a term that can be misunderstood because it does not apply exclusively to Jesus Christ but defines anyone in Jewish tradition who served as an anointed one. Among the reasons for later Jewish rejection of claims that Jesus of Nazareth was a Messiah is the notion that such individuals were envisaged as dropping from the sky with the Covenant in one hand and a conquering sword in the other. Jewish scripture did much to impress upon ordinary people that military leaders had been sent by God to render salvation at times of national crisis, and the biblical writers were capable of building the characters of these messianic figures to near-superhuman proportions. The confrontation between David and the Philistine strongman Goliath may or may not ever have taken place, but it was introduced as an object lesson to demonstrate that, with God guiding the Messiah's fighting arm, anything was possible.

Saul was neither superhuman nor long-lived as king. He died in a losing battle with Philistine forces at Mount Gilboa. The writer of Samuel, however, attributed his downfall to the 'transgression factor', the principle that if the Children of Israel, king or commoner, did not carry out the militant instructions of God to the letter they would suffer the same degree of punishment as any other idolators. Saul's problem had lain initially with the Amalekites. He had become squeamish about the severity of the order handed down from his God to 'spare not' the Amalekites and he resisted a demand for anathema or herem, their ethnic cleansing from the Promised Land down to the last man, woman and child. Saul opted to spare the Amalekite king, Agag, and, presumably for economic reasons, kept the best of the domestic stock from having its collective throat slit. Not everyone agreed with this bending of the rules. The prophet Samuel, still wielding de facto control over the Israelites, was in no doubt that a grievous sin had been committed against Yahweh through Saul's lack of obedience, and he was not slow to remind Saul of his failed duty. 'The Lord sent thee on a journey, and said, Go and utterly destroy the sinners the Amalekites and fight against them until they be consumed. Wherefore then didst thou not obey the voice of the Lord?'14 For Saul's transgression Samuel took it upon himself, on instruction from God, to strip Saul of his kingship and to take over as Agag's executioner. In spite of Samuel's attempt to complete the process of attrition, a remnant of the Amalekites escaped and during the reign of David continued to cause problems until they were allegedly wiped out by 500 warriors belonging to the Simeonites in a battle at Mount Seir.15

After the initial demotion of Saul, Samuel was instructed by God to anoint David, the youngest son of Jesse, as a new king and deliverer. It was a policy decision guaranteed to trigger a jealous feud between Saul and David. The latter is alleged to have spent many years as little more than a refugee evading retribution until Saul's death opened the way to his return and coronation. King David ruled over a united Israel for thirty-three years, and during the time made best use of an international situation in which Egyptian influence had all but evaporated, the Hittite hegemony was long past, and the serious rise of Assyrian power had yet to materialise. David immediately went on the offensive, conducting brutal campaigns of repression against the Philistines in the west. He then turned his army to the east and attacked the tribes of Edom, Moab and Zobar. If Old Testament accounts are to be trusted the Edomites in particular fell victim to a familiar level of total slaughter when David's army killed 18,000 in company with their Syrian allies in the Valley of Salt and, during a separate campaign, 22,000 Syrians sent in from Damascus. During a six-month period of systematic bloodletting the Israelite senior army commander, Joab, claimed to have 'killed every male' Edomite.[16] A chance rift with the Ammonites provided an excuse to mount a new offensive until in effect they, and all the surrounding nations, were paying tribute to Israel. Peace of a kind ensued but David suffered a succession of internal rebellions until his death at the age of 71, when the reins of power were taken up by Solomon, the illegitimate offspring of an adulterous tryst with Bathsheba, the wife of Uriah, while her husband was away campaigning on David's behalf against the Ammonites.

The reign of Solomon effectively marked the end of the Israelite expansion. Consolidation might have followed, but in reality the nation split into two feuding and increasingly weak political and religious camps, Judah in the south and Israel in the north. Intertribal clashes had actually gone on between the Israelite tribes intermittently for much of the time since their arrival in Syrio-Palestine. An infamous episode, probably much embellished by writers, took place at Gibeah during the time of the Judges between the clans of Benjamin and Israel, when 26,000 men of Benjamin allegedly engaged 400 armed men of Israel over the rape and murder of a concubine.[17] Much of the disagreement after the schism of the two nations, however, concerned religious differences. The northern state of Israel almost immediately lost faith with Yahwism and reverted to idolatry. Judah retained its loyalty to the religion of Moses to a greater extent, though it also dallied from time to time with pagan practice, partly in response to public pressure and partly out of political expediency. The two sides almost came to blows at the outset when the Judahite king Reheboam assembled an army to attack the forces of Jeroboam's ten northern tribes but was dissuaded by the prophet Shemaiah and was obliged to rely on verbal polemics against Jeroboam sympathisers.

'and [I] will take away the remnant of the house of Jeroboam as a man taketh away dung, till it all be gone . . . Him that dieth of

Jeroboam in the city shall the dogs eat; and him that dieth in the field shall the fowls of the air eat.'[18]

It was not long, however, before any pretence of constraint was abandoned. The Judahite king, Asa, sent his General Ben-hadad at the head of a considerable force to attack a succession of Israel's key towns, including Ijon, Dan and Abel-beth-maachah. The Israelite king was not slow to respond and in the third year of Asa's reign managed to have him assassinated after a prolonged bout of skirmishing. The religious differences between the two nations came to something of a bizarre climax when the Yahwist prophet Elijah challenged Ahab, the King of Israel to put 450 priests of Baal to the test against himself. Legend has it that the Baal prophets lost the wager, whereupon Elijah encouraged the people to commit an act of mass slaughter beside the brook Kidron.[19]

For much of the era of internal Israelite conflict, neighbours to the east, the Assyrians, dominated the political and military stages beyond the borders of Syrio-Palestine. Assyria looked covetously towards the region and was set to become the new power-broker, followed by her southern neighbour Babylonia. Unlike the fanatical campaigning spirit of the Israelites in the past, the motives of the Mesopotamian overlords had little to do with religion, although religious circumstances played a significant part in determining whether the region was at peace or war.

The Assyrian and Babylonian despots remained confident in the potency of their own pantheon of deities and adopted the view that one more added to the celestial ranks made little difference. They had no reason to fear the wrath of Yahweh, whose proclaimed omnipotence, in their eyes and practical experience, was simply a frivolous notion. The intention of the Mesopotamians was purely strategic, to extend the boundaries of their respective empires in the most productive way. Syrio-Palestine represented not only an important intersection of trade routes but also a source of valuable commodities including, notably, the timber of the cedars of Lebanon. Trees other than palms were a scarce asset in Mesopotamia. Nonetheless, from time to time issues rooted in religious ideology played on the minds of Assyrian and Babylonian strategists in determining whether or not they went to war in Syrio-Palestine. When the north lost its sovereignty between 733 and 732 BCE, becoming the Assyrian province of Magiddu, its government formed an alliance with Syria and the combined forces made threatening advances towards Judah, which at the time was under the rule of King Ahaz. Perhaps unwisely Ahaz turned to the Assyrian overlord Tiglathpileser III (745–727 BCE) for military assistance. Hitherto the Assyrians had merely forayed intermittently into Syrio-Palestine to gather tribute from cities nominally under Assyrian control. Tiglathpileser had other strategic objectives in mind and his purpose in mounting offensive campaigns was to achieve permanent conquest. No doubt grateful for the opportunity, he obligingly marched his forces into Israel to thwart Mesopotamian ambitions there and at the same time reduced Judah to being little more than a vassal state.[20]

According to the Second Book of Kings, Ahaz then embarked on a diplomatic mission. 'And king Ahaz went to Damascus to meet Tiglathpileser, king of Assyria, and saw an altar that was at Damascus; and king Ahaz sent to Urijah the priest the fashion of the altar, and the pattern of it, according to all the workmanship thereof.'[21] The harder reality is that Ahaz was summoned to attend Tiglathpileser in order to discuss Assyrian settlement terms with the Judahites and was recommended to install the trappings of Assyrian religion in the Temple of Jerusalem as a suitable expression of fealty. The presence or absence of the Assyrian religious cult alongside that of Yahweh determined Israelite chances of peace and quiet for the next two centuries, because Tiglathpileser and successive Mesopotamian overlords recognised that Yahwism and nationalism were inseparable. Biblical accounts tend to leave us with a distorted impression about root causes in the rise and fall of Judah's fortunes. The general tone is that installing pagan trappings in the Temple resulted in an outburst of wrath from Yahweh directed upon Jerusalem. 'Therefore will I cast you out of this land into a land that ye know not, neither ye nor your fathers; and there shall ye serve other gods day and night; where I will not shew you favour.'[22] This incidentally was a reference to the plight of the large number of inhabitants of the former northern kingdom who had been deported and resettled in a form of ethnic cleansing by Tiglathpileser III. A tablet fragment of the time records that 13,150 people from the former kingdom of Israel were forcibly exiled to Mesopotamia and replaced by Aramean and Chaldean tribes from Babylonia.

A more objective view of history, however, finds cause and effect different to those implied in the Old Testament observations of Jeremiah. In about 701 BCE the militant Assyrian general Sennacherib faced a rebellious uprising fomented by Pekah of Israel and Rezin of Damascus. It gave Hezekiah, one of the more reformist-minded leaders of the Judahite kingdom in the south, a rash opportunity to dump the entire Assyrian cult out of the Temple in a clear snub to Assyrian suzerainty and in the hope of freeing Judah from Assyrian political and religious domination. Sennacherib was not amused. This flexing of Yahwist muscle was seen in the Mesopotamian power base to the east to be little more than open rebellion among a people who had achieved a progressive reputation for making themselves a nuisance and who now needed to be dealt with severely.[23] Sennacherib was to extract payment for Hezekiah's intemperate behaviour. He sent a chilling message to the Judahite king: 'Let not thy God in whom thou trustest deceive thee, saying, Jerusalem shall not be delivered into the hands of the king of Assyria. Behold thou hast heard what the kings of Assyria have done to all lands, by destroying them utterly.'[24]

And so it was. When Sennacherib ascended the Assyrian throne in 705 BCE his army marched on Syrio-Palestine, wiped out an Egyptian expeditionary force that had come to Judahite assistance and put the city of Jerusalem under siege. Hezekiah sued for terms and as a gesture of goodwill presented several of his daughters to Sennacherib to use as concubines. Jerusalem, however, experienced a lucky escape because by 701 BCE Sennacherib had laid waste forty-six other Judahite cities.

Stripped of all but nominal power Hezekiah died in 687 and his son Manasseh, labelled as a safe Assyrian loyalist and whom history records as one of the more extreme pagan rulers of Judah, restored the Assyrian cult. 'For he built up again the high places which

Hezekiah his father had destroyed; and he reared up altars for Baal, and made a grove as did Ahab king of Israel; and worshipped all the host of heaven and served them.'[25] For this demonstration of loyalty, Manasseh was rewarded with a fifty-year spell of peace.

The harmony was not to last. From 612 BCE onwards the power-brokers in the ancient Near East became the Neo-Babylonians, who had smashed their way into the key cities of Assur and Nineveh, thus ending Assyrian domination. When in 640 BCE Josiah, another Yahwist reformer, took over the Judahite throne from Manasseh's short-lived pagan successor, Amon, he attempted to bring the country back to the pure religion of Yahweh. But the critical eye of Babylon was immediately focused on the renegade kingdom. By the time of the coronation of Josiah's equally reformist successor, Zedekiah, in 598 BCE, the Babylonian king, Nebuchadnezzar II, had decided enough was enough. He attacked Jerusalem the following year and by 587 BCE Judah was obliterated, with large numbers of the Israelite aristocracy removed to languish in the so-called Babylonian Exile.

From the point of view of the Assyrian and Babylonian authorities the justification for invading Syrio-Palestine was entirely materialistic. The Israelites had demonstrated their own imperial ambitions to be a regional superpower and, when the occasion arose, had been as brutal and thorough in their policy of mass murder as the most tyrannical Mesopotamian despot. Though reduced to the status of a tribute-paying vassal state they still presented a higher risk of rebellion than many other conquered territories, and their intermittent determination to observe Yahwism exclusively and to the letter could only be interpreted on each occasion as a fresh sign of militant posturing. Rejection of the Mesopotamian cult therefore amounted to a threat of political insurrection that had to be curbed.

The biblical approach to recording these momentous events in Israel's history for posterity was to couch the whole process in terms of religious backsliding. It was essential to interpret the misfortunes of Judah and Israel as a direct outcome of failure to maintain Yahwist unanimity. According to the biblical texts, first the Israelites in the north then the Judahites in the south had brought military defeat upon themselves by reneging on their covenant with Yahweh. It was, in effect, a propagandist exercise orchestrated by the prophets and religious leaders, the cream of the Judahite hierarchy, in a fraught attempt to keep Israel's remnants together under one banner. To a superstitious mind the threat of divine retribution loomed large and carried a potent message. The harsh reality was that the Israelites were never going to be a match for the strength of Assyria and Babylonia, and so first the north and then in the final outcome the Judahite kingdom succumbed. This was hardly because of failure to respect the religious covenant – precisely the reverse! Nonetheless the biblical interpretation of history persisted and became a key part of Jewish religious tradition.

The restoration of the Babylonian exiles in 539 BCE did not bring an end to the plight of the Jews. They were to be dominated successively by the Persians, the Macedonian Greeks of Alexander the Great, the Seleucids and finally the Romans. Throughout all of this the regular message to the suffering communities from their religious leaders was that backsliding from Yahwism had brought defeat in the past and continued to bring calamity in the present, and the only way to avoid further disaster in the future was to stand firm in honour of their God-given faith.

Later Jewish rabbinical literature, including much to be found in the pseudepigraphal works of the Old Testament, hammered home the message that observance of the 'ways of the Lord' was the key to survival. These texts are often drawn in terms of 'kill or be killed', and a constant emphasis in the more apocryphal books is placed on the struggle of Israel with its enemies, generally the historical adversaries who live 'to the east'. Among these works 1 Enoch is a composite of manuscript sources probably drawn from various earlier periods. The compilation, as we know it, is thought to have originated somewhere in Judaea and to have been in use in the reclusive religious settlement at Qumran before the beginning of the Christian period. It typifies the mood of many similar writings. In Book IV, the so-called dream visions that Enoch relates to his son Methuselah, the prophet harks back to the time of the Judges and speaks of 'rams' leading the 'sheep' of Israel against enemies depicted as the lowest forms of predatory beast. 'Now the dogs, foxes and wild boars began to devour those sheep till the Lord of the sheep raised up another sheep, one from among them – a ram which would lead them. That ram began to fight on all sides those dogs, foxes and wild boars until he destroyed all of them.'[26]

After the catastrophe of the Maccabean revolt and under evermore punitive Roman domination, the Judaeans realised that military restoration of Israel was a forlorn dream and their hopes reverted back to the idea of salvation through the righteous arm of a god-king. They came to believe in the idea of deliverance in the form of a freshly minted and heavenly Messiah who would descend to Earth and, rather than fight on mortal terms, would deliver divine judgement, a final arbitration from an all-powerful throne, the destruction of the wicked ones and the resurrection of the righteous to eternity. The Messiah would then found his kingdom centred upon the city of Jerusalem. It is this grandiose vision, kept alive by Jewish orthodoxy down the centuries, that explains some of the impassioned resistance to Gentiles, followers of foreign cults, ever taking control of even part of the holy city. Jerusalem is not merely bricks and mortar. It is the place wherein the divine throne of God will be established in the event of another messianic coming.

One of the most fascinating and extraordinary of all religious war documents to emerge from archaeological sites in the ancient Near East is the so-called War Scroll, dated to the first or second century BCE and allegedly preserved among many other texts by an Essene community at Qumran as one of the Dead Sea Scrolls. These austere and remote sectarians dispensed with the more typical anticipation of deliverance in that they considered the possibility of two Messiahs: a warrior who would slay the ungodly and defeat nations,[27] and a more priestly divine who would serve to interpret the law.[28] In 1948 the ruins of Khirbet Qumran lying on the western shore of the Dead Sea about 8 miles south of Jericho in the wilderness of Judaea yielded up a treasure trove of ancient Hebrew and Aramaic manuscripts, discovered in eleven scattered caves. Nineteen heavily damaged columns of the War Scroll were discovered in Cave 1, and another collection of fragments was discovered a little to the south in Cave 4. Some of the War Scroll is clearly original while other parts, including an introduction to the entire work and a narration of a final battle against an enemy called the Kittim (written as 'Chittim' in the King James version of the Bible), are thought by scholars to be based on the closing verses of the Old Testament Book of Daniel. These describe the downfall of the Seleucid ruler of Palestine, Antiochus Epiphanes, in the second century BCE and represent a blatantly militant call to arms.

And at the time of the end shall the king of the south push at him; and the king of the north shall come against him like a whirlwind, with chariots and with horsemen, and with many ships; and he shall enter into the countries, and shall overflow and pass over . . . he shall stretch forth his hand also upon the countries; and the land of Egypt shall not escape . . . but tidings out of the east and out of the north shall trouble him: therefore he shall go forth with great fury to destroy, and utterly to make away many. And he shall plant the tabernacles of his palace between the seas in the glorious holy mountain; yet he shall come to his end, and none shall help him.[29]

Biblical scholars interpret the Hebrew name Kittim not as a people but a place, Kition (modern Larnaca in Cyprus), once an important Phoenician port. This they propose is why biblical reference is usually in the context of ships.[30] By the Maccabean period of Judaean history, and as Cyprus became strongly influenced by Greek culture, the application of the word was extended to describe the whole of Greece and, finally, to include Rome. The War Scroll envisages an attack by the sons of light against the sons of darkness, and the writer goes on to prophesy that the archangel Michael will rise up on behalf of Greater Judaea and vanquish her oppressors. When the Dead Sea Scrolls were written, therefore, Kittim stood for the Gentile 'enemy' in the shape of the Romans and the previous occupants of Palestine, the Seleucid Greeks. The War Scroll beats the drum, citing a list of Judah's enemies, past and present, including the old adversary Assyria. In the Proclamation of War it speaks of 'the unleashing of the attack of the sons of light against the company of the sons of darkness, the army of Belial; against the band of Edom, Moab, and the sons of Ammon, and the Philistines, and against the bands of Kittim, of Assyria and their allies the ungodly of the Covenant'.[31]

There is, however, a twist in the tale, because Antiochus Epiphanes had successfully encouraged the Jewish people to pursue pagan practices, much as they had done in the past. According to the Jewish historian Jason of Cyrene the response was one of widespread support and enthusiasm. 'Many in Israel took delight in his [form of] worship and they began sacrificing to idols and profaned the Sabbath. Furthermore the king [Antiochus] sent letters . . . that they should build high places and sacred groves and shrines for idols . . . and many of the people joined themselves unto them, all those who had forsaken the law; these did evil in the land.'[32] Judah's enemies on whom war must be unleashed are therefore also seen to include the enemy within.

In at least one respect the experience of the Israelites during their expansionist phase differed markedly from that of both Christians and Muslims. Beyond their territory, according to the Deuteronomist, they could rape and pillage to their souls' content, though they could not slaughter indiscriminately. 'Of the cities of these people, which the Lord thy God doth give thee for an inheritance, thou shalt save alive nothing that breatheth.'[33] Within the confines of the Promised Land, however, the rules handed down to them were somewhat more stringent, allowing them only to anathematise alien cults.

There is no evidence that the children of Israel ever sought to convert their enemies, although a degree of gradual social and cultural assimilation took place over a long period of time.[34] It was only much later in the history of the Jews, during the Hellenic period, that conversion to Judaism gained acceptance. Christians on the other hand were intent on conversion from the outset, as were early Muslims, since this was the only way in which they could gain numerical strength. But in both of these situations there was no clear ethnic separation between the founding fathers of the movements and the idolatrous people around them.

The glossing over of violence in the biblical texts should not disguise the fact that the leaders of ancient Israel from Moses onwards, through Joshua and David down to the priestly Hasmonaeans, were hard men, greedy for material power. They are depicted as the enforcers of a holy covenant, but the evidence of this militant pact with God came only from their own mouths. There is of course no miraculous artefact; no archaeological treasure; no inscribed tablet to prove that the Yahwist God ever promoted the shedding of blood in his name beyond the claims of those who delivered the instructions. Jewish historians dispense with the 'commanded by God' notion as something of a modern-day embarrassment and focus instead on the superior tactics of the Israelite military leaders. Moses apparently thought nothing of ordering his Levite brethren to take a sword and slaughter 3,000 fellow Hebrews, 'every man his brother, and every man his companion and every man his neighbour', for the crime of a brief dalliance with idolatry.[35] Joshua is portrayed as Moses' military henchman, who after the death of his patron spent much of his adult life engaged in indiscriminate killing in order to rid the land of anyone and anything that did not conform to the object of his own ideological zeal. David was a shrewd, out-and-out imperialist probably little different in character from the most tyrannical of the Mesopotamian dictators. From an early age he showed brutal tendencies and apparently relished butchery on a grand scale. To obtain the hand of Saul's daughter Machal he had thought little of not only massacring 200 Philistines in order to present Saul with a grotesque tribute, but of taking the lives of twice the hundred that Saul had originally demanded. 'David arose and went, he and his men, and slew of the Philistines two hundred men; and David brought their foreskins and they gave them in full tale to the king, that he might be the king's son in law.'[36] David undoubtedly understood the religious significance of removing the foreskins of the slain, yet he was also sufficiently unconcerned about the commands of his covenant that he happily committd adultery with the wife of one of his generals, whom he then had assassinated. The acts of all these men often defied recognisable norms of humanity but were supposedly committed in answer to divine authority.

Modern interpreters of Jewish biblical history tend to hurry through these matters and play down acts of aggression, interpreting them as defensive responses, with the result that biblical history is distorted still further. When discussing the battles of Deborah and Barak, the fourth and fifth Judges, against the Canaanites, A. Malamat reports that 'like other Israelite wars under the Judges, this was fundamentally a war of defence thrust upon the people. The Canaanites were apparently attempting, in a last comprehensive effort in the north of the country, to turn back the clock of history.'[37] Other neighbours of the Israelites earn similar labels. Towards the end of the twelfth century, during the lifetime of the Israelite commander Gideon, the Midianites are painted darkly 'in the style of desert predators [who] descended on the cultivated areas at harvest time plundering and destroying the crops'. This provided Gideon with ample excuse to launch a 'daring long-range pursuit' as far as the 'recalcitrant town of Penuel, killing its inhabitants and razing its citadel, all this because the populace had declined to supply his troops with food for fear of Midianite reprisal'.[38]

The Philistines are frequently claimed to have been the ultimate warmongers against the Israelites. But the Books of Joshua and Judges do not have to be scrutinised too closely for it to be appreciated that Philistine immigrants had a fair claim to residency in the region and merely resisted efforts by the Israelite tribes to dislodge them from their city bases in the south-west. Malamat, however, writes glowingly of how, 'awakening to its own latent potential in the struggle for life and death against the Philistine oppressor, the nation of Israel constituted itself as a monarchy in the final quarter of the 11th century'. In the retrospective view, it was always others who launched aggression against a moderate Israel. It is not hard to find claims made by modern Jewish historians to distort the facts. It has been argued, for example, that it was not King David who initiated a bloody war against the Ammonites but the reverse.[39] In a more dispassionate analysis, the Philistines having realised that David was driven by imperialist ambition and was now looking expectantly in their direction, the Ammonite leaders had called on the assistance of the Syrian Aramaeans in order to defend themselves against impending Israelite assault.

Those who dominated the Israelite clans during the period of biblical history had adopted a revolutionary and partly effective method for obtaining obedience from their subjects that relied on the power of religious superstition. They took their armies to war and obliged them to commit atrocities that made some, such as Saul, rationalise and draw back. Violence was urged with the justification that an omnipotent and unseen hand was steering the course of events and scrutinising behaviour, ready at any time to deliver a mailed fist to those who wavered or slid away from the imposed ideology. The books of the Old Testament thus read as an unremitting catalogue of violence, always in supposed obedience to the will of God. 'The name of the Lord' was called upon to explain and indemnify conquest and control involving extreme methods of suppression and including the most extreme forms of ethnic cleansing. Moses and his successors can be said to have invented the terrifying but ingenious device of 'Big Brother is Watching You'. They conjured up words from God to endorse their actions much as a modern advertising campaign for a proprietary brand of curative informs us that it is 'recommended by doctors'. Who says so? For a time the strategy worked, but throughout history priests have rarely made successful generals, and so it was with the ancestors of today's state of Israel.

FIVE

The Christian Counter-attack

Where Judaism went in terms of earning a belligerent reputation, Christendom would shortly follow. Anti-Christian sentiments received a serious body blow after the rise to power and coronation of Constantine the Great as Roman Emperor of the West in 312 CE. Pagans, knowingly or otherwise, now faced the slow downhill road towards oblivion throughout Europe, and, although Christianity was still not quite the official religion of the Roman Empire, the tide of public opinion had turned in its favour. The leading lights of Rome knew which side of their non-secular bread was being buttered, and by joining the new religious elite they were assured not only of a place in heaven but also of a short cut to secular prominence beforehand. In 386 CE, by the time that one of the leading pagan aristocrats died as consul-designate, he was being best remembered for an anecdotal remark made within earshot of the papal secretary of his day, St Jerome. The pagan is said to have exhorted the pontiff, Damasus I, who reigned from October 366 to December 384, 'Make me Bishop of Rome and I will become a Christian at once.'[1] Damasus actually acquired something of a dubious reputation during his pontificate for endearing himself to upper-class pagan families through lavish hospitality, particularly where wealthy women were concerned, and he was gleefully dubbed 'the matron's ear-tickler' by Roman gossips; but, at the same time, Damasus was relentless in his pursuit and condemnation of heretics.[2]

It was during the fourth century that patterns of violence in Christendom also changed. Now that the constant threat of persecution had been lifted, Christian leaders began marshalling their forces not only to thwart internal dissent but also to confront

95

pagan enemies. The first military engagement against the pagan rump was not long in coming. Shortly before his assassination in 383 the Western Emperor, Gratian, repudiated the title of Pontifex Maximus, much resented by Christians, terminated the salaries of the Vestal Virgins, who earned their pay not least by displaying themselves decoratively around the gardens of their retreat in the Forum, and blocked other subsidies to the official pagan cults in Rome. In a particularly contentious move during 382 he had instructed that the Altar of Victory, the arch-symbol of pagan devotion, be removed from the Senate House, although he was content to leave in place a statue of the winged Victoria, whom he decided that the Christian flock could conveniently interpret as an angel.[3] Conservative opinion was not long in condemning the altar outrage and in the following year, after Gratian's assassination, his eastern counterpart, Valentinian II, was presented with a petition from the pagan elite of Rome – now marshalled by one of their more influential lights, the scholarly Quintus Aurelius Symmachus – to restore the altar. After a barrage of objection from Ambrose, the no-less energetic Bishop of Milan, Valentinian turned down the request and also ignored pleas from a delegation of pagan priests. However, Valentinian was himself destined for assassination in 392 and Eugenius, the new Augustus, while generally being regarded as a usurper, endeared himself to the conservative pagan community during his brief two-year reign by bringing back the Altar of Victory and initiating private sponsorship of a number of pagan cults.

With Eugenius temporarily in charge, the pagan community of Rome was sufficiently confident of its position that the ancient festivals were celebrated anew in the spring of 394 under the management of another of their leading lights, Virius Nichomachus Flavianus the Younger, whom Eugenius had installed as the Prefect of Rome. This was too much for the Christian camp, which howled for forcible cancellation of the order. Later in that year the army of the Emperor Theodosius I, temporarily excommunicated in 390 by Ambrose for his part in a massacre at Thessalonica before being restored to a state of grace, clashed with that of Eugenius on the banks of the River Frigidus. Cult statues of Jupiter and Heracles led the way for the pagan contingent in the hope that their presence would bring weather conditions adverse to the Christian forces. It was not to be. Eugenius was slain and Theodosius triumphed over the 'army of unbelievers'.[4] The course of future imperial policy in favour of Christians was now firmly set. Theodosius found himself increasingly under the thumb of Ambrose, one of the most hard-line and thuggish of the early Christian lights, and from 391 until Theodosius' death in 395 a succession of edicts against both paganism and the heretical sects that claimed to be Christian or part-Christian started to flow from the imperial legislative machine.[5]

There is no simple or single explanation of why at around this time Christendom began to adopt a new and expansionist militancy, but rather a number of factors – spiritual, strategic and solidly materialistic – came to bear. The interests of Christendom, with the backing of the Holy Roman Empire, were now directed towards extension of its spiritual clout beyond the imperial frontiers, and one of the chief preoccupations of the pontificate was consideration of the Muslim threat. By the end of the seventh century, some 300 years after the reign of Constantine, the rampaging forces of Islam had not only seized the Holy Land from the perennially weak eastern wing of the Christian Empire, but had also taken over North Africa and much of the Iberian peninsula from its western counterpart. During the eighth and early ninth centuries, however, Charlemagne, the leader of an administration that was now officially in its post-Classical period, conquered most of Western Christendom and in 800 was crowned 'Emperor of the West' by Pope Leo III. Centres of anti-Muslim resistance soon began to form from which, initially, the Christian reconquest of Iberia would come, although for a long time any such military advances were spasmodic and localised. There is a brief note of success under the leadership of the King of Asturias, Pelayo, whom history records as the first Christian hero, in 718, of the Spanish Reconquista against the Muslim occupiers. Raids to the south as far as Lisbon were then carried out under the Portuguese King Alphonso II (791–842). The first of the more significant victories involved Charlemagne's forces taking Gerona during 785 and restoring Barcelona to Christian rule by 801. Between 850 and 866 Ordono I was responsible for recapturing the area that would later become known as Aragon.

On the whole these military pluses were of limited scope, and in the age that followed Christendom had to be defended more or less constantly against attacks from quarters other than the 'Islamic front'. The Northmen (who later became known as the Normans) and the Hungarians chiefly plagued Christian frontiers further north. In was in the defence of all that was holy to Christendom in this tumultuous era that the warring medieval knight came into his own and the notorious and at times utterly bizarre phenomenon of the Crusades emerged. At first the strategic objective of the Christian knight-at-arms was merely to defend the Church and protect the weak. This tallied with a doctrine promoted by St Augustine, widely respected throughout Europe, which drew clear distinction between offensive and defensive war. Although fighting pagans was not part of the initial job description of a knight of the Cross, and any such exercises were officially viewed as defensive, sometimes it was convenient to draw on Augustine's contrasting imagery of light and dark, the city of God and the city of the Devil, to provide good reason for Christians attacking non-Christian neighbours. This both ensured the justice of making war on the unholy and also allowed for a departure from the old ecclesiastical rule that 'penitents should not bear arms'.[6] The purely defensive policy gradually changed until 'pagan-bashing' became an important aspect, perhaps the most important, of knightly conduct and the Church was prompted to take direct responsibility for waging war in the name of God. By the ninth and tenth centuries religiously inspired attacks against the heathen wherever he was found on the borders of Christendom, whether threatening the empire or minding his own business, took on a subtly different status to those secular campaigns that were waged strictly to acquire booty and territorial gain.

Suitable bastions from which the knight on his charger could sally forth arose across medieval Europe, quasi-military institutions that also stood to unite the diversity of Christian peoples and, optimistically, to bridge the conflicts that too frequently divided them. These were the mighty monastic houses, the religious orders that had first been reorganised under the system developed by the monks of Cluny near Lyons. By the mid-eleventh century Cluny was the largest monastic institution in Europe. It was also the most influential in the years before the monks of Citeaux in Burgundy, that other great mother house founded in 1098 and belonging to the Cistercian Order, undertook a series of critical reforms. These institutions now came to represent the military backbone of the Holy See as clearly as they served as cloistered religious retreats. Their military brethren largely managed to escape jurisdiction through privileges granted by local bishops, and their abbeys provided resting places for those participating in the pilgrimages that travelled incessantly along the roads of the Christian world.[7] The general attitude to military activity as one of the central functions of such establishments began to change early in the tenth century when an influential work, the *Vita of St Gerald of Aurillac* compiled by Odo, the Abbot of Cluny, identified militarism in the name of God as a way of life possessing spiritual and redemptive value. This point was further reinforced by a monastic contemporary, Bonizo of Sutri, who devoted a full section of his *Liber de Vita Christiana* to explaining the chivalrous responsibilities of remaining faithful to and protecting the name of the Lord, to the extent of disregarding personal safety.

From about the mid-tenth century the temperature of Christian militarism was clearly rising. Bishops were receiving pontifical instruction about precise rituals for blessing weapons of war and military banners. Such incantations included, 'Hearken O Lord to our prayers and bless with the hand of Your Majesty this sword with which your servant desires to be girded in order to defend and protect churches, widows, orphans and all the servants of God against the cruelty of the pagans and in order to be the scourge of all those who lay ambushed for him.'[8] The military religious knight was thus given carte blanche to hunt down heretics and schismatics in addition to protecting the poor and needy and abstaining from pillage, instructions that were not, of course, always applied evenly.

Across Europe the Christian knights and their followers, answering to the great religious orders, were savouring the prospect of taking the campaign to the enemy, and at the close of the century the idea of purely defensive Christian warfare had become distinctly passé. Even so it would be a full 700 years after Constantine that the first major offensive of Christendom against another religious ideology would take place in the East with the marshalling of the First Crusade.

Keen to add his voice to the ever-louder martial strains, the influential monk, Abbon (*c.* 945–1004), who ruled over the abbey of Fleury in present-day St-Benoît-sur-Loire, had proclaimed emphatically in his *Apologeticus* that the objective in life of a knight should be to turn his weapons against the enemies of the Church. The military knights needed little persuading to interpret this as encouragement for a rather more adventuresome scrap than merely defending Christendom against pagan assault. Officially, these actions would not be described as wars to eliminate paganism or force conversion, although there was much enthusiasm in clerical quarters for trotting out a particular gospel simile attributed to Jesus, 'Go out into the highways, and compel them to come in, that my house may be filled.'[9] In *The City of God* St Augustine had seized on this instruction and applied it specifically to heretics within the Christian community, but another reforming medieval ascetic, Brun of Querfurt, one of an intimate coterie surrounding the Italian King Otto III, had decided that Jesus was in fact referring to all sorts, including pagans. He raised the complaint that only a few monarchs since Constantine the Great had bothered to drive pagans into the Church and most had been far too interested in fighting for territorial gain.[10]

Brun of Querfurt's interpretation of the gospel message was but one of an assortment of honourable reasons put forward in favour of offensive war. These generally followed the line that the protection of Christians 'from the fury of the enemy' was a necessary task, while also implying that Christendom was never the aggressor.[11] The coronation orders of several medieval emperors included the pontifical command, 'may you cast out all the adversaries of Christ, the pagans and bad Christians . . . for a lasting peace of all Christians'.[12] And so in Germany the knightly forces wasted little time in attacking the pagan Slavs, while in Italy they began to think seriously about restoring Christian pride to Muslim-held lands in the East.

The duty of the Christian Emperor was to protect the Church from danger, and if this necessitated attacking pagan neighbours, who automatically qualified as a danger, nobody could complain. It must also be said that Holy Roman Emperors saw little wrong in the hypocrisy of recruiting pagans as occasional allies when it suited them. At one stage the German Emperor Henry II (973–1024) entered into a questionable deal with pagan Slav tribes, collectively named the Liutizi, that if they felt inclined to lend support in a protracted conflict against Polish Christian forces, who were threatening the purely secular interests of the German state, Henry would ensure the preservation of the Liutizi pagan cult. Strategic issues were not, of course, the only factors in Christian aggression. More pecuniary excuses were to be found, especially among those who had watched enviously as Venetian merchants made colossal sums of money trading with Muslims in the lands bordering the Eastern Mediterranean. During the latter part of the tenth century, as the European military situation altered, and particularly when the principal barbarian threat, the Normans, had become settled and Christianised in France, attitudes began to shift even more enthusiastically in favour of outright aggression against the forces of Islam occupying the Holy Land. In the early part of the eleventh century some enterprising French barons reached the sanguine conclusion that there were rich pickings to be had by organising military assaults against Muslim-held territory.

These militant rumblings against 'the infidel' took time to develop into anything approaching full-scale holy war, and for much of the era following the foundation of Islam there had been reasonable cooperation between Christian and Muslim cultures. Since the ninth century, however, the coastal cities of Italy had been obliged to fend off occasional plundering raids by Muslims coming across the Eastern Mediterranean and at around the turn of the millennium some of these cities, with Venice leading the way, opted for a more aggressive posture beginning with the relief of the Byzantine city of Bari in 1003. The Venetians, under the captaincy of their Doge,

Peter Orseolo, assembled a fleet and set out to liberate the people of Bari from 'the cruelty of the heathen'. When the Venetian fleet hove into view, some of the besieged residents of the city believed that they were witnessing a miracle, and this particular incident probably marked the start of that phenomenon described as Christian holy war. The interest in launching a full-scale assault against Islam received a boost when in 1008 reports began to come back to the European leaders that the Muslim caliphate had been weakened by internal strife, and, with this in mind, the Spanish King, Alfonso VI, advanced a series of raids against tottering local emirs in Iberia, resulting in the fall of Toledo on 25 May 1085. More or less at the same time the redoubtable El Cid took Valencia.

From about the close of the eleventh century another factor came into play. European Christendom had been seized by a peculiar religious fervour that was to last for several centuries and has rarely been seen since. This undoubtedly helped to stir public sentiment and raise passions about the prospect of recovering the most sacred Christian site, the Holy Sepulchre, from pagan hands. The chief inspiration came from one exceptional pontiff, Innocent III, who reigned from 1198 to 1216. Determined not only to apply papal spiritual dominance in all areas of secular government and to subordinate temporal rulers to theocratic rule, but also to extend the boundaries of European Christendom overseas, Innocent III believed passionately in the vision of a grand Christian republic. More than all other medieval incumbents of the papal throne he envisaged a world in which states that were otherwise more or less independent from one another would look to the supreme authority of the Church of Rome in all matters. The choice of subject taken for his coronation sermon, drawn from the Old Testament Book of Jeremiah, is not without significance: 'See, I have this day set thee over the nations and over the kingdoms, to root out, and to pull down, and to destroy, and to throw down, to build and to plant.'[13]

Innocent III, however, may not claim credit for conceiving the idea of the Crusades. This must go to the great reformist pontiff Gregory VII, who reigned from 1073 to 1085. Gregory had been the first pope to claim universal jurisdiction over the whole of Christendom – laity and religious clergy, prince and pauper. It was he who first dreamed of liberating the Holy Sepulchre by armed aggression and restoring union with the Eastern Church.

How does one define the medieval Crusades? Religious historians boil them down to a series of collective actions on the part of Christendom that can be interpreted as armed pilgrimages, not to convert pagans but specifically to reclaim the holy places of the Bible for Christendom. This, however, is a narrow and thoroughly inaccurate definition, because between the twelfth and sixteenth centuries a series of Christian Crusades took place with other destinations and objectives in view. Less well known are the northern Crusades, largely mounted by the Teutonic knights against the pagan Slavs and Russians. There is also the matter of the notorious Albigensian Crusade into southern France and the unmitigated brutality of the Spanish Crusade to the Americas that followed.

The most thoroughly recorded of the campaigns, it has to be agreed, are those that set out to liberate the Holy Land. At least, this was the optimistic idea, because, although most began with the best of intentions, in nearly all cases they ended in failure or having been seriously sidetracked. Dragging on for some 200 years between the eleventh and thirteenth centuries, and designed to take back from the Arabs the lands which they had seized in Palestine and Syria in the seventh century, these Crusades were vicious, strategically unsound and at times ludicrous in their mismanagement. They became known in European circles as the Wars of the Cross, but to Arab historians they were the Frankish Wars or Frankish Invasions, mounted by people soon tagged as *franj*, a word applied in colloquial Arabic even today to designate Westerners in general and the French in particular. The Franks had originated in what is now the western part of Germany, and towards the end of the fifth century had successfully migrated into the northern part of Gaul following the retreat of the Romans. By 500 they controlled a vast area north of Paris, and by the mid-eleventh century they were challenging Byzantine control over the lands of the Eastern Mediterranean.

In 1073, the Byzantine Emperor in the East, Manuel VII, had appealed to Pope Gregory VII for military assistance in defence of his realm, but Gregory did little by way of response due to a continuing ecumenical spat that had begun in mid-century between Greek Eastern and Latin Western wings of the Church. At the time the balance of power between the two had shifted profoundly, with the Eastern Byzantines now a shadow of their former selves. They had lost land, political and military control of the Eastern Mediterranean, and commercial affluence. Their financial reserves were depleted, which meant that Constantinople's military resources were also substantially weakened. The Byzantine Patriarch was smarting over the suppression of Greek customs that had come about under Gregorian reforms in the West, and by way of retaliation he had closed down Latin visitors' churches in the city. With the Byzantines in this enfeebled condition the Pope in Rome saw an opportunity for gain and dispatched a delegation to Constantinople with the intention of asserting papal dominance once more. The Byzantines, however, were having none of it, and matters became increasingly heated until the Patriarch of Constantinople found himself opening a letter of personal excommunication conveyed by one of the senior members of the Roman curia, Cardinal Humbert. Not to be outdone the Patriarch cried 'foul', dismissed the letter as a fake and excommunicated its author.

A further plea for help aimed at Gregory's successor Urban II, who reigned from 1088 to 1099, fell on more receptive ears. Papal attitudes towards the Muslims had hardened after the pontiff had learned of a restriction imposed by the Seljuk Turks that prevented pilgrims from visiting the holy city of Jerusalem. The Seljuks had wrested control of the Middle East from the Fatimid caliphs of Egypt in 1065 and, although the Fatimids had laid obstacles in the path of Christian visitors, it was to be the Seljuks who finally stirred Europe into decisive action. A vociferous and influential monk named Peter the Hermit was also doing his part to stir public sentiment by trumpeting the moral value of an armed adventure to liberate the Holy Sepulchre. Born at Amiens in 1050, tradition has it that Peter the Hermit was first enthused for his mission by a vision obtained in the Church of the Holy Sepulchre. Encouraged by divine revelation he toured Europe preaching the urgency of rescuing Jerusalem from the Seljuk Turks, the 'Saracens', and his undoubted powers of oratory drew the crowds and inflamed emotions at street level. His exhortations eventually brought about such a degree of agitation that the public angst could not be ignored.

The period between 1095 and 1291 saw no less than seven major offensives and a host of minor military exercises, all undertaken in the name of Christendom and with the banner of the faith, the Cross, flying high. It was not, however, the immediate situation in the Holy Land or even the ranting of Peter the Hermit, to which the root causes of the Crusades can be attributed, but political issues at home. The First Crusade, conducted over a roller-coaster four-year period from 1095 to 1099, was triggered and controlled directly by a papacy that found itself in deepening internal trouble. Throughout much of the eleventh century the Church of Rome had been developing an ever-greater thirst for secular as well as spiritual power, and the implications of this came to a head with Pope Innocent III. Already, prior to his reign, various pontiffs had acquired what the historian R.W. Southern describes as a 'litigious thirst', a yen to see all parties, archbishops, bishops and ordinary litigants come to Rome for government as part of the optimistic dream of a great Christian society bound together by loyalty to St Peter, with kings, princes, bishops and monks looking to a single leader, the Pope, for a single end.[14] Not all European policy-makers were in sympathy with this grandiose vision, and certainly not the secular Emperor of the Holy Roman Empire, Henry IV, who sat on his German throne bristling with indignation. Vexed by a pronouncement of *Dictus papae* on the part of Gregory VII in March 1075, which effectively awarded the papacy massively increased powers including the prohibition of princes and other secular rulers in the appointment of bishops, Henry decided to place a man of his own choosing in Rome.[15] It resulted in Gregory being deposed at the Synod of Worms in January 1076 by twenty-six carefully selected pro-German bishops. Gregory was not amused and promptly responded by excommunicating Henry. The feud escalated, with relentless hatred building on both sides. In 1090, after launching an Italian military campaign, and having seen Urban II succeed Gregory VII, Henry chose to oust Urban, who largely supported the policies of Gregory VII, and to throw his weight behind an anti-pope in the shape of Clement III. Urban wisely fled Rome and sought refuge with the Norman kings of southern Italy.[16] Having seen Clement illegally installed in the papal seat, he then became desperate for a common cause to deflect attention away from the schism that now seemed virtually unavoidable. With Henry experiencing military setbacks and having become bottled up with his army in the region of Verona, Urban made his way back to Rome and managed, through generous bribery, to recover the Lateran Palace in 1094 (the Vatican Palace did not become the official papal residence until 1288). Nevertheless the imperial court was still heavily backing Clement, with little sign of wavering, and Urban II needed to find a solution to what was already a protracted political conflict between rival Christian factions.[17]

Urban II reached the logical conclusion that there was a pressing need to unite Europe in a suitable cause célèbre, and the most obvious contender, although not necessarily the wisest, was the Holy Land and its plight. The sensible course, and one that probably would have achieved far greater success, would have been to mount a military campaign against the Greek Empire in the East in order to reunite Christendom. General opinion regarded the Greeks as thoroughly schismatic and heretical, having proclaimed themselves optimistically the inheritors of the Roman Empire. An assault on the Byzantine powers would undoubtedly have won much popular support, particularly since militarily they were also in a weak position. Byzantium had been in decline for fifty years. It had lost all of its Italian possessions, and its army, emasculated by decades of internal crisis, had not managed to stem the Muslim advance. In 1071 when the Byzantines surrendered the town of Manzikert, the Turkish forces also captured the Emperor, Romanus Diogenes. In the aftermath of one of the Byzantines' worst military debacles, the Seljuk Turks gained effective control over the whole of Asia

Minor, and the loss of Antioch in 1085 completed the rout. The Byzantine Christians had limited resources at their disposal and were now quite incapable of war against the Muslims or anyone else. Yet the papacy elected to have Christendom remain divided, prop up the tottering Eastern Empire, and lavish vast efforts and money on the military campaigns against Islam, the strategic importance of which from the outset was far less convincing.

The religious establishment envisaged that the launch of a Christian assault on Islam would serve as a useful device to get the secular communities of Europe to forget their troubles and unite in a common inspirational cause. In reality Western civilisation was beset by rather deeper social and economic problems than any political ructions arising from excessive papal ambition. The general population, as distinct from the nobility, gradually became resentful about its lot and increasingly restive for change. Famine was never far from the doorstep because agriculture had not kept pace with the population explosion that began in the twelfth century, and successive onslaughts of the plague added to the miseries of existence. The ordinary subject viewed the noble knight, in whose wake and service he and his fellow hordes of impoverished peasants struggled along, as unreasonably well fed and well shod. For this reason in the minds of the European establishment, revolution was emerging on the horizon as a distinct and ominous possibility. Crusading was seen as the ideal distraction. The tempting prospect for the would-be conqueror of Jerusalem with his stave, ragged clothes and worn-out shoes – the winning of the city of the Revelation – was to be able to imitate the suffering of Christ on the Cross and to commit to a kind of mass sacrifice to be rewarded by a mass apotheosis. In his *Europe* Norman Davies succinctly describes the phenomenon of the Crusades as a collective *imitatio Christi* and 'the messianism of the poor'.[18]

In March 1095, believing that at last he had sufficient popular backing to launch a Crusade, Urban II summoned a synod in the convivial setting of Piacenza in Lombardy, near the confluence of the Po and Trebbia rivers. There, and to resounding cheers, he first robustly declared Clement III's ordination invalid. Next, while retaining Gregory's edict over the German ruler, Henry, to keep out of Church affairs, then delivered a shrewd sop to the powerful Norman kings of England and southern Italy by restoring them to full control over their own churches. The atmosphere was the right one in which to broadcast a more official rallying call to Christians than that of Peter the Hermit, to wage holy war against the 'infidel'. An ideal excuse arose when the Eastern Emperor, Alexis I Commenus, appealed to the Western powers to go to the aid of a chronically beleaguered Byzantine Church now increasingly pressed by the Muslim hordes. It was the nearest that the Western arm of the Church ever came to a rapprochement with its Eastern counterpart.

In order to give the matter official sanction Urban II convened a further synod at Clermont-Ferrand in France, where on 27 November 1095 the signal for the First Crusade was formally broadcast. Whether Urban simply wished to restore the security of the pilgrim routes to the Holy Places or to recapture the land of Palestine was never made clear. The volume of response is an indication of the renewed popularity that Urban had earned on behalf of the papacy, but, before any level of order could be achieved, the news brought chaos. Initially, the reaction of the lay populace was passionate but wholly lacking in organisation, and, although no prudent admirer of the German Emperor and his court dared show support for the papal initiative, nonetheless thousands of fervent pilgrim enthusiasts, including large numbers of women, gathered together and armed themselves with a motley assortment of weapons with which to batter the infidel into submission. The German Emperor meanwhile harboured grave personal suspicions about the motives of the Crusade leaders and made them swear oaths of allegiance before he agreed to hand over a measly amount of cash backing. His daughter Anna summed up the mood when she allegedly remarked of the knights that she admired their bodies but despised their minds.[19]

With virtually no food or other material supplies to sustain them, four virtually anarchic hordes now headed east towards the Balkans and en route thought fit to plunder much of the countryside for sustenance and whatever else of value they could lay their hands on.

This, however, was not the worst of their marauding activities. Fired up by rabble-rousers clamouring for revenge against those who had insulted Christ, the mob turned on the first offenders that vaguely fitted the charge and, as they advanced through the Rhineland, pursued the apparently senseless policy of murdering some 8,000 Jews. It marked the earliest major European pogrom against the Jews and amounted to a crime that even St Bernard was compelled to denounce.[20]

The collective behaviour of this raggle-taggle army triggered sufficient resentment among the local populace in Bohemia, Hungary and neighbouring Bulgaria that the majority of would-be Crusaders fell victim to reprisals before they had even reached Constantinople. Once there, the capital of the province of Bythinia perched on the eastern shore of Lake Ascanius, the tattered remnant congregated and circled the walls of nearby Nicaea in a supposed show of force, chanting what would become the familiar Crusader rallying cry, 'God wills it'. It was a useful reminder that the Almighty was still very much in command when it came to the violent shedding of blood. In a climate of religious superstition it was perhaps inevitable that some of these 'warriors' would acquire supernatural powers. There are reports of a specially recruited band known as the Tafurs manning the vanguard devoid of armour, fortified only with sticks, religious ecstasy and probably a little extra something, who terrified the Turks because they were alleged to eat the bodies of the slain.

During the autumn months, however, the Turkish army progressively dispatched the besiegers, culminating in a massacre on 21 October 1096, reported somewhat improbably by Arab historians as involving as many as 26,000 slain. The sources describe witnessing thousands of women, children and old people parading in rags 'like an evicted tribe'. All are said to have worn strips of red cloth in the shape of a cross, sewn on the backs of their garments.[21]

The next strategic advance of the First Crusade was organised in more recognisably military style but with somewhat diffuse motives. The knights who joined the march, well fed, well armed and well provided with horses and retinues, envisaged spiritual benefits and material advantages coming their way in the form of blessings and booty once they arrived in Turkish-held lands. Thus the heady mix of power, politics and greed once more merged inseparably with religion. These back-up Christian forces advanced towards Constantinople in five expeditionary groups led by a coterie of French nobility including Hugues de Vermandois, the brother of the French King, Godfroi de Bouillon, the Duke of Lorraine, Raymond de St Gilles, the Count of Toulouse and Robert Curthose, the son of William the Conqueror.[22]

On the Muslim side a youthful and woefully inexperienced 18-year-old Turkish general named Kilij Arslan, a son of the great Suleyman, is said to have ignored warnings about the fresh contingents arriving at Constantinople. A gradual build-up had started in 1096, but it was not until April 1097 that Arslan began to prepare for decisive confrontation, moving his army to Malatya, an urban centre north-west of Diarbekir. The Frankish build-up was completed in the summer of that year and in June the barons attacked and overwhelmed Nicaea. Arslan abandoned any hope of retaking the city and took his force to Dorylaeum, where he met the Crusaders and was beaten decisively.

The European barons led their combined victorious army into Syria and on 21 October 1097 they laid siege to the major city of Antioch. Christian commentators were jubilant. In November Anselm of Ribemont wrote a letter to the Archbishop of Reims: 'Be it known to you that we have certainly conquered for our Lord two hundred castles and cities. May our mother Church in the West rejoice that she has borne men who have won for her such a glorious name and have succoured the Church in the East in such a marvellous fashion.' Meanwhile, the Arab historian Ibn al-Athir reported that the ruler Yaghi-Siyan, fearing sedition, had thrown any Christians out of the city.[23]

Surrounded by massive walls, Antioch was claimed to be virtually impregnable, and it also encompassed a substantial area of cultivated land that fed the city. Nonetheless, during the siege, which lasted for seven months, disease and famine took their toll on both sides, so much so that Peter the Hermit, the original rabble-rouser who had subsequently attached himself to the army of Godfroi, chose to desert the campaign and return to Europe, where he founded an Augustinian monastery at Huy near Liège. In February 1098 an Aleppan force arrived on the scene supposedly to aid the Antiochian defenders, but their leader Ridwan delayed any action, with disastrous consequences. Bottled up in a narrow strip of land between the Orontes river and Lake Antioch, his army was attacked and slaughtered. Antioch itself fell in June and the inhabitants were massacred in what was to become a familiar round of brutality on the part of the Crusaders. The Christian forces suffered a temporary siege fending off the regrouped Muslim army, but the Turks were finally routed. English mercenaries, especially English mariners, became involved in some of these actions to an extent that has not been clearly appreciated until recent times. An assortment of pirates, pilgrims and traders with a fleet of about thirty ships seized the important Asia Minor trading centre of Laodicea from the Turks in 1097, and they also contributed to the siege of Antioch by keeping marine supply routes open from Cyprus on behalf of the besieging forces.[24]

Much depleted, in 1099 the Crusaders advanced on Jerusalem, the ultimate objective of the next and final siege of the campaign. Of more than half a million soldiers who had assembled in Nicaea, less than 40,000 witnessed the capture of Jerusalem on 15 July. A few days later, at the end of the month, Urban II died, ignorant of the victory on which he had staked so much of his reputation because the news did not reach him in time. During the rape of the city it was reported that some 70,000 of Jerusalem's inhabitants suffered the same appalling fate as the civilian population of Antioch, slaughtered in cold blood.

At least for the time being, victory resulted in the establishment of a Christian kingdom in Palestine, based on Jerusalem, with Godfroi de Bouillon as its crowned head. Another of the crusading French knights, Bohemund, was awarded sovereign rights over Antioch. Within a month of the capture of Jerusalem the vizier of Fatimid Egypt, al-Afdal, had assembled an army of 50,000, which he pitched against 10,000 Crusaders. In spite of the odds weighing against them, the Crusaders dispersed the Muslim forces on 11 August and chased them as far as Ascalon, where the final decisive and victorious battle took place.

After Ascalon Godfroi de Bouillon had as little as 300 knights and 2,000 infantry at his disposal. He received practically no reinforcements from the West, yet during the next fifty years the Christian kingdoms of the Near East were set to grow at the expense of the Muslims. Jerusalem was substantially enlarged in the hands of its ruler, Baldwin I, early in the twelfth century, and by 1135 under his successor, Baldwin II, the Latin states seemed reasonably safe. This sense of security, however, was illusory and possession was short-lived. The Syrian leader, Saladin, took the city back into Islamic control at the Battle of Hattin in 1187. It was to change hands at least twice more, the Muslims finally gaining control in 1244, after which Jerusalem did not return to Christian hands until 1917, when the British held it under mandate prior to the creation of the state of Israel in 1948.[25]

From before the time of the First Crusade the effective defence of the Holy Land was managed by two orders of military knights, the Knights Templars and the Knights Hospitallers, and it was these institutions that generated much of the later opprobrium against the ethical conduct of the Crusades, or, more precisely, the lack of it. The so-called Knights of the Order of the Hospital of St John of Jerusalem, also known as the Knights of the Holy Sepulchre but usually referred to as Hospitallers, were founded sometime in the middle of the eleventh century, their original purpose being to provide protection for pilgrims travelling to and from Palestine and wishing to visit the Holy Sepulchre. Initially, members of the Order included an eclectic mix of men with military, medical and pastoral backgrounds. After the cessation of the First Crusade in 1099, however, the order was enlarged, received papal recognition and was exempt from various taxes and all episcopal controls, so that effectively it became autonomous. Under its first leader, Gerard, it proceeded to benefit from a generous number of donations of both land and money from crusading benefactors determined to earn their place in paradise. It professed to be essentially religious in nature but was pre-eminently a military institution. Its massively fortified bases first appeared in the Holy Land from about 1118, but most of their occupants were forced to retreat to Cyprus after the fall of Acre. They governed the island of Rhodes between 1309 and 1522 and eventually migrated to Malta, where they remained until 1801.

The Knights Templars were founded in 1119, shortly after the Hospitallers, by Hugues de Payen and Godfroi de St Adhemar along with seven others, and first went under the title of The Poor Knights of Christ and the Temple of Solomon. Like the Hospitallers they were pledged to defend pilgrims en route to the holy places in Palestine and took solemn vows of chastity, poverty and obedience, formulated by Bernard of Clairvaux but not always strictly adhered to. They received their official authority at the Council of Troyes in 1128 and obtained their name after Baldwin II granted them residential quarters in his palace in Jerusalem, which had been built on the site of the Jewish Temple. In 1172 they were granted virtual autonomy from any secular power, indeed any authority other than that of the Pope, and like the Hospitallers they paid no taxes. In time they acquired a substantial amount of wealth through donations from the nobility, much of which was invested in the construction of castles in the Middle East. The fortifications they built were massive both in construction and in the amount of money they consumed. One of the most impressive, Les Krak des Chevaliers in Syria, was about twenty times the size of Dover Castle.[26]

The Templars also gained their store of enemies, who lost little time in impugning the Knights' morals and their adherence to orthodox Christianity. The Order was suppressed in 1312 after charges had been levelled by the King of France that included such diverse misdeeds as heresy, witchcraft and sodomy. To what extent any of this was true remains a matter of conjecture. That they were thoroughly maligned is well documented, and some of this criticism was unquestionably justified. Yet they suffered greatly for the cause they fought for, and to their credit the Templars formed the backbone of the crusading forces over 200 years. As many as 20,000 perished during the campaigns to liberate and secure the Holy Land from the 'infidel'. In the space of a hundred years no less than five Masters of the Temple died with sword in hand.

The Second Crusade was launched in 1147, having been promoted by another eccentric religious figure, Bernard of Clairvaux, whose powers of persuasion were sufficient to coerce the two most powerful European monarchs, Louis VII of France and Konrad III of Germany, into gathering an immense new army and leading it across the Bosphorus back to the gates of Constantinople. The indignation of the occidental powers had been stirred not least by the fall of Edessa, the ancient biblical city of Ur, which returned to Muslim control in 1144. As with the First Crusade this second venture included a rabble of foot soldiers, pirates and not a few members of the European nobility, though often these were men of anarchic mentality, opportunist adventurers with little sense of scruple and a surfeit of brutality to be exploited. Some of the forces embarked from the English port of Dartmouth on 23 May, but matters did not go well. The incumbent Byzantine Emperor, Manuel Commenus, plotted treachery and the campaign met with little short of disaster. The German force in particular was ambushed and decimated by the Sultan of Iconium, and what was left of the expedition then mounted a doomed attack on Damascus in 1148 before struggling back to Europe.

Saladin, who had proclaimed himself as the Sultan of Muslim lands in Egypt in 1175, exploited the chronic inability of the Byzantines and the current weakness of the Latin forces, taking the opportunity to invade Palestine from the south. He crushed Christian forces at Tiberias and recaptured Jerusalem in October 1187. The only accountable success of the Second Crusade turned out to be the liberation of Lisbon from the Moors. The fleet of vessels transporting the Crusaders had reached Oporto, en route to the Straits of Gibraltar, at which juncture the Portuguese King, Alfonso I, approached the leadership for help. He managed to strike a deal that placed Lisbon under a seventeen-week siege until the Muslim forces surrendered on 24 October 1147. For this reason the Second Crusade also became cynically dubbed the 'Portuguese Crusade'.[27]

It is unquestionably the Third Crusade, led this time by three crowned heads of Europe, the German Emperor Frederick Barbarossa, Philip II of France and Richard I of England, that has captured most of the romantic attention of later historians. Barbarossa launched the Crusade in 1189 and Richard I, affectionately known as Richard the Lionheart, joined forces with him in 1190 shortly after being crowned King of England. Apart from a brief return to England for six months, Richard spent the rest of his ten-year reign away from home, either fighting or incarcerated, and died of his wounds in France in 1199. Barbarossa (not to be confused with the sixteenth-century Turkish pirate of that name) concentrated much of his career on a bitter struggle with the papacy. He was the first to engage the 'infidel', but drowned before reaching the Holy Land when attempting to cross a river in Pisidia in 1190. The climax of the campaign was the siege of Acre, which lasted for twenty-three months, and, despite all the military skills of Saladin, the city fell to the Christian forces in July 1191. It turned out to be a hollow victory for the Crusaders. They resorted to squabbling among themselves and the campaign fizzled out, with Philip II abandoning the enterprise altogether. In September of the following year Richard alone was left to negotiate a questionable truce with Saladin in exchange for the rights of Christian pilgrims to visit Jerusalem without being subject to taxation or Muslim harassment.

When Innocent III gained the pontificate in 1198, the conduct of the Crusaders became even more brutal than it had been thus far. His edict to those who joined the various Crusades that took place during his pontificate was crude but effective. It involved unrestricted remission of sins and unrestricted authority to loot and plunder. The passions generated by earlier endeavours encouraged Innocent to sanction the Fourth Crusade of 1204, in which the Crusaders never reached the Holy Land at all but managed to sack Constantinople, not once but twice. This, according to some historians, marked the apogee of the political might of the Church of Rome, and in terms of European influence the papacy probably did indeed reach the height of its powers under Innocent. He was a man with a remarkably exalted opinion of his own position; it was Innocent who popularised the title Vicar of Christ. He saw himself as 'set midway between God and man. Below God but above man and given not only the universal church but the whole world to govern'.[28] The 'whole world' included the Muslim lands, and since Innocent was also concerned with rooting out heresy and heathendom, effective crusading became one of his abiding concerns. But he was not a military strategist, and as an offensive against Islam the Fourth Crusade was abortive to the extent that it became known as the Great Betrayal. It would never reach the Holy Land and was destined to stop short 1,000 miles from Jerusalem.[29] More significantly perhaps for Christendom's future, the exercise inflicted such material damage on Constantinople that neither the city nor its feelings about the West ever recovered.[30]

The crusading army gathered in Venice prior to moving towards the Bosphorus. Here it became subject to the political intrigues of two influential men, both of whom savoured personal gain in the taking of Constantinople and therefore discouraged the Crusaders from viewing Jerusalem as their prime objective. Instead they offered the generous hire of the Venetian fleet to transport the troops to attack the Byzantine capital in return for a half share of the booty and some specific political support. For his part the aged Venetian Doge, Enrico Dandolo, relished the idea of Venetian possessions being enlarged in the Levant at little cost to the Venetian Republic. Dandolo also had a personal score to settle. Some thirty years earlier he had suffered grievously at the hands of the Christian Byzantines in an incident the causes of which can probably be traced back to the tenth century. At that time the Venetians were technically part of the Byzantine Empire and had earned the lucrative right to act as trading intermediaries between Europe and Constantinople. By the mid-twelfth century the Venetians had exploited their position and become the major trading nation in the Eastern Mediterranean, with commercial interests in a number of port cities, both Muslim and Christian. In Constantinople they had initially established themselves as a small ex-patriot waterfront community. As time passed, however, Venetian families began to expand throughout the city and the Byzantine authorities became increasingly unnerved by their influence. Eventually matters came to a head, and on a tumultuous night, unannounced, Byzantine enforcers rounded up and imprisoned many of the Venetian families. Enrico Dandolo had established himself as the most powerful maritime trader in Venice, and as a man of some influence he was sent as an envoy to negotiate the release of the prisoners. He was not well received. The Byzantines tortured and blinded him, and sent him home without reward. Subsequently elevated to the rank of Doge, he finally saw the opportunity for revenge. He was supported, though more for reasons of nepotism, by the German King, Philip of Swabia, who was married to the Byzantine Empress, Irene. Philip anticipated the chance to restore his nephew, Alexius IV, deposed following accusations of being too much in the pocket of the Venetians, to the Byzantine throne.

Dandolo set out with the Venetian fleet and its Crusader cargo, ostensibly bound for the Levantine coast, but midway he ordered a change of course and headed north-east towards the Bosphorus. The Crusaders found themselves with little option but to launch an attack, at Dandolo's behest, against the Byzantine capital in July 1203. The Venetians were more or less guaranteed that the assault would take place since it had been discovered that roughly half the expected number of Crusaders were present for duty and the payments for Venetian transport fell far short of the mark. The Crusaders thus found themselves reluctantly indebted to the Venetians. Against the wishes of Innocent III the force stormed the seaward fortifications of Constantinople, having passed through the Dardanelles without incident. Unfortunately for the strategists a palace revolution took place shortly afterward in which Alexis, having first grudgingly been accepted, was assassinated by strangulation, and the entire assault had to be repeated in the spring of 1204. This resulted in a new Western-based administration being created in the city under Baldwin, Count of Flanders and brother of Godfroi de Bouillon. From Good Friday until Easter Monday 1204, as an overture to his enthronement in the basilica of St Sophia by a patriarch who was actually a self-styled Venetian nobleman, the

Crusaders saw to it that the city was thoroughly ransacked, churches stripped of their valuables, icons destroyed, a priceless imperial library burnt and its citizens systematically raped and slaughtered. This was not, however, quite the end of the saga of the Fourth Crusade. In April 1205 at Adrianople the Bulgarians extracted appropriate revenge and massacred the Crusader force. It effectively created two Latin empires in the East, the so-called Empire of the Straits at Constantinople and the Byzantine rump at Nicaea in Asia Minor.[31]

Innocent then oversaw an exercise in sheer military lunacy when in 1212 some 50,000 adolescents were persuaded to march in two separate expeditions from France and Germany to the Middle East, with the intention of capturing Jerusalem through the so-called Children's Crusades. The ideology was simple and compelling, if somewhat perverse in modern thinking. Children benefited from worldly innocence and would therefore, through the will of God, be able to accomplish what men who were sinful were not permitted to achieve. History records that the first expedition was led by a shepherd child, referred to as either Etienne or Stephen, who came from the village of Cloyes near Vendôme.[32] He announced that he had been ordained by miraculous means to 'crush the Saracens', and so charismatic was his religious fervour that he was promptly joined by a ragtag army of some 30,000 French children. They assembled in the port of Marseilles, from where they were embarked in seven ships of which no more than five would make landfall at Alexandria, the remaining two destined to sink off the Sardinian coast. Moreover, none of these children reached their objective. Some perished en route, but the majority were rounded up in Alexandria and sold into slavery. Very few ever set foot in their home countries again, and then only seventeen years later when the Holy Roman Emperor Frederick II negotiated a treaty with the Egyptian Sultan El-Kamil. More or less simultaneous with Etienne another child, Nicholas, was encouraged to deliver the same propagandist message of a miraculous victory in store for his under-aged German troops. He gathered together about 20,000 children and led them, or at least those who survived the ordeal, across the

Alps, arriving in Genoa on 25 August 1212. The city's archbishop, appalled at the prospect of what might be in store for this juvenile flock, persuaded them to go back. As a consequence some were abducted into slavery and many more died of exposure in the mountains, although Nicholas is said to have survived and returned to live in Cologne.

The launch of the Fifth Crusade was delayed for nearly a quarter of a century until 1228, this time organised by the German Emperor Frederick II. He managed temporarily to recover a large part of Palestine, including Jerusalem, after negotiating a truce with the Egyptian Sultan. However, his efforts were shortly to be undone by a new hostile element, the Kharesmians, who took Jerusalem in 1244. The Germans returned home bloodied, and next it was the turn of the French knights under Louis IX to mount the Sixth Crusade. Faring little better Louis and most of his army were either slain or captured by Muslim forces having been distracted into laying siege to Damietta in Egypt. Louis eventually bought his freedom after negotiating a heavy ransom. He was, however, clearly a general easily distracted since, when he mounted the final Seventh Crusade in 1270 in the company of Edward I of England, he was again lured away from the objective of the Holy Land. Under pressure from his brother, Charles of Anjou, to conquer Tunis on his behalf, Louis turned his attentions to a North African conquest of no religious significance whatsoever, and while there succumbed to the plague.

The final outcome of all this shed Christian blood was that Palestine remained firmly under Islamic control, and the limited Christian acquisitions of Acre, Antioch and Tripoli were in the hands of the Knights Templars for only a few more years, until 1291. Militarily the Crusades amounted to a disaster with little visible achievement. Religious fervour constantly got the better of common sense and ultimately the enterprise failed in its stated objective to recover the holy places of Palestine from occupation by the Muslim Arabs. It is worth noting perhaps that in the entire history of armed conflict no theocratic power or government has ever achieved enduring military success. On the whole the Crusades had a negative effect on the world, in that they raised massive barriers between an already mutually hostile Islam and Christendom, while they also left a legacy of extreme brutality and inhumanity in the name of the Christian God, and raised the moral stock of both feudalism and militarism. The temporal power of the papacy was substantially aggrandised to the advantage of little else than the papacy. The conduct of the Latin Western arm of the Christian realm served to heighten the opprobrium of the Greek East, who were appalled by the litany of massacre in the service of Christ. It also rendered the reunification of Christendom a distant dream. Nonetheless, the Crusades brought profound and sometimes more positive changes that affected the policy and progress of the West in ways as radical as those of the later Reformation. Some of the more lawless and reckless European barons were enticed away never to return, and the perceived perils of the East encouraged a new sense of solidarity and national identity in Europe. Many of the modern European nations owe the beginnings of their consolidation to the effect of the Crusades. The conflicts brought Westerners for the first time into close contact with the higher standards of comfort and luxury to which the East had become accustomed, and this triggered a trade boom. The experiences of the Crusaders were destined to open up the Eastern Mediterranean to travel and a vibrant commerce. Especially for the Italian mercantile republics, including the seaboard cities of Genoa and Venice, this brought a new-found affluence. Yet the Crusades were also the prelude to a period of internal strife and hatred during which Christendom turned to an orgy of violent self-mutilation.

SIX

Jihad

It is difficult to make any kind of meaningful or direct comparison of the expansion periods of Judaism, Christianity and Islam, because each went through this stage of its evolution under different social, political and strategic conditions. The fathers of Judaism were not interested in imposing either their brand of religious ideology or a political dominance beyond their own self-prescribed frontiers, and this outlook has never radically changed. Early Christianity was almost a bystander to its own expansion, which was carried out by the post-Constantine Roman Empire. The founders of Islam anticipated an expansionist policy from the outset, but this did not necessarily include imposing their ideology. We should bear in mind that the current phase of near-fanatical activity within Islam to impose Muslim ideology on others is a distinct phenomenon, one that has arisen at about the same stage of Islamic history as the Crusades came about in the history of Christianity. At the start of 2006 this phase is not hard to detect each time one opens a newspaper. At the Old Bailey court in London at the time of writing, the radical Islamic cleric 'Abu Hamza is facing an array of charges including incitement to murder. *The Times* reports that he has told his followers that it is their religious duty to kill Jews and other non-Muslims (11 January 2006). Elsewhere in the Islamic world the story is much the same, and one can select from innumerable examples. In February 2003 the *South Asia Tribune* reported that 'Bangladesh has built hundreds of thousands of Mosques and madrassahs that constantly foment violence against non-Muslims and the country's progressive groups and cultural institutions. There are 64,000 madrassahs or so-called religious schools where the unsuspecting Muslim youths are recruited and

121

trained to be the foot soldiers for a Taliban-style Bangladesh. They espouse hate and bigotry against anyone that does not conform to their brand of militant Islam.'

Christendom went on the offensive in much the same fanatical degree some 1,200 years from its foundation, as Islamic fundamentalists are doing now after roughly 1,400 years. The peak era of aggressive religious bigotry in Christendom began in the twelfth century. Islam was founded in the sixth century. In both cases the renewed activity came after a period of relative stagnation. An impartial observer viewing the levels of atrocity committed, in each case in the name of God, would find difficulty in making any clear distinction.

The story of the initial Islamic expansion, like that of the Patriarchal Age in Jewish history, is sketchy and not infrequently romanticised. Although a rich store of material about the early period is to be found among classical and medieval Islamic sources, contemporary accounts that would corroborate much of this material tend to be scarce. For this reason the same caveats that applied to surviving literature about the early Jewish heritage also apply here. What we know of the Islamic patriarchs and the early dynasties is generally included in composite works whose editors collected together sources that may have been compilations of still earlier writings. Typical of the 'universal' histories of Islam is the *Ta'rikh al-rusul w'al muluk* of al-Tabari. One can also encounter extensive local histories such as Ibn 'Abi Tahir's *Kitab Baghdad*. Among the best-known early works about dynastic families is al-Baladhuri's *Ansab al-ashraf*. But separating fact from romance is fraught with difficulty, because a book of this nature typically consists of a jumble of historical reports, traditions and anecdotes, together known as *akhbar*, all mixed up with Hadith.

For many Westerners Hadith will probably be an unfamiliar term. The close friends of the Prophet are believed to have drawn from him and committed to memory a collection of sayings and practices. These entered the oral tradition of early Islam, and it was only many decades after the death of Muhammad that any attempt was made to compile the word-of-mouth lore into a written structure, by which time it was, of course, difficult to verify which of the lists of sayings were authentic and which amounted to innovative fabrications. During the ninth century learned Muslim opinion trawled through some half a million known and alleged utterances of the Prophet. Scholars placed them in groups of ascending credibility on the basis of what they contained and who had originally recorded the information, much as early Christian arbiters sifted and separated what they regarded as orthodox, apocryphal and heretical literature. Today two collections of Hadith, the *Sahib Moslem* and *Sahib Bukhari*, are among those considered to be most reliable. It is therefore the Hadith in particular that gives works such as the *Ansab al-ashraf* a label of authority, emphasising their kinship with the Prophet by advertising an intimate knowledge of his sayings, and it is true that at least some of such early collections can shed light on the way in which attitudes developed in the early Islamic past.

The dearth of non-Arabic editions has tended to leave Islamic origins as a 'grey area' in the eyes of many Westerners, and clearer understanding is hampered no less by what non-Muslims are taught, or rather not taught. Although the bias is becoming less acute, the curriculum in most schools in Europe and North America still concentrates on the history of the last 2,000 years primarily from a European, then a Christian, perspective. The record of Islam largely involves neither, though over the centuries since its birth Islam has impacted not only on the Christian heartlands of Europe but also on the Bible lands of Western Asia. Our understanding is also impeded by the tortuous course of history in the Middle East. The geography and economic significance of the lands in which Islam arose have always guaranteed that they would be a political and military melting pot. Arabia constitutes a strategic crossroads between three continents, Europe, Asia and Africa. It is the stepping-off point for the Mediterranean countries and the lands of the Caucasus in the north, as well as providing the land routes into India and the vast hinterland of Central Asia. Not surprisingly, Arabia has seen constant comings and goings of power-brokers from all over the globe fighting for possession of its territory during the 1,400 years of Islamic history. The region has been squabbled over by Europeans, Persians, Mongols, Turks, Afghans, Abyssinians and, more recently, a Western civilisation anxious to safeguard a wealth under the desert sands not recognised in the lifetime of Muhammad the Prophet.[1]

Until recently, particularly before the advent of the Internet, the only sources of information for someone outside the faith were to be found in academic libraries and specialist bookshops. Many of these literary offerings are written from an Islamic and, one might dare to suggest, romanticised perspective that does not always correspond to a more objective view of history. Mythology has contributed a considerable amount to the causes of modern disagreement between Jews, Christians and Muslims in parts of the Near East. Jerusalem stands as a holy city in the traditions of all three faiths. Jewish history records it as the one-time capital of the southern state of Judah and, later, of Greater Judaea. Its sanctity in the eyes of generations of Christians has been assured by it being the place of the Crucifixion. Its Islamic connections are less well known outside the Muslim world. According to tradition, in 620 Muhammad was transported to Jerusalem during the space of one night as part of a mystical and dreamlike experience in which he also ascended briefly to heaven. Known in the Islamic world as Al-Quds al-Sharif it is part of the land identified in the Qur'ān as being 'blessed for all human beings', and indeed some archaeologists contend that the earliest Islamic holy sanctuary was not in the south-west of Arabia but somewhere further to the north, in which case Jerusalem becomes a strong contender. The most sacred part of the city for Muslims is a complex known as Al-Haram al-Sharif, the Noble Sanctuary, at the heart of which stands the Al-Quds, the Golden Dome of the Rock. Extending over 35 hectares some of the buildings may have been commissioned in 691, according to some historical records, by the Umayyad caliph 'Abd al-Malik ibn Marwan to commemorate Muhammad's nocturnal journey from Mecca to the Rock, an event that Muslims celebrate annually during the month of Ramadan. The complex also includes the slightly smaller Al-Aqsa mosque, completed in 715 and distinguished by its silver dome. The name means, literally, 'The Furthest' and stems from a qur'ānic verse:

> Glory be to him who made his servant go by night
> From the sacred temple [of Mecca] to the farther temple
> Whose surroundings we have blessed
> That we might show him some of our signs.[2]

For us in the West much of this is unfamiliar territory. The Muslim past and its traditions can easily amount to little more than a two-dimensional portrait on which certain names and events are sketched without any clear background, connection or purpose. A trawl of the available volumes on Islamic history in such major repositories as the British Library provides a stark eye-opener on how little is available to a European reader in languages other than Arabic. The *Cambridge History of Islam* published more than thirty years ago still amounts to staple fare. It is this shortage of objective up-to-date information that lends to our occasional bafflement. Why have fundamentalists like Osama bin Laden viewed the stationing of American troops in Saudi Arabia during the Gulf War as a sacrilege, a pollution of holy ground, leading to his adoption of such a catastrophic course of retaliation against the United States? Why do Palestinian Arabs, Christians and Jews defend their respective rights to other sacred sites such as Jerusalem with such passionate fervour? The root causes, in each and every case, are embedded in the histories and most profound traditions of the three religions.

Dissecting the history of Islamic expansion, as we know it, indicates that aggressive behaviour towards the wider world developed more or less side by side with internal strife. However, the internal problem is a subject to be dealt with in a later chapter. Here the focus is on the holy war against unbelievers, sometimes misleadingly referred to as jihad, which Islam declared from the very outset. This did not imply that all Muslims were actually to be in a constant state of aggressive bloodthirstiness, but that unlimited expansion of the Islamic religion, if necessary by violent means, had been ordained and was to be fulfilled.

The founder of Islam, Muhammad, did not actually envisage setting up a political state, or at least it was not foremost among his objectives; he was merely advocating a universal religion. But his successors fostered more ambitious targets, committed first to the development of an Islamic state in Arabia and then to becoming an imperial world power. In their eyes there was to be *dar-ul-Islam*, 'the abode of Islam', the world of the believers, and *dar-ul-harb*, 'the abode of war', the world of the infidel or unbeliever, which in practice meant all those states and communities that did not bend to the will of Allah as prescribed by his chosen apostle, Muhammad.

In Muhammad's lifetime the political situation in the Arabian peninsula was confusing. During the centuries between the death of Jesus Christ and the birth of Muhammad in about 569, there had been momentous changes in the region. At the dawn of the Christian era most of the ancient Near East had found itself under the military control of the Roman legions which in turn were administered from Rome. The only other significant imperial power in the area was Persia. Early in the third Christian century a new aggressive dynasty, the Sassanids, arose and galvanised a new round of empire-building in which Rome steadily lost ground until in 260 the Persian overlord Shapur I conquered Roman-held lands as far west as Palestine.

Control of the northern part of Arabia thus ebbed and flowed between two major imperial power-brokers, but in the south the political situation remained much less organised. Other than in the far south-west, which tends to be more fertile, southern Arabia represented a desolate landscape of desert and flat arid grassland punctuated by occasional oases, and neither the Romans nor the Sassanid Persians had been able to annex these somewhat lawless lands. The pre-Islamic history of the southern part of the peninsula hence reads as an unremitting catalogue of intertribal strife and bloodshed between small city states retaining ancient tribal loyalties between which groups of insurgents, loosely known as Saracens, roamed at will.

In the beginning of the fourth century the northern and western parts of the Middle East were affected by the rise of the new Roman strongman, Constantine the Great, who moved the empire firmly in the direction of embracing Christianity. By that time 'Roman' was a slightly misleading term because the seat of Roman secular power had moved to Byzantium, to be renamed as the city of Constantinople (modern Istanbul) in 330, and although the Visigoths conquered Rome in 410, bringing the Western wing of the empire effectively to an end, in the East the Byzantines maintained power as the Christianised Holy Roman Empire.

Confrontation between the Byzantines and the Persians was largely down to secular disagreements, but there was a second element to the strife because the Persians, while not being pagan, certainly did not support Christianity. They followed a religion peculiar to themselves known as Zoroastrianism, based on the revelations received by their founding father, the prophet Zoroaster, sometime between 6000 BCE and 600 BCE, a timescale that offers slightly improbable provenance for the cult. Whatever the start date, which will always lie in the realms of romance, three successive Persian dynasties, the Achaemenids, the Parthians and finally the Sassanids, embraced the faith.

Thus in the north of Arabia the land was carved up between the Byzantine Christians in the west and the Sassanid Persian Zoroastrians in the east. On the frontier with the politically less well-defined southern part of the peninsula, Bedouin tribes, often in imperial Byzantine pay, patrolled a form of buffer zone. But in the meantime the warring southern clans needed to trade with the north and to this end they were in regular contact with the outside world from about 400 CE onwards. Arabia thus became important in terms of commerce, and as different business enterprises moved in so the populations became increasingly cosmopolitan. Christians and Jews found themselves living side by side with traditional polytheists, and an uneasy laissez-faire developed.

In a transfer of power that took place in 547 the area technically came under the provincial control of Abyssinia after a campaign of repression against both its own nationals and the Christians living in southern Arabia had resulted in an Abyssinian military backlash supported by Byzantine forces from the north. One further twist was to take place during Muhammad's childhood when the Abyssinian colonial ruler, Abreha, chose to launch a military strike against the Persians in the north. This eventually permitted the Persian Emperor Chosroes II to throw the Abyssinians first out of Yemen, where a pro-Persian faction had arisen, then between 597 and 598 out of the whole of southern Arabia, which became a Sassanid province administered by a governor known as a satrap. In 613 Chosroes II took the Christian city of Antioch and, with his army beating the drum on the borders of Palestine, the Jewish resistance prudently joined him for a renewed attack against their old Christian enemy. In the spring of 614 this resulted in the delivery of Jerusalem into Persian military hands, and Chosroes shrewdly handed the city back to the Jews, who promptly took over the Christian churches and expelled their members from the country.

The balance was destined to shift yet again when the Byzantine Emperor Heraclius acquired a renewed military strength. In 629 he mounted a major counter-offensive against the Persian forces, which saw Jerusalem restored to Christian control in the spring of that year, although much of northern Arabia was destined to remain under Sassanid control at least for the time being.

It was from this mêlée during the early part of the seventh century – in particular from the southern and western area of Arabia known as the Hijaz in which lie the holy cities of Mecca and Medina – that Muhammad was to recruit most of his initial support. Mecca, in which he spent much of his early life, lies about 80 kilometres east of the Red Sea and, according to whichever scholarly view you believe, may or may not have been an important stopping-off place on one of the main caravan routes. Medina, formerly known as Yathrib, is some 300 kilometres to the north and in the seventh century amounted to little more than a fertile oasis inhabited mainly by pagan Arabs and some Jews, whose former local political dominance was by then on the wane. The Medina area was not a tranquil region. It had experienced a hundred years or more of fighting between clans, and this seething hostility had culminated in a pitched battle in about 618 at a place identified in the records only as Bu'ath, with nearly all the clans involved.

Muhammad had correctly recognised that the long-standing culture of local intertribal conflict in southern Arabia was a potential weakness to be exploited. If he could unite a sufficient number of clans under one inspirational banner, following the logic of 'united we stand, divided we fall', it would provide him with a secure power base from which to export his new religion. Mecca, dominated by the Quraish tribe from which Muhammad stemmed, solidly wedded to conservatism and the traditional strength of polytheism, was hostile from the outset. Medina, on the other hand, offered greater potential for the Muslims, not least because through rubbing shoulders with the Jewish community and the teachings of Moses, its Arab population had become familiar with the romance of an inspired religious leader.

In 620 a deputation of six leading Medinans made encouraging overtures to Muhammad during their annual pilgrimage to Mecca, and the following year twelve civic leaders from the most important tribal factions based around Medina expressed more emphatic readiness to accept Muhammad as a veritable prophet. This pledge of allegiance would become known as the Aqaba Oath. Muhammad was initially sceptical, however, and sent an envoy to Medina in order to gain some clearer idea of the state of internal politics there. During the 622 Meccan pilgrimage the pro-Muslim deputation from Medina swelled to seventy-five and these men, confirming that attack was the best means of defence, pledged to fight on behalf of the Prophet under the second Aqaba Oath.

The increased level of support was finally enough to persuade Muhammad to pack his bags in September 622 and flee north with his Muslim faithful. But even in the comparatively safe surroundings of Medina, where they found refuge among somewhat more amenable tribes, security was far from assured. The Meccan authorities continued to rattle sabres in their direction and demanded Muhammad's capture and return. So the initial objective in this precarious environment was to extend and consolidate Islamic cohesion among the tribes centred in and around Medina in order to provide a defensive 'wall'. The second Aqaba Oath effectively welded a number of powerful tribes into the foundation of this strategic alliance, one that would shortly begin its fight for the Islamic cause further afield. The oath committed those who took it to what became known as the 'red and black war', red being the symbolic colour adopted by the Christians, black being that of Islam.[3]

First, however, there were scores to settle closer to home. The indications are that from an early stage Muhammad contemplated armed conflict in the name of Allah against the Quraish in Mecca. Effectively, this amounted to a continuation of the traditional style of intertribal warfare that had largely characterised life in Arabia for as long as anyone could remember. It involved sending out armed raiding parties or *ghazwa* against Meccan caravans commuting to and from Syria. The first of these attacks took place at Badr on 15 March 624 and involved some 300 Muslims pitched against a much larger force of about 900 Meccans who had rapidly assembled to protect the caravan once news of the offensive had spread. Against the odds the Muslims achieved a decisive victory, interpreted by many as God's vindication of the Islamic cause.

The caravan commander was not amused and promptly assembled a force of some 3,000 infantry and 200 cavalry, taking them to a hilly vantage point, Uhud, just to the north of the Medina oasis. On 6 March 625 they clashed with the Medinans. The fighting finished up with a virtual stalemate, little advantage being gained by either side, although Muhammad was wounded. The absence of a Muslim victory was blamed on poor discipline and an overenthusiastic interest in collecting booty.

On 31 March 627 a large Meccan force backed by a motley of Jewish and Arab tribal insurgents and allegedly amounting to as many as 10,000, made an abortive siege assault on Medina in the so-called Battle of the Allies, which lasted for about two weeks and ended in frustration for the Meccans. Their defeat was enough to accelerate the pace of recruitment to Muhammad's cause. By the following year it is reported that he and his second-in-command, 'Abu Bakr, had at their disposal a force of some 10,000 fighters made up of Medinan Arabs and nomadic Bedouins. Having acquired this military muscle, Muhammad effectively became head of state in Medina and in the spring of 628 he signed a peace treaty with Mecca. Almost immediately, however, he confronted the town with a large expeditionary force and the townspeople capitulated on 11 January 630.[4]

The Islamic conquest of Arabia was completed shortly afterwards. Its success was boosted in part by problems that had developed in Persia. In February 628 the Persian Emperor died, which in only a few years led to collapse of the Persian Empire, with pro-Persian factions in Arabia then turning to Muhammad for support. The remaining measurable opposition amounted to a group of tribes pledged to support the Hawazin clan and based on the town of Ta'if. The Muslim army met the Hawazin forces at Hunayn, an unidentified battleground somewhere east of Mecca, and roundly defeated them. With the exception of small pockets of resistance on the Syrian and Iraqi borders, still closely wedded to the Byzantines, there was now no armed group in Arabia capable of taking on the Islamic forces, and Muhammad was in a position to sign a series of non-aggression pacts, resulting in a federation of tribes with Islam as its common bond.

Islam thus conquered Arabia much as the Israelites had suppressed Syrio-Palestine, and initially the experiences of the Muslim Arabs mirrored quite closely those of a loosely bound gathering of Semitic tribes on their way to founding a religious state in Syrio-Palestine some 2,000 years earlier. Divergence from that historical Jewish precedent came during the next chapter of events, not least because the custom arose that fighting should be prefaced by 'invitation to Islam' or the payment of appropriate financial dues. The Arab commanders would detail the options before fighting began, and one could agree or one could be slaughtered. Unlike the Israelites, the Muslim leaders offered their opponents a degree of choice.

Islam completed its establishment as a religious entity, and began the real programme of expansion, after the death of Muhammad. With his demise came the main change of outlook from intertribal warfare to conflict with the outside world and true jihad. We should, therefore, take time out from history and establish what jihad is and why it has remained of such significance. Jihad is a word that has come into frequent use in recent times in the Western press, being made to appear synonymous with 'holy war'. At times in the recent past it has been very difficult to separate the two, but in reality the Christian Crusaders first coined the expression 'holy war' when referring to the conflict with Muslims. It is not a definition of jihad and probably has no equivalent in the Islamic glossary. Majid Khadduri has defined jihad not as a casual phenomenon of violence but a product of complex conditions existing while Islam worked out its doctrinal character. To these conditions are to be ascribed the peculiar Muslim conduct of relations established with other peoples.[5] The precise interpretation of the word jihad, which derives from *jahada* (meaning 'struggle'), is that of personal exertion in the way of Allah, according to the Qur'ān it involves material support but also, if necessary, violent sacrifice of one's life. In return, paradise beckons, a heady prospect for the faithful embarking upon battle.

> Believers! Shall I point out to you a profitable course that will save you from a woeful scourge? Have faith in Allah and His apostle and fight for the cause of Allah with your wealth and with your persons. That would be best for you if you but knew it.
>
> He will forgive you your sins and admit you to gardens watered by running streams; He will lodge you in pleasant mansions in the gardens of Eden. That is the supreme triumph. And He will bestow upon you other blessings that you desire: help from Allah and a speedy victory.[6]

Jihad did not evolve immediately in this way. During the early days in Medina it probably amounted to little more than a propaganda exercise aimed at converts, but as the Muslim power base grew and Islam earned its position as a state religion, jihad was woven into a more elaborate doctrine. It became an instrument of state, one imposed on the whole community rather than individuals. For this reason the duties of the caliph also included calling the believers to battle. This gave war in the name of Allah a legal status, and believers were committed to respond to the call. The Arab historian Al-Baladhuri records that on the eve of expansion 'Abu Bakr was obliged to write to the tribes that had consented to join the Islamic cause, calling them to battle and formally requesting their consent to take the field.[7] The exertions of the faithful were now directed towards the ideal of converting the entire world into an idealised Islamic state through a more or less permanent warfare punctuated only by limited periods of tranquillity. As Khadduri points out, jihad can only end when the world at large constitutes one Muslim community.

Expansion beyond the borders of Arabia, following the principles of jihad, was begun by 'Abu Bakr, elected to become the immediate successor of the Prophet, the first Khalifa or Caliph. A former Meccan merchant whose daughter 'A'isha became Muhammad's favourite wife, 'Abu Bakr had not emerged from a clan of any major importance in pre-Islamic Mecca, and it was perhaps not least for this reason that Muhammad, with social reform close to his heart, had placed considerable reliance on him. According to tradition 'Abu Bakr had assumed the role of leading deputy during Muhammad's lifetime and had taken over increasing levels of responsibility, including leadership of the faithful in prayer when the Prophet's infirmity increased. It was he who broke the news of the Prophet's death on 8 June 632.

'A'isha's description of 'Abu Bakr's physical appearance is hardly flattering. 'He was a man with fair skin, thin, emaciated, with a sparse beard, a slightly hunched frame, sunken eyes and protruding forehead.' Nonetheless, he seems to have had a sound grasp of military strategy. Initially, he set about eliminating any remaining opposition to Islam in Arabia. This was a comparatively straightforward exercise given that any non-Muslim clans remained under the control of petty tribal chiefs constantly scrapping with one another and in consequence were comparatively weak.

'Abu Bakr confirmed the obligation of all Muslims to pursue jihad during his inaugural address, declaring that Allah would humiliate those who abandoned its principles.[8] With some shrewdness he courted the hitherto questionable support of the tough and well-armed northern Arabs, and once he had attracted this additional backing he found little difficulty in persuading any isolated and still polytheistic clans to abandon their traditional gods and join forces under the Islamic banner. With the dreams of his founder in mind 'Abu Bakr now set his sights on wider empire-building, and thus he launched the first foreign expansion programme, ordering one of his more accomplished generals, Khalid bin al-Walid, to make an assault on lands outside Arabia. Beyond the northern borders of the developing Muslim hegemony the two mighty imperial institutions of Byzantium and Persia posed a technical threat to Islamic sovereignty. Whether the threat was real or imaginary matters little; it offered a good excuse to launch an offensive military campaign. 'Abu Bakr's intention was to dismantle the Christian presence in Syria, Iraq and parts of North Africa including Alexandria and Libya. The first success came in Iraq where Khalid bin al-Walid attacked the capital, Hira, and only agreed to save it from armed Muslim occupation after its authorities consented to hand over a large cash sum. Overall the campaign proved successful, helped by the agreement of the Bedouin tribes to come under Muslim command. Less successful was the offensive in Syria, where the Muslim army came up against stiff resistance to the extent that Khalid bin al-Walid had to leave the Iraq theatre in the hands of his deputy commander, al-Muthanna.

It is possible that other factors also played a part in encouraging the Arabian Muslims into empire-building, not the least of which was the need for migration because of changing climatic and geological conditions. From time to time these had affected the Arabian tribes, bringing unrest and causing them to transfer into more fertile lands outside the Arabian peninsula when the land became too arid to support the adequate cultivation of harvests. Some scholars contend that this alone triggered a demand for imperialistic expansion, but others maintain that it could not have happened without the added incentive brought by religious and political pressures.[9]

The offensives were always required to follow a code of conduct. This was accountably more tolerant than the one delivered in centuries past to the forces of the Israelites, which effectively amounted to an order to kill anything that moved. The early Islamic instructions for jihad included, 'Do not desert your posts or your comrades and do not be found guilty of disobedience. Do not kill old men, women or children and do not damage date palm nor cut down fruit trees. Do not slaughter sheep, cows or camels unless to provide food. Do not molest holy men who live in monasteries but leave them in seclusion.'

Not all Muslims were obliged to undertake jihad in the violent sense. Aside from being a believer the jihadist was assumed to be male since the Qur'ān refers only to *mu'minin* (masculine) and not *mu'minat* (feminine). He was expected to be able-bodied, of maturity and sound mind. Muhammad specifically excused children and lunatics from such duty until mature or cured, and he reportedly refused 'Umar bin al-Khattab – who in time would become the second Caliph – participation in a major battle when he was only 14.[10] The jihadist must also be of independent means and free from debt unless specifically excused by the debtor; thus a slave was under no obligation to join a jihad. Perhaps most significantly, he must go about his obligation with good intentions, following the Prophet's maxim that deeds are judged by intentions.[11]

'Abu Bakr would also have ordered an assault against the Persian Sassanids, whose new Emperor, Yazdigird III, had raised a formidable army, but 'Abu Bakr died in 634, two years after Muhammad. His recommendation for the new leadership post was 'Umar bin al-Khattab. Here was another experienced military man who had been involved in early campaigns during Muhammad's lifetime and who had also supported the election of 'Abu Bakr. Like his predecessor, he came from a clan of minor importance in the Meccan social hierarchy, but in spite of this he received the clear backing of the army and became no less committed to the expansion programme. 'Umar's first priority was to send reinforcements to the Muslim commander al-Muthanna facing the Sassanids in Syria. In spite of this the campaign resulted in a major Muslim defeat in 634 in the Battle of the Bridge, so-called because the main fallback position was held for some time at a bridge spanning the Euphrates. During the next two years, however, fortunes were reversed. 'Umar persuaded more of the northern Bedouin tribes to come under his command and with substantially enlarged forces he was poised to overthrow a succession of non-Islamic regimes.

The war was effectively conducted on two fronts. The Christian Byzantine power bases to the west included Damascus, Jerusalem and Alexandria, while the Zoroastrian Sassanid rulers still firmly controlled Persia and parts of Syria. 'Umar attacked Damascus in 635, and although his initial assault failed he was not long in defeating the Byzantine forces defending the city. The Patriarch of Jerusalem sued for peace and eventually handed over control without further bloodshed. The following year 'Umar faced a regrouped Byzantine army in Palestine but again emerged victorious. More or less simultaneously, other regiments of his Islamic army attacked the Sassanids, and this resulted in major successes at Buwayb in 635 and Qadisiyya (modern Najaf) in 636, with 'Umar gaining control over the whole of Iraq. The Muslim army chased the retreating Persians into the Zagros Mountains in the north of the country, then into the western part of Persia. Six years later 'Umar routed the remainder of their forces near the town of Nihavand, and the Sassanid ruler, Yazdegird, only narrowly escaped capture or death, fleeing first to Khurasan to the south-east of the Caspian Sea then to Istakhr (ancient Persepolis), where he was assassinated in about 652. The Muslim conquerors adopted a programme of repression under which any Zoroastrians who refused to convert to Islam were persecuted and forcibly repatriated to remote desert areas where they could only cling to a meagre existence. 'Umar was assassinated in 644 allegedly by a slave carrying a personal grudge, and was succeeded to the third caliphate by a general from an altogether different mould, 'Uthman ibn 'Affan, who ruled for the next twelve years.

As a prominent member of one of the long-established aristocratic houses of Mecca, the Umayya tribe, 'Uthman negotiated a series of political deals and compromises that achieved a temporary cessation of local skirmishing. Perversely, this lull gave the tribal leaders time on their hands and an excuse to stoke up fresh grievances against one another. In 656 civil war broke out during which 'Uthman was also assassinated and replaced by 'Ali ibn Abi Talib, the cousin of the Prophet and the husband of his daughter Fatima. A strong Medinan faction backed him, determined to put an end to twenty years of aristocratic nepotism and what they saw as unwarranted religious innovation coming out of Mecca. But 'Ali too proved unpopular, lost vital support and suffered a premature end at the hands of an assassin. With his death the first phase in the history of the Islamic peoples, the elective caliphate that might be compared loosely with the era of the patriarchs and judges in Jewish history, came to an end. In its place there arose a new dynastic leadership, that of the Semitic house of Umayya. Its first Caliph, Mu'awiya bin 'Abu Sufian, a former governor of Syria, came to power in 661 and lost little time in moving the Islamic state back towards the traditional style of a monarchy. At this juncture the Islamic 'state' amounted to a gathering of separate tribal identities in a single body politic held together largely by the same ideology. It was not yet an empire of separate nations in the modern sense.

By revitalising the old tribal loyalties that early followers of Islam had resented, the irony is that the Umayyad caliphate held power for almost a century. Mu'awiya moved the Muslim capital from Arabia to Damascus in the newly conquered territory of Syria and from there took a firm grip on parts of the Byzantine Empire including Palestine, while also having the pragmatism to conclude a truce with the Holy Roman Empire that was to last through his reign. Umayyad policy had its distinct pros and cons. On the positive side it permitted the unity of Islam to be maintained and it was also generally tolerant of other religious beliefs. The army also came to be organised along more professional lines, influenced by contact with the forces of Byzantium, so that it ceased to be divided among generals who did not always see eye to eye, becoming a single compact entity. But the rise of the Umayyad caliphate was not without cost. The old Arab aristocracy that came to dominate non-Arab communities did so along imperial lines, and, when it suited, this went so far as engaging the practical assistance of officialdom from empires that had been superseded by the new Islam. The Umayyad caliphs also amassed slave labour, much of which was put to work in the armed forces. These aspects generated smouldering dissent that would eventually lead to schism and civil war during the eighth century.

A new phase of Muslim expansion had begun during the reign of Abd-al Malik ibn Marwan, who came to power in 685. He pushed the frontiers of the Muslim Empire west along the coast of North Africa, taking the city of Carthage in 698 and eventually reaching the shores of the Atlantic. But it was under the hand of his successor Walid I that the Umayyad dynasty achieved the zenith of its might. His forces crossed the Caucasus northwards into southern Russia while also gaining a bridgehead across the River Oxus to open up a route to Central Asia, including the fabled cities of Bukhara and Samarkand, reaching as far as the Chinese frontier. In the East the Muslim armies troubled India and only halted their campaign in the Indus Valley. By 713 Spain was firmly in the grip of Islam, as was southern France as far north as Narbonne and Toulouse.

Yet just when the Umayyad rulers seemed unstoppable in their quest for world domination, they were becoming weakened by increasingly bitter internal conflicts. Great caliphs of the past were succeeded by weak men, and at sometime prior to 747 disaffected factions began to gather in a rebel base at Khorasan in Persia. Under the authority of Abdullah as-Saffah or 'Abu al-'Abbas, they would become known as the 'Abassids. At sometime between 747 and 750 their main expeditionary forces headed west towards Syria and Damascus where they engaged the Umayyad army and defeated it. Known as the Battle of Zab, this was a particularly vicious encounter during which all the princely Umayyad families were slaughtered, bar one whose members escaped to Spain, where Umayyad rule was set to continue at least for a time.

The incoming dynasty of the 'Abassid caliphs amounted to an altogether different breed of rulers. Essentially a Persian-based non-Semitic Muslim dynasty, they had backed the cause of 'Ali ibn Abi Talib. They were less interested in expansionism than their predecessors, but, nevertheless, within a year of 'Abu al-Abbas taking office a Muslim force had penetrated beyond the Oxus, routing the Chinese and replacing their administration in Transoxus with that of a local clan, the Samanids. The 'Abassid dynasty was set to rule for some 500 years from 750 until the mid-thirteenth century, but after its initial coup it proved less successful either politically or militarily and from the tenth century its authority was nominal. Major changes in the style of government rapidly became apparent and the new binding element among a more cosmopolitan Arabic-speaking administration was one of which Muhammad would no doubt have approved – the faith of Islam.

Islamic expansion, to both east and west, thus came to a fairly abrupt halt in the first half of the eighth century. Having finally acquired control of the Iberian peninsula, the Muslim forces were defeated in decisive fashion at Tours in 732. They also found themselves impeded in Transoxus and on the banks of the Indus. Muslim power had effectively reached its geographical limits. On the home front the 'Abassids had to contend with internal squabbling and administrative inefficiencies, and these negative factors drove the caliphs to revise their ambitions. They chose to consolidate their borders with the Christian world in the north and west, China in the north-east and India in the east. They signed peace treaties with foreign rulers and, although in theory these were temporary measures, the concept of jihad changed. It had become untenable in terms of any Islamic dream of world domination. An indication of their steadily weakening position can be gained from the transfer in 750 of the imperial capital from Damascus to Baghdad, where the 'Abassids enjoyed their strongest support. There came about a general lessening of Arab racial supremacy within the empire. As the prestige of the dynasty diminished its caliphs came to rely too heavily on recruitment of mercenaries in order to maintain authority. The army lost its old Arabic spirit of chivalry and eventually the caliphs succumbed to the will of their mercenary protectors. They had relied heavily on Turkish guards, who came to play much the same role as the old Praetorian Guard in Rome.[12]

During the next century qur'ānic passages were judiciously reinterpreted by Islamic scholars, and the propagandists were forced into conceding that permanent fighting for the cause was no longer in the general interests of the Muslim community at large. It became fashionable to assert that mere preparation for conflict in the future was sufficient to fulfil the obligation to jihad. Violent exertion was 'put on hold', ready to be revived at any time under the authority of the caliph or the imam, should he deem it appropriate. Eventually the 'Abassid caliphs became little more than symbolic heads of state, with the real power passing into the hands of a motley of sultans and princes. Control of the Muslim Empire was about to be seized by a non-Arab dynasty from Persia, starting in about 930 when they took the cities of Isfahan and Kerman. By 945 they were at the gates of Baghdad.

One of the fundamentals of early Islam that radically distinguishes it from early Christianity is that it is not something to be found *within* the community, it *is* the community. In the eyes of his people Muhammad was the realisation of a dream that first-century Jews had hoped but then failed to discover in Jesus Christ. Thus there is no parallel to be found in Islam with the utterance of Jesus, 'Render to Caesar the things that are Caesar's and to God the things that are God's',[13] and there is no sense of division between the religious and the secular. When, during his own lifetime, he became the sovereign leader of the first Islamic state, Muhammad was delivering not merely a culmination of all that had gone before but inaugurating a new beginning and a new nation. Henceforth, for a Muslim all of life became wholly subservient to the will of Allah as the word 'muslim' implies.[14]

This vision of Islam as a political force, set to function universally at all levels of society and in all activities, has never been abandoned by some members of its congregation. The dream is still very much alive, and, for the modern Muslim fanatic with the Qur'ān in his head and Semtex on his chest, it translates into a quest for world domination through violent conduct. Yet it also includes a vicious war of attrition *within* Islam that time has done nothing to erase and which if anything is strengthening in its intensity. Today the actions of Muslim religious fanatics claim the lives of more of their fellow believers than of 'infidels', and to explain how this can be we need briefly to retrace our steps to the time of the Israelite patriarchs.

SEVEN

Internal Conflict

In one respect the progress of a religious movement is not unlike that of a marriage. The interested parties come together with a fervent pledge of loyalty to a common future; they go through betrothal, a ceremonial union, a honeymoon period and the enthusiasm of home-building. But, when these things are past, history suggests that strife and ultimately divorce become all the more likely. So it has been with all three of the monotheistic faiths, which uncannily resemble each other in this respect. Each has been blighted by dissent and heresy from within, either during their expansion phases or shortly afterwards. Once expansion has taken place, the consolidation phase that follows becomes marked by vicious internal abuse and an orgy of bloodletting, which the followers claim to be a necessary spiritual cleansing.

Much can be attributed to an unhealthy mix of creed and greed. In the history of the Jews the split was fairly clear-cut when it emerged. During the reign of Solomon the northern tribes dissociated themselves from David's single kingdom and formed into the state of Israel (distinct from the modern state of that name) under the rebel leader Jeroboam I. From that moment in time Israel more or less abandoned Yahwism, the religion of Moses, and reverted back to popular paganism, with a few monolatrous elements included, until the Assyrians dismantled the state in 722 BCE. The southern kingdom of Judah remained faithful to Mosaic beliefs at least to a degree, although it too was guilty of not infrequent bouts of apostasy and idol worship.[1]

In Islam internal ideological differences leading to a succession of civil wars began almost immediately after Muhammad's death and progressed for some 200 years with a dizzying list of comings and goings. These are as convoluted as those of Old Testament history or of early medieval Europe and thus can only be summarised in this chapter; but they also do much to explain the perennial conflict between Shi'as and Sunnis that has become so newsworthy in recent times. During the final years of the Prophet's life and for much of the caliphate of 'Abu Bakr, the so-called wars of apostasy were fought with tribes that refused to abandon either Christianity or any other forms of religious belief that did not conform to the developing Islamic code. Jealousies also arose between the Medinan clans, who collectively earned the title of *ansar* or 'helpers', and whom the Meccan migrants referred to as the *muhajiroun*. As if this was not enough, 'Abu Bakr was obliged to deal with the rantings of false prophets and their followers. Most notably, these clerics spouting their unorthodox brands of Islam included one Musaylima from the tribe of Hanifa in central Arabia, who emerged briefly into the limelight in 632, and 'al-Aswad, who was energetically promoting his personal claims of divine revelation in the Yemen in the same year. The collective ideologies of the unorthodox factions were promptly condemned by the mainstream and became known as *firaq*. The term 'heresy', incidentally, has no comparable significance in Islam.[2]

Deeper schism, more strictly Islamic in nature, would become fully apparent from the time of the 'Abassid dynasty, although in reality the germ of conflict had been present from the outset and was probably evident in a minor sense even during the lifetime of Muhammad. In the reign of 'Abu Bakr the supporters of 'Ali ibn Abi Talib were starting to air occasional differences in their approach to spiritual and moral guidance, and it is from these historical divisions that the entrenched differences between factions developed, accounting for much of the slaying of Muslims by fellow Muslims in the world today. A fundamental problem for the successors of Muhammad lay in his ambivalence about who should succeed him, and in this respect early Islamic experience differed markedly from that of Christianity. The Christian faithful of the first century CE experienced no such dilemma because Jesus Christ had clearly entrusted the 'keys' of succession to St Peter.

On Muhammad's death, however, a clear rivalry came to the fore between 'Abu Bakr, his most trusted lieutenant, and 'Ali ibn Abi Talib, the man to whom Muhammad's only surviving daughter, Fatima, was married. The majority of activists among the Prophet's followers, the original Muslim electorate, considered that he had indicated 'Abu Bakr as the rightful heir and so in 632 they voted overwhelmingly for him as their first Caliph. Others were unhappy with this decision, on the grounds that Muhammad had allegedly presented 'Ali to the close circle accompanying him on his final journey to Medina with the advice, 'Everyone whose patron I am, also has 'Ali as their patron.' A disadvantage for 'Ali in his campaign to assume the leadership was that the position of son-in-law in a society used to polygamy carried little weight.

The effects of electing 'Abu Bakr over 'Ali were felt in other ways that would contribute to the emergence of squabbling divisions within Islam. 'Abu Bakr's caliphate guaranteed the Quraish tribe a privileged position but at the same time it provided him with the absolute authority to disinherit the family of the Prophet, the *ahl al-bayt*, from its former special status. This would have economic repercussions. Under Arab convention Muhammad's kin included the descendants of his great-grandfather, Hashim, and at least some of the dependants of Hashim's brother, al-Muttalib. It was mutually agreed during Muhammad's lifetime that neither he nor members of his family should be required physically to handle charitable donations, or zakat, because they were deemed to be unclean. Under qur'ānic decree the family of the Prophet became legally entitled to receive material handouts, including one-fifth of all collected war booty, known as *khums*, and other unearned property or *fay*'. Once these had been denied by 'Abu Bakr, the position of the *ahl al-bayt* became precarious.[3]

At the same time a distinct mood of resentment was growing among the Arab public against dynastic institutions. For centuries past the tribal clans had lived with the imposition of hereditary succession and rule by divine right. The legitimacy of this arrangement may have been challenged infrequently, but few people were under illusions that dynastic kingship did other than encourage despotism. Many of the rank and file had become disenchanted with the very principle of monarchy, and they resented the old-style aristocracy, which they felt had enjoyed too much of a cosy relationship with the monarchy. Hence they reached the conclusion that it might be better to elect heads of the Muslim state on the basis of personal qualities of leadership and their ability to engender loyalty among subjects. 'Abu Bakr had already earned a degree of popularity, and, although he came from the Quraish tribe, he was not a member of its elite, which made him an ideal choice. After his short-lived reign, the second caliphate went to 'Umar, chosen not least because he came from a similar social background, but in spite of this 'Umar's lot was to be slain by a grudge-ridden Persian slave. The election of the third Caliph, 'Uthman, amounted in some ways to a retrograde step, since he was firmly positioned as a member of the aristocracy. 'Uthman promptly became a target of detractors who criticised him for introducing innovations that had no place in the Qur'ān.[4]

During the rule of these first three elected Caliphs, all of whom had been voted into power by the Meccans, 'Ali and his supporters in Medina were obliged to await their chance. Already deep cracks were showing in the unity of the Muslim community, and during the first half of 'Uthman's caliphate a popular movement supporting the election of 'Ali had also begun to take shape in Kufa. A comparatively modern city, built out of empty desert on the banks of the middle branch of the Euphrates on the eastern margin of the Arabian steppe, Kufa would become synonymous with early Muslim radicalism, and would act as a stronghold of the breakaway Shi'a element. The Kufan pro-'Alid faction began to agitate for the removal of 'Uthman, and there were strident calls to restore the rights of the family of the Prophet. Matters came to a head when one of the voices of the radicals, Malik bin al-Harith al-Ashtar, organised a local armed revolt that resulted in the overthrow of 'Uthman's city governor, Said bin al-As.[5] His replacement was a man more sympathetic to the 'Alid cause, and, encouraged by this shift in administrative politics, the Kufan rebels then joined up with units from Egypt and Basra before converging on Medina to demand a mixture of better pay, social and religious reforms, and the resignation of 'Uthman. When they did not receive the desired response, the palace of the caliphate was placed under siege by the Egyptian force and 'Uthman was assassinated. Significantly, he was slain by the hand of a fellow Muslim.

'Uthman's violent removal provided the opportunity for the Medinan 'Alids, fed up with more than twenty years of Meccan domination, to launch 'Ali into office as their fourth Caliph. However, his accession was viewed as counter-caliphate in that, having received acclaim to be the legatee of the Prophet, his supporters promptly placed the legitimacy of the three previous Caliphs in question. An approximate parallel can be drawn with the situation that prevailed in Christendom during the Avignon papacy, each side insisting that its man possessed entitlement to head the relevant movement. 'Ali's camp lost no time in broadcasting accusations amounting to a catalogue of misdemeanours that allegedly fouled the record of the previous administrations, including nepotism, favouritism, government failures and unwarranted religious innovation. It was, they clamoured, time for change. Yet 'Ali's election to the caliphate, when it came, did not earn a consensus of popular support. On the contrary, it was destined to trigger the first full-scale Islamic civil war.

'Ali paid lip service to diplomacy by restricting his criticism of previous caliphates to 'Uthman's while praising the policies of 'Abu Bakr and 'Umar. But his unbending view was that the family of the Prophet should lead the community so long as any of its members survived who could competently recite the Qur'ān, had studied the Sunna – the correct code of behaviour laid down by Muhammad – and adhered to the true faith. This determination had the effect of colouring the already fraught political situation with a religious dimension, and before long 'Ali's opponents were talking of *din 'Ali*, the 'religion of 'Ali', in less than reverential tones.[6] 'Ali was also hesitant to condemn the rebels who had laid siege to 'Uthman's headquarters, insisting that 'Uthman had brought his execution upon himself. Members of the Umayyad tribe and their supporters, already seething over the assassination, lost little time in branding

'Ali complicit in 'Uthman's slaying, and hence the stage was set for internecine violence. The time-honoured culture of intertribal bickering that Muhammad had sought to bring under control, a key requirement for Islamic expansion, had now returned with a vengeance.

Within a short time of 'Ali's election two influential former companions of Muhammad, Talha bin 'Ubaidallah and al Zubayr, broke ranks in open revolt and went over to the Meccans, agreeing to support the widow of Muhammad, A'isha, who had never been a strong admirer of 'Ali. 'Uthman's killers, they clamoured, must pay the price for their crime, and the rumour grew ever louder that 'Ali had blood on his own hands. The Meccan defectors gathered a substantial body of insurgents and, for his part, 'Ali raised a force in Medina. The two sides advanced to meet near Basra in a clash that became dubbed the Battle of the Camel because A'isha chose to watch the course of events from a palanquin perched on a camel's back.[7] 'Ali managed to come away victorious, with the added satisfaction that both Talha bin 'Ubaidallah and al Zubayr had been killed. 'Alid success, however, was short-lived because it was then the turn of Mu'awiya bin 'Abu Sufian, the Umayyad military governor of Syria, to cry vengeance for the death of his compatriot 'Uthman. In the spring of 657 Mu'awiya confronted 'Ali at a place known as Siffin near the great bend of the Euphrates in Iraq. It resulted in a prolonged military stand-off, with neither side able to claim decisive victory, and even when the matter went to arbitration no agreement was reached. The decision of those elected to arbitrate went against 'Ali, but he protested that it had not been carried out in accordance with qur'ānic law and refused to submit. It proved a negative reaction that immediately lost him much of his popular support and, realising on which side their bread was buttered, the Syrians shrewdly handed their allegiance to Mu'awiya as the legitimate Caliph. The stalemate continued for several months until, at Adhruh in Transjordan, large numbers of the faithful gathered to witness a further abortive attempt to arbitrate for a new caliph. But a similar stand-off resulted, with 'Ali relying on the qur'ānic instruction, 'If two parties of believers take up arms one against the other, make peace between them. If either of them unjustly attacks the other, fight against the aggressors till they submit to the judgement of Allah.'[8] In the view of 'Ali the aggressor was indisputably Mu'awiya, so any further decision about who should officially succeed 'Uthman had to be postponed indefinitely.

Some of the 'Alids found sufficient disagreement with the arbitration process that in 657 they migrated to the city of Nahrawan and within two years had become known as the Kharijis, from the word *kharaja*, meaning 'to rebel' or 'to go out'. In more recent times they have taken the name Wahhabi. The embryo of the Islamic state, this became partitioned for a while, with 'Ali exercising limited control from the city of Kufa, the Kharijis going their separate way in Nahrawan, and Mu'awiya using his strengthened position to administer large parts of the Muslim territory, including Egypt, which was now an Islamic province. 'Ali continued to lose ground and eventually controlled little more than central and southern Iraq among the occupied territories. A disaffected supporter from among the Kharijis assassinated him in the Kufa mosque in 661.

In the immediate aftermath, 'Ali's backers having demanded that the caliphate must go to another member of the *shia't 'Ali*, the legacy passed to al-Hasan, 'Ali's eldest son. He, however, seems to have anticipated shrewdly that the odds of survival for any length of time were stacked against him and, shortly afterwards, he abdicated in favour of Mu'awiya. This critical decision not only launched a century of Umayyad rule, but also brought to an end the 'golden age' in which the Islamic patriarchs were elected by the people for the people. The Umayyads reverted to precisely the hereditary form of dynastic government that the early followers of Muhammad had so strongly resented. Mu'awiya's accession may have resulted in some two decades of comparative peace and prosperity yet in the longer term, for the next hundred years, the Umayyad dynasty did little to dissipate old-style factional loyalties. They also imposed on Islam what, in the eyes of modern Shi'is, has amounted to more than 1,000 years of illegitimate government.

As part of his deal for resigning the caliphate al-Hasan had negotiated a treaty that supposedly granted full amnesty and safety for the *shia't 'Ali* while depriving Mu'awiya of the right to appoint his own successor. Mu'awiya tore up the treaty. Notwithstanding his departure from the caliphate, Al-Hasan's luck was also destined to run out because he died prematurely in 669 or 671, allegedly poisoned by one of his concubines acting on behalf of Mu'awiya.

The next contender for the caliphate urged on by the Shi'a followers was 'Ali's younger son al-Husayn (also spelt Hussein or Husain), but he, like his older brother, fought shy of assuming office while Mu'awiya was alive. His decision proved wise. In 671 he witnessed a bloody reprisal by Mu'awiya's forces against the Shi'a when they rioted in Kufa, resulting in several of the Shi'a leaders being executed as an exemplary punishment aimed at curbing future insurrections against Umayyad rule. To add a sombre religious impetus, Mu'awiya personally instructed that 'Ali should be cursed from the pulpit during Friday prayers.[9]

At the same time the Umayyad authorities, with an eye to strengthening their position as the only credible authority in Islam, were urging contemporary Arab historians to dispense even with the traditional view that 'Ali had founded the Shi'a movement. Instead propagandists were encouraged to spread a story that its founder was a disreputable Yemenite Jew named 'Abd Allah bin Saba', who had not only stirred up the anti-'Uthman revolt but also invented a spurious doctrine that 'Ali was the rightful heir to leadership of Islam. By way of a counterblast a rumour went around, possessing clear echoes of the Christian Passion story, that 'Ali had not actually died but ascended to a paradise as an incarnate deity.

Mu'awiya died in 680 and matters came, once again, to a point of bloody crisis. Predictably, his followers ignored the treaty made with al-Hasan and in the spring of that year Mu'awiya's son, Yazid I, was elected on a wave of popular support. As the sixth Caliph since the death of Muhammad, Yazid proved to be a man with a mission, determined to stamp the authority of the Syrian-based Umayyads even more firmly on Arabia. On taking office he instructed his Medinan governor, 'Ubayd Allah, that al-Husayn must now acknowledge him

The dramatic death scene on the wall of a vertical shaft in the cavern system at Lascaux in the Dordogne region of south-west France clearly has profound significance. Dating from the Magdalenian period some 20,000 years ago, it may represent an early case of ritual slaughter to an unknown spirit guardian. (© *Charles and Josette Lenars/CORBIS*)

At Bamiyan, a high valley in the Hindu Kush of eastern Afghanistan, two massive images of the Buddha dating from the third century CE once reposed in niches on the face of a sandstone cliff. From 38m to 55m tall they fell victim to man's religious intolerance in 2001 when Taliban forces used high explosives to reduce them to rubble. (© *Paul Almasy/ CORBIS*)

The Christian-inspired medieval Crusades launched against the forces of Islam were intended to recover the Holy Land and the sacred places of the Bible to Christendom. By and large they were ill conceived, poorly executed and in spite of reliance on impressive war machines such as these, rarely achieved any lasting success. (© *Leonard de Selva/CORBIS*)

The capture of King Cuauhtemoc in 1524 by the forces of the Spanish Conquistador, Hernando Cortés, signalled the end of effective opposition by the defenders of the Aztec capital Tenochtitlan. Cortés waged the last of the great Crusades ostensibly spreading the Christian message. It was, as were its predecessors in the Holy Land, immensely brutal and bloody. (*Bettmann/CORBIS*)

The wheel was a popular instrument of torture used by the inquisitors of the Papal Inquisition. The application of these devices in order to extract confessions or recantations in the name of God was accompanied by gross hypocrisy. The Church of Rome professed reluctance about getting involved in torture and death but this amounted to nothing short of cant and its hands were well and truly bloodied from the outset. (*Bettmann/CORBIS*)

The Spanish Inquisition was an especially bloody affair and one of its most notorious henchmen, Torquemada, administered a form of rough justice that was neither Christian in spirit nor in execution. Defendants were not informed of the specific charges against them, nor were they allowed to confront their accusers. A lawyer for the defendant could be penalised if they were found guilty. (*Bettmann/CORBIS*)

The inquisitors relied on a range of devices for extracting confessions. The use of the *strappado* involved tying the victims hands behind the back and attaching to a rope by which he or she was hauled up to the rafters before being dropped to just short of the ground. The effect was to dislocate the shoulder and arm joints and the degree of suffering could be enhanced through tying weights to the legs. (*Bettmann/CORBIS*)

The ancient Israelites often resorted to extremes of ethnic cleansing known as *herem*. When King Ahab battled with the Syrian Aramaeans he chose not to execute their king and was severely reprimanded by a 'prophet of the Lord' for his leniency. (*Historical Picture Archive/CORBIS*)

The Israelite warrior Gideon offered no leniency when he attacked the Midianites in the valley of Jezreel in about 1200 BCE. According to the Book of Judges his military action resulted in the excessive slaughter of 120,000 of the enemy. (*Historical Picture Archive/CORBIS*)

One of the most horrific examples of religious violence in modern times took place in the jungles of Guyana at a sectarian compound known as the Jonestown People's Temple. In November 1978 the cult leader, James Jones, exhorted 911 followers to mass suicide by swallowing poison and ordered the execution of any who attempted to evade their fate. (*Bettmann/CORBIS*)

formally as Caliph, to which Al-Husayn responded by packing his bags and fleeing to a stronghold in Mecca. Having declined to offer allegiance to Yazid I he was now fearful for his life and, as it turned out, was right to be so. On hearing of Yazid's demand for a show of subservient allegiance, many of the Shi'a supporters in Medina and Kufa bridled, encouraging al-Husayn to mount a revolt. But treachery was afoot and the situation was to come to a bloody climax that eventually took on legendary proportions, and for which the Shi'is have never forgiven their Sunni brethren.

At the outset the prospects looked good for al-Husayn. The Kufan tribal leaders made contact with him in Mecca and formally pledged their loyalty. Having thus tested the water, and in the confidence that he would soon be able to head a successful revolt against the Umayyads, al-Husayn assembled a small rebel force and advanced on Kufa. Unbeknown to him, however, the city governor persuaded the majority of local supporters in the meantime to switch sides, and on 10 October 680, at Karbala, Al-Husayn and his party found themselves confronted by a much larger hostile force under the command of 'Ubayd Allah. Al-Husayn's loyal troops, along with more than twenty of the Prophet's *ahl al-bayt*, were surrounded and, in spite of fanatical resistance, massacred. Finally, al-Husayn, who had observed from a distance, was captured and executed. The date of his death is recorded variously as 680 or 681.[10]

Out of this single act of treachery, this blatant volte-face by tribes and individuals who had invited al-Husayn to Kufa, a movement grew calling for revenge and self-sacrifice. Al-Husayn became recognised as the third of the great imams, and thus was fashioned the ancestor of today's suicide bomber. Sometime between 684 and 685 a pilgrim army of some 4,000 volunteers assembled in Kufa before heading for Karbala, where ostensibly they were to lament and make vows of attrition on the tomb of al-Husayn. The Umayyad army, now essentially orthodox in its adherence to Sunna, awaited them, and most of the 4,000 were slaughtered. The outcome of this attempted revolt was disastrous for the Shi'a, but it also probably made intractable some of the ideological splits that were already deepening within Islam.

At this juncture none of the various factions that had taken shape was clearly identifiable by name, although during the caliphate of 'Ali, under the conditions of the first civil war, his supporters, including all his family of 'Alids, became known as the *shi'at 'Ali*, to distinguish them from the opposing *shi'at 'Uthman*. The full title *shi'at 'Ali* is conventionally abbreviated to Shi'a, and its members are referred to as Shi'is or Shi'ites. Later on the supporters of Mu'awiya would become known as the *ahl al-sunna* or *al-sunnah wa-l-jamaa*, 'the people of the traditions of the Prophet', where Sunna means literally 'practice' or 'tradition', and from which Sunni is derived. The term was probably coined by a *muhaddith* (a scholarly authority on the Islamic canon) named Muhammad bin Sirin, who died in 728 or 729 and who had done much to categorise Muslims by dividing them into the *ahl al-bida*, effectively heretics, and the *ahl al-sunna*, representing the growing orthodoxy. The eighth century saw intense theological argument between rival Islamic groups about the interpretation of the Qur'ān and the Hadith, culminating in a series of *mihna*, or theological trials. It was after these had taken place that *ahl al-sunna* became applied as a more widely recognised term.[11]

Some smaller breakaway groups – the Ithna, 'ashariyya, Ismailiyya, Zayudiyya and others – emerged during the late Umayyad and early 'Abassid period, all wearing politico-religious coats of one colour or another. Other more blatantly heretical factions included the Rafida, Mu'tazila and Murji'a. All of these small parties whose traditions were labelled 'unorthodox' were known to the Muslim mainstream under the collective and rather derogatory title of *ahl al-bida*. The divergence of views was often borderline in nature. The Mu'tazila promoted the idea of free will rather than destiny being preordained, while the Murji'a argued in favour of deferring to the judgement of Allah on the complicity of certain companions leading to the death of 'Uthman and the later assassination of 'Ali. There was also a level of interest in Manichaeism, which involved a belief in some kind of dualism that conflicted starkly with the mainstream Islamic view of one God, Allah. Interest in this form of apostasy was known as *zandaqa* or *zandiq*, and to be accused of such a crime could cost the offender his or her life. But the term also came to be used more loosely for anyone following too liberal a lifestyle or in some way flouting Islamic beliefs and practices. It has been suggested that the young Islamic state was validating its Muslim credentials through persecution of *zandaqa*. Since it stood for many things it could be hurled at a wide variety of opponents.[12] Eventually, the more obscure factions disappeared and Islam was left with three sects driven by a mix of politics and religion, the majority Sunna, the minority Shi'a and the somewhat smaller congregation of Kharijis.

Tribal conflict continued unabated during the reign of Yazid I. In 682 the Medinans staged another revolt against the Umayyad government by expelling the Umayyad residents from the city. This insurrection prompted the arrival of reinforcements from Syria, and the two sides met in a bleak volcanic wasteland known as al-Harra. Once more the Medinan army suffered defeat and, in order to discourage any further attempts at insurrection in Arabia, Yazid I ordered his troops not only to occupy Medina but also to place the city of Mecca under siege. It was during this operation that the most sacred site, the Ka'ba, was burnt down.[13]

Yazid I died unexpectedly, replaced in 685 by Abd al-Malik ibn Marwan. Now a radical Shi'a faction with a distinctly more messianic ideology, headed by al-Muktar bin 'Ubayd al-Thakafi, began to clamour ever more vociferously for revenge against the killing of al-Husayn. The Shi'is were dependent on promoting 'Ali's only surviving son, Muhammad bin al-Hanafiyya, who although not a child of Fatima was nonetheless heralded as the new Imam and the Mahdi. Imam means 'model' and therefore became attached to any exemplary Muslim figure of good standing and character, but also to religious leaders. Mahdi translates as 'a divinely guided one', but the term gained distinct meanings for both Sunni and Shi'a. Among mainstream Sunnis it would be applied to occasional revivers of the faith when the Islamic community had grown impotent or found itself unduly oppressed. For the Shi'a the ideology of the Mahdi was also still to evolve fully, but it was already being identified with al-Husayn and the myth that he had not died but disappeared. He was the hidden Imam due to return as a messianic figure, not unlike Jesus Christ, and rule over the Islamic world by divine ordinance.

He on the other hand was reluctant, and declined either to assume personal leadership of the Shi'a movement or to come to Kufa. In his absence al-Muktar seized the city by armed revolt. For a time there was a degree of internal conflict, because al-Muktar's decision to bring a number of non-Arabs into his civil administration did not meet with the approval of some of the more conservative tribal chiefs; but the revolt was suppressed and the rebels who survived fled to Basra. Al-Muktar's radical supporters took over full control of Kufa, determined to avenge the death of al-Husayn, but the Basran faction became equally determined to oust al-Muktar from power. They attacked and took Kufa in 687, resulting in a massacre that allegedly claimed the lives of between 6,000 and 8,000 of al-Muktar's followers, including al-Muktar himself.[14]

In spite of this disastrous setback the movement established by al-Muktar survived, continuing with its messianic message that al-Husayn would return as the Mahdi. It venerated an empty chair said to be a sacred relic from 'Ali himself. Popular among the lower classes, it earned the title Kaysaniyya from one of al-Muktar's former bodyguards who next took on the leadership, 'Abu 'Amfra Kaysan. The alternative name of Sabiyya derives from that of another contemporary messianic teacher, 'Abd Allah bin Saba.

Muhammad bin al-Hanafiyya continued to be recognised by the bulk of Shi'is as the Imam and the Mahdi until he died in 700. But, in common with the traditions that developed about al-Husayn, many of his supporters believed that he had retired to an occult state and was destined to return in a blaze of glory at some time in the future.

Beyond the confines of Kufa, Abdullah al-Malik ibn Marwan managed to bring civil war to an end, and, although persecution of the Kharijites continued, the Muslim Empire entered another period of expansion before his death in 705. Abdullah al-Malik was succeeded by Walid I, who oversaw the zenith of Umayyad power, beyond which the dynasty entered a slow decline. The last of the great Umayyad caliphs is generally regarded as Hisham, the fourth of Abd al-Malik's sons, who held office for nineteen years. After his death no outstanding statesman emerged during a short period of weak and chaotic government by a succession of Marwanid caliphs. A resistance movement sprang up in the Hijaz and caused ongoing difficulties for the administration, first in Arabia, then over the course of time spreading through North Africa and into the Iberian peninsula. The takeover by the 'Abassid dynasty that ended Marwanid rule came in either 747 or 750 (accounts remain contradictory).[15]

The momentous events of the Umayyad era left behind a bitter legacy of disagreement about the rights of inheritance of Muslim leadership. Traditionally, the Sunnis have had no problem with the history of succession and have accepted the legitimacy of the first four elected leaders, whom they regarded as the 'rightly guided caliphs'. Shi'is reject the legitimacy of the first three and recognise only 'Ali as Muhammad's chosen if largely thwarted successor. It has been their uncompromising position that 'Abu Bakr, 'Umar and 'Uthman usurped the entitlement of 'Ali and that the original companions of the Prophet were complicit in denying him his rightful inheritance. It is this above all else that underpins the historical grievance between Sunnis and Shi'is, although it was specifically the killing of al-Husayn that led to a tradition of glorious martyrdom among Shi'is. Sometime during the eighth century the term *al-rafida*, 'the deserters', ceased to apply exclusively to a heretical breakaway faction and came to be used as a term of abuse directed at all members of the early Shi'a movement.[16] The term is still applied in a derogatory manner. A modern Islamic commentator (unnamed) publishing his views on the Internet, notes that, 'Among such bad names, which are often repeated in books written by the enemies of the Shi'as, is the misnomer 'Rafidis', rejectionists. Any uninformed reader will instantly consider the possibility that they are the ones who rejected the Islamic principles and who did not act upon them, or that they rejected the Message of Prophet Muhammad. But the truth of the matter is quite different. They were called "Rafidis" simply because early Umayyad and 'Abassid rulers, as well as evil scholars who always tried to please them, wanted to misrepresent them.'

153

From the viewpoint of the mainstream Sunnis, 'Ali was bypassed for the caliphate more because of his own deficiencies than by any illegal usurpation on the part of the early electorate. In the popular view he was also implicated in the plot to murder 'Uthman. These aspects were probably widely aired in street conversation and would, in time, be recorded in a letter from the 'Abassid Caliph al-Mansur to a rebel leader from among the Hasanids named Muhammad al-Nafs, or al-Zakiyya.

The 'Alid camp and its embryo Shi'a movement eventually saw a way to bring the 'Abassids to power by backing the anti-Umayyad revolutionaries, who by then were operating from a secure Persian power base. But ironically, in this move to rid Islam of dynastic succession and for the rights of the family of the Prophet to be restored, the losers were destined, once more, to be the 'Alids and their supporters. When the first 'Abassid Caliph, the Prophet's uncle 'Abdullah bin al-'Abbas, took over in 749, he was at pains initially to emphasise family links with the Prophet and to demand vengeance for past wrongs. He could point piously to having backed the caliphate of al-Hasan and to having consistently dismissed claims by 'Abu Bakr's daughter A'isha that her father had been the favoured companion of Muhammad. Al-'Abbas reminded detractors that he had gone so far as to support 'Ali's historical claims about legitimate right of succession and had warned al-Husayn about the dangers of leading an uprising.

But this was largely a shadow play, and as time went on the 'Abassid administration became openly paranoid about 'Alid claims to the caliphate. The rightful entitlement of the 'Abassids to rule took on such political sensitivity that within a short time they had distanced themselves from the 'Alids, their stance shifting to the extent of doing a U-turn, arguing that 'Ali had never been a legitimate contender for the throne. According to the incoming caliphs al-Mansur and his successor al-Mahdi, the 'Abassid claim to political legitimacy was based on hereditary descent from al-'Abbas, whom they regarded as having a stronger legitimacy than Fatima, since she was a woman and for the purposes of Arab inheritance the uncle was akin to the father. Meanwhile the 'Alids became known

154

collectively to their followers as imams, a title which in their eyes denoted the religious leadership of Islam but which, in the view of the 'Abassids, amounted to little short of insurrection. In 786 internecine violence flared again, this time in Mecca where the Shi'a population rebelled. The uprising amounted, in part, to a reaction against the dismissal of some of the Shi'a's deeply held principles by the 'Abassid caliphs, and it resulted in another massacre of their number. The survivors were forced to flee to an area of West Africa known as the Maghrib, which today includes Morocco, Algeria, Libya and Tunisia, where they set up an independent Shi'a kingdom ruled by the Idrisid family.[17]

At least some of the internal conflict during the 'Abassid period was caused by dilution of Arab authority. The caliphate, which by then had moved from Damascus in Syria to Baghdad in Iraq, was no longer in full control of the empire. Government had been decentralised and in many cases was now in the hands of local non-Arab overlords. By the turn of the ninth century a number of powerful barons were running what amounted to rival states: the Fatimids in Egypt, the Ayyubids in Syria and the Mamluks in Palestine. This antagonised Muslim conservatives, who saw a renunciation of basic Islamic principles unfolding. In 809 civil war erupted for the fourth time in the short history of Islam, involving a vicious succession struggle between the sons of the fifth 'Abassid Caliph, Harun al-Rashid. One of these rivals, al-Amin ibn Harun, seized control of the sixth 'Abassid caliphate, but within four years another brother, al-Ma'mun ibn Harun, mounted a successful coup. He and a third sibling, al-Mu'tasim ibn Harun, reached the timely conclusion that, in order to safeguard against such events in the future, the caliphate needed to secure itself with a loyal imperial guard. The present Muslim army, largely made up of Persian and Arab troops, could no longer be relied on to support the 'Abassid administration and so sometime after 833 al-Mu'tasim ibn Harun, who by that stage had taken over the caliphate, began to recruit a force predominantly made up of Mamluks. These former Turkish, Slav and Berber slaves – in effect mercenaries – had been seconded into the armed forces over a period of time and proved to be formidable warriors. Not surprisingly, their presence was highly unpopular among the Arab and Persian contingents of the Muslim army, and nowhere was the resentment felt more strongly than among the Khorasanian faction in Persia that had been instrumental in bringing the 'Abassids to power.

During this period of strife the caliphate steadily lost ground and eventually found itself more or less sidelined by a new civil authority, the sultanate. The empire was held together by its common use of the Arabic language and by the key sinews of its religion, the Qur'ān and the Hadith. But it was not a united force, although many Muslim scholars argue otherwise. Some claim that since all Muslims recognise the unity or oneness of Allah, accept that the Prophet Muhammad received the divine revelations from God and believe that the souls of the dead will be restored at the Day of Judgement, it is unrealistic to say that they are divided along sectarian lines. Nonetheless, the inescapable reality is that within the first hundred years of Islam's foundation Sunni, Shi'a and Kharijite factions had each assumed distinct and identifiable loyalties that would rarely see eye to eye in the future. Each still views its own position as the legitimate one, and that of the other as unorthodox, much as Catholics and Anglicans consider that they have unalienable rights to the true faith of Christianity. From time to time the smouldering resentments between Sunni and Shi'a would erupt into violent feuding.

Today the Sunni branch of Islam, by far the most traditional and conservative, includes about 90 per cent of the faithful and extends into North Africa and east through India, Central Asia and Indonesia. Since the Shi'a movement went its own way in 661, Sunni has effectively dominated the Muslim world, and the view of its majority community is that, since Muhammad did not appoint a successor, the source of guidance for Islam must rest strictly in the words and instructions of the Qur'ān. Rejecting any claim that 'Ali and his descendants were the exclusive executors and upholders of the traditions established by the Prophet, Sunnis continue to accept the legitimacy of the first four caliphs and believe that the office, not necessarily elected from Muhammad's own clan, rightly took over the leadership of the Muslim world. They have left the caliphs and their successors to safeguard the principles of Islam in government. The ulemas, the body of Sunni religious scholars whose most significant centre of learning is the al-Azhar university in Cairo, bears responsibility for interpreting Islamic religious law. In terms of practical devotion Sunnis hold an annual pilgrimage, or hajj, to Mecca and accept this as the major event in the religious calendar.

Modern Shi'is continue to reject the first three caliphs as guardians of the prophetic legacy and recognise only the legitimacy of 'Ali. They also consider that Muhammad initiated a special category of men from within his own family to carry forward the responsibility for guiding the faithful, beginning with 'Ali and continuing with his male offspring from Fatima. These are the venerated imams, the incontrovertible messengers of Allah who assume their authority irrespective of time and place. Shi'is attach more or less equal importance to other pilgrimages. However, even in this common ideology there has been an element of dissent between two Shi'a factions, the Ismailis, the dominant group, and the smaller branch known as the Ja'faris or 'Twelvers'. On the death of Ja'far bin Muhammad 'al-Sadiq' in 765, a squabble arose over which of his sons should succeed him. The main faction gave their support to his eldest son Ismail and his descendants, which they trace to the present-day incumbent of the imamate, Karim Aga Khan. The splinter group rallied behind al-Sadiq's younger son, Musa al-Kazim, and today support his direct line of descent, which ended with al-Mahdi, the 'hidden' Imam. In the meantime the guidance of the twelve is obtained through the meditation of clerics known as *mujtahidun*, experienced in the interpretation of Islamic Shari'a or law. Their most senior ranks include the ayatollahs, whose pivotal role in Islamic states like Iran is well reported.

Twelve of these imams are recorded during the early period of Islamic history, and the number provides an interesting comparison with the twelve disciples of Jesus Christ. The most significant among them was probably al-Husayn, the third Imam, martyred in 680, since it was his violent death at the hands of the Umayyads that proved the inspiration for much of the suicide attacks that occur today. His untimely fate epitomises the Shi'a view of the world, with its mood of dispossession and interest in martyrdom. Another notable was the sixth Imam, Ja'far bin Muhammad 'al-Sadiq', who is acclaimed as the scholarly leader who formalised much of the Shi'a doctrine and made serious attempts to weld the Shi'a community together. Another, Muhammad bin Abdallah 'al-Nafs al-Zakiyya', was the radical extremist who led an abortive revolt during the caliphate of al-Mansur. He was supported by at least some of the learned body of ulemas, and in a move to deter future uprisings by setting an example, the 'Abassid administration had these clerics flogged, tortured, imprisoned and in some cases executed. By and large, however, the imams adopted a moderate position in society and tended to dissociate themselves from extreme activities, though nonetheless they counted extremists among their followers.

The twelfth Imam, Muhammad abdul Qasim, also known as al-Mahdi al-Muntadar (which translates roughly as 'the guided one and the awaited one'), occupies an unusual place in Shi'a tradition. It is believed that he was born in Samarra in Iraq in about 868 during the caliphate of the 'Abassid ruler al-Mu'tamid. His mother is said to have been the granddaughter of a Byzantine emperor, abducted by the eleventh Imam, Hassan al-Askari, who kept her as his concubine. As a child al-Mahdi was hidden away from the community, perhaps for his own protection, since his inheritance of the imamate was energetically challenged by one of the brothers of Hassan al-Askari and the lives of two previous imams had already ended in assassination. The tenth Imam, his grandfather, had met a violent end and his father was also murdered in 872. To avoid further persecution from the 'Abassids, who were also hostile to his claims of leadership over the Shi'a community, he is supposed to have gone into hiding as an adult in an incident known as 'Occultation of the Twelfth Imam'. He may, in reality, have been assassinated like his forebears, but in the romantic imagination he disappeared down a well and became a *ghaybat*, an occult being. Deputies known as *bab* or *na'ib* took over his duties, and over a period of seventy years he appeared to them from time to time to issue instructions. These seven decades became known as the *ghaybat-i sughra,* or Lesser Occultation, ending in 941 with the death of the fourth *bab*. Shortly before the end of his life he allegedly produced a letter from al-Mahdi instructing that no more deputies were to be enrolled and that all tangible representation of the imamate was to cease. *Ghaybat* is a term to which Shi'is attach particular significance, because it implies not merely that Allah has ordained the concealment but in doing so has miraculously prolonged the life of the imam for an indefinite period. Al-Mahdi is thus believed to be hidden from the world in a kind of immortal time warp, the *ghaybat-i kubra* or Greater Occultation, which will end at the Day of Judgement or at some other time in the future and therefore equates loosely with Christian belief in the Second Coming. Shi'is envisage al-Mahdi as being like the sun behind clouds, hidden for the time being but still possessing the power to warm the spirits of the faithful, and that one day he will lead his people to a restoration of their status, much as some believe that Jesus Christ will appear to re-establish a world of justice and peace. Very little, however, can be said about al-Mahdi's life with any degree of historical certainty, and indeed much of the popular lore about his future re-emergence in an event known as *raj'a* stems from words attributed to the Prophet:

> The world shall not end until a man from my family and of my name
> Shall be master of the world.
> When you see standards of green coming out of Khorasan
> Then join with them for the imam of Allah will be there.
> He will be called al-Mahdi.

Tradition has it that the rightful place of the Shi'a in taking the faith of Islam forward will only be resolved when the twelfth Imam returns to complete the 'cycle of prophethood', and therefore Shi'is apply the term Mahdi in a specific context. Sunnis also recognise Mahdi, but use it in a looser sense to identify unusually gifted men who are divinely inspired and who have appeared at different times in history to lead Muslims during periods of oppression and conflict.

Although the current level of bloodshed in Iraq dominates the news at the time of writing, Iran provides a tacit example of how the conflict between Sunni and Shi'a factions is still very much alive elsewhere in the Middle East. Persia, which after the 1979 revolution became the Islamic Republic of Iran, has represented a continuous stronghold of Ja'fari Shi'ism. This branch of Shi'a has been the official religion of the country since the sixteenth century, and following the revolution its leading clerics took important political roles in the new Islamic government. After the abdication of the Shah, Muhammad Riza Pahlavi, the radical Ayatollah Ruhollah Khomeini returned from exile in France to head a new and fundamentalist Islamic government which removed all Western influence from the country and instigated a cultural revolution as a step toward founding a new Shi'a religious state. In encouraging militant extremism, however, many people considered that Khomeini's zeal was somewhat overplayed, and that he was responsible for extending the Gulf War against Iraq.

About 93 per cent of the Iranian population is Shi'a, with the remaining minority predominantly Sunni and Baha'i, and in urban areas this mix has often led to the rise of religious tensions.[18] Iranian Shi'is feel that they are witnessing an unwelcome shift away from political Islam and towards secular nationalism, particularly since Akbar Hashemi Rafsanjani's second term as President, which began in 1993. Early in 1995 Rafsanjani ordered the Islamic Republic News Agency to establish a newspaper entitled simply 'Iran', without any reference to Islam, and large advertisement hoardings appeared comprising the Iranian flag minus any Islamic logos. In the mid-1990s the political debate about the appropriateness of Islam as a political ideology became increasingly heated, and leading Iranian clerics were routinely berated for putting religion to political use. Younger elements in Iran came to the view that Islam was ill suited to the demands of modern statecraft.

Yet the use of religion as a political tool has, if anything, increased. In December 1997 the League of al-Assunah (the Iranian Sunni League) obtained a highly sensitive letter emanating from the Cultural Revolutionary Shura Council and in September 1998 the

160

letter was published through the London offices of the Sunni League. The document is entitled 'Iran's Fifty Year Plan to Export the Revolution and Spread Shi'ism'. The Sunni League seized on this as a propaganda tool to further its own political interests, and distributed copies of the leaked document to the heads of various states, noting that it represented further confirmation of their previous warnings about attempts to introduce Shi'a 'protocols', if necessary through violent means, not only into Sunni regions of Iran but beyond its borders.

The document is prefaced with an uncompromising statement:

There is no doubt that if we are not capable of exporting our own revolution to the neighbouring Islamic countries, their culture which is mixed with Western culture will attack us and be victorious on us. As we have achieved an *ithnai-ashareiah* state in Iran [apparently a reference to the twelve Ja'fari imams] after many centuries of struggle we therefore carry a serious and heavy duty in exporting our revolution. But because of the current global situation and the present international laws it is not possible to simply export the revolution, for the major destructive risks that we might encounter. Therefore . . . we have set a fifty-year plan which comprises five phases of ten years, to export the Islamic revolution to every neighbouring country so that we can first unite Islam. Because the hazards facing us from the Wahhabi and Sunni rulers are by far greater than those from the East or the West; because [these] oppose our movement and they are the genuine enemies of the rule of the *faqeeh* and the infallible imams, to the extent that they consider recognising the Shi'a school of thought . . . as a heresy. By doing this they have split Islam into two contradicting branches.[19]

The document vehemently criticises the religious discipline of several neighbouring countries, including Turkey, Iraq, Afghanistan, Pakistan and various Persian Gulf states whose 'social and cultural corruption and non-Islamic way of life are apparent'. The strength of Shi'a antagonism against Sunni becomes clear when the letter describes modern Shi'is as the 'inheritors of millions of martyrs, whose blood has been running from the day the Prophet Muhammad died, killed at the hands of the false Muslim devils (Sunnis). This blood will not dry until every Muslim testifies that Shi'is are the true inheritors of Islam.'

The overall objective during the fifty-year period includes the immigration of Shi'a families into cities where there is a Sunni majority. This is to be followed by the strategic placing of Shi'a agents in military and executive positions. The plan is then to foment strife between governments and leading clerics. 'We have to secretly enrage the Sunni and Wahhabi [formerly the Kharijis and also known as Salafis and Najdis] scholars against the social corruption and non-Islamic trends in these societies . . . suspicious incidents will occur, which will lead to the suspension or replacement of some government officials. These incidents will be the cause of distrust.' By taking away what they describe as security, tranquillity and comfort, 'the ruling authorities will appear like a ship in the middle of a storm . . . and will accept any suggestion to rescue themselves. The atmosphere will then be ready for revolution and ready for a takeover of power.' The final somewhat daunting paragraph in the document proposes, 'We will then advance to the world of disbelief and we will decorate the world with the light of Islam and the light of Shi'ism until the appearance of the longed-for al-Mahdi.'

An interesting aside from the above is that Osama bin Laden has been rumoured to be a member of the Wahhabi sect, which has some of its strongest support in Saudi Arabia and other Gulf nations supporting the Saudi regime,[20] and the rumour was apparently triggered through an article written by the BBC's Middle Eastern correspondent, Roger Hardy, in September 2001, entitled 'Inside Wahhabi Islam'. According to Hardy, 'Osama Bin Laden, named by US officials as the main suspect in the 11 September attacks against America, is Saudi-born and a Wahhabi.' However, this has been strongly refuted as a superficial conclusion based on the fact that bin Laden was born and bred in Saudi Arabia. In his book *The Wahhabi Myth*, Haneef James Oliver notes that bin Laden has shown that he is not concerned with the same matters of belief and worship that a Salafi would concern himself with, because the sect he belongs to does not distinguish between matters of belief, as long as people adhere to their movement.[21]

The sectarian disputes that have plagued Islamic history may seem pedantic and pointless to an outsider. By most logical arguments they were, and still are, wrangling over ideological minutiae. Yet the internal strife of Islam pales into insignificance when set beside the bloody conflict that tore one of the most devout strongholds of Christendom apart during the medieval period and became known as the Albigensian Crusade.

EIGHT

Heresy

One could be forgiven for believing that sectarian warfare is a modern phenomenon notably affecting Islamic society and accounting for limited Catholic and Protestant bloodletting in Northern Ireland as well as prompting other local ideological disputes. But there came a moment in the past when Christendom turned upon itself and waged a massive and violent conflict against its own members in pursuit of differing religious principles. In this it shares much in common with the present-day troubles between Muslims of opposing Shi'a and Sunni sects. Like today's Islamic strife, the cause of Christendom's self-abuse can be traced back to the early years of the faith.

At more or less the time that Pope Innocent III was having increased doubts over the direction taken by the Fourth Crusade in 1204, deflected from its original goal against his instincts and wishes, other problems were mounting closer to home. Innocent III, born Lotario di Segni and raised in an aristocratic Roman family, was just 37 years of age when he inherited the throne of St Peter, and was destined to become one of the most important and powerful pontiffs in the entire history of the Church. Yet among his flock a counter-Church was on the rise, and the already polluted air of Europe was becoming tainted further with a distinct whiff of Christian heresy. This was indeed an unwelcome situation for a pontiff whose ambition was to realise a European Christian republic marching with one doctrine in its breast and under one spiritual banner, with the Church of Rome leading the way.[1]

A special brand of Crusade in which medieval Christian armies marched not against the Saracens but against their own European kind was driven by a number of developments that took place from the eleventh century onwards. There emerged two conflicting political currents, on the one hand an evermore hostile public attitude to the decadent conduct of at least some of the priesthood, and on the other a raft of radical reforms proposed by one of Innocent's forerunners in the papacy, Gregory VII, the intention of which was to strengthen the power of the Church over all earthly things. The catastrophic events that were destined to unfold owe their ultimate cause, however, to an obscure ideological deviance that arose in the fourth Christian century, known as the Donatist heresy. It earned its title from one of the founders of the doctrine, the Galician bishop Donatus,[2] becoming what one Catholic commentator has described as 'perhaps the ugliest phenomenon in early Church history'.[3]

The natural tendency in the early centuries of Christendom may have been towards diversity, but this was not quite what the first ecclesiastical policy-makers in Rome had in mind. Their interest lay more in prescribing a uniform regime of belief and behaviour enforceable from the top. One of the landmarks in that process of centralisation was the ruling of the Council of Constantinople in 381 which set out the terms of the Nicaean Creed.[4] In so many words the council decreed that anyone who leaned towards beliefs at odds with this rigid statement of faith was to be branded a heretic. It's important to appreciate that, although fine points of deviation from official religious ideology seem of little consequence today, up to the end of the Christian Middle Ages heresy was a crime of immense importance. There is also a common misconception that heresy always involves something un-Christian or sinful. St Thomas Aquinas may have identified it specifically as a sin,[5] but more realistically it amounts to nothing more innocuous than freedom of thought over matters of faith.

The heretical doctrine of Donatism first surfaced in North Africa as an indirect outcome of the persecutions of the Christian community that stemmed from the authority of the Roman Emperor Diocletian. Its ideology ran along the lines that the deity who had created the imperfect material world of humankind could not possibly be the true and perfect God, and thus there must surely be not one but two separate numinous entities, one perfect and the other imperfect. This amounted to a concept of divine dualism. Physical matter, created by the imperfect principle, followers argued, was both intrinsically evil and the source of evil. This reasoning, of course, flew in the face of the Catholic dogma of one God in three aspects, the Trinity, and amounted to blatant heresy, if not actual full-blown blasphemy.

During Diocletian's reign, the North African Christian community had actually fared better than many others, due in no small part to the tolerance of the Roman provincial governor. Christians were expected to do little more than make a symbolic repudiation of their faith by handing over their scriptures and, as a convenient way of avoiding personal repercussions, the wealthier members of the sect were content to oblige. When, however, the persecutions came to an end, a group of zealous reactionaries chiefly drawn from the poorer classes promptly lambasted these turncoats and demanded that they should be expelled from the Church. The criticism against the so-called *traditores* was extreme: they were no longer proper Christians and the priests among them were not fit for office! The zealots began to sound the 'Donatist' cry, arguing that the *traditores* had succumbed to the evil and materialistic principle and that only those of pure spirit, men cast in the image of the true God who had resisted Diocletian's repression, were suitable administrators of the sacrament. The mood encouraged the formation of a group of breakaway ascetics who were suddenly threatening to usurp the priesthood of the Church of Rome. From the viewpoint of the ecclesiastical establishment this, needless to say, was the stuff of revolution and of such concern that by the fifth century it prompted St Augustine to issue a swingeing rebuttal.[6] But his arguments, and indeed those of the Emperor levelled in similar vein, failed to move or remove the sect despite the threats and the actual beginnings of persecution. Its members, effectively the first puritans and soon to be dubbed the 'pure spirits', gradually went underground so that after the Muslim conquest they seem to have disappeared from view.

They were to re-emerge in the West during the second half of the eleventh century, but the reasons for this revival of sectarianism are rooted in events that took place in the mid-tenth century, when a new criticism of the clergy began to gain momentum. The rumblings of discontent amounted to a reaction against the establishment priesthood, which had been falling into a state of evermore deplorable laxity from the ninth century onwards. The mood of antagonism against these slothful clerical ways seems to have begun in Italy and spread from there into the region that is now southern France.

In the face of deterioration in the quality of various holy orders, a reforming and thoroughly radical Tuscan-born Cluniac monk named Hildebrand began to demand higher standards among the wider community of priests, monks and priors. But this was coupled with a new and, in Hildebrand's eyes, excellent proposition by which the powers of the Church would be vastly strengthened. Hildebrand's armoury included a letter purporting to have been written on 30 March 315 by the Emperor Constantine to Pope Sylvester I, the so-called 'Donation of Constantine'. The letter stated that the Pope was not only entitled to pre-eminence over all the other churches of the Roman Empire but over secular governments, their kings and emperors as well.[7]

Today there is a general consensus of scholarly opinion that Constantine the Great probably issued no such donation and that the letter was faked sometime after 750 on the instructions of Pope Stephen II in order to prove his authority to hand over large areas of former Byzantine territory in Italy to the Frankish King, Pepin III.[8] But, whether knowingly or otherwise, for sometime after the reign of Stephen II the papacy treated the forgery as entirely legitimate. Then in the mid-tenth century the papal notion of supreme temporal authority was abruptly challenged. In 962, after uniting a bevy of squabbling German princes under a single flag, Otto the Great launched the new Holy Roman Empire, effectively the German Empire that had arisen out of the ashes of the old, short-lived Carolingian Empire founded by Charlemagne on Christmas Day 800. In 962 Otto was crowned Emperor of the new imperial order, and the German aristocracy lost no time in demanding to know where ultimate sovereignty lay, with the Pope or the Emperor. Matters came to a head when Otto issued his own Donation, superseding that purporting to be from the hand of Constantine. It confirmed the right of the papacy to its Italian possessions but added the proviso, 'saving in all things our own power and that of our successors'. In short order the German Emperor was staking his claim. Observing these developments the ecclesiastical voice opted for prudence, at least for the time being, and said nothing.

Matters remained thus until after 1050, when the team of cardinals surrounding Pope Leo IX (1049–54) set out to make the papacy a transparent force in European politics after centuries of German tyranny had worn away much of its former prestige. From 1059 onwards, as if to reinforce the point, popes were crowned with the tiara, a tall cap that allowed a royal crown to be added to an ecclesiastical mitre.[9] In 1073 the pace accelerated when the radical cardinal Hildebrand was inaugurated as Pope Gregory VII following the death of his predecessor Alexander II, and thus began the so-called Age of Gregorian Reform. Almost immediately Gregory hauled out key sections of the dubious Donation of Constantine in a snub to the imperial court and declared, for the first time in history, that the pope had the right to universal jurisdiction over clergy, princes and paupers alike. There was, however, one significant distinction. The old Donation had represented the emperor giving authority to the pope. Gregory, on the other hand, saw papal authority as a direct gift through Christ from God alone. No more than two years into his reign he issued a famous bull, *Dictatus papae*, legitimising these unprecedented changes.[10] The Church of Rome would gain complete freedom from state control, the authority of kingship to transmit and receive divine grace would be revoked, and the papacy would have the last word over any and all temporal rulers, including the power to remove them from office. The secular rulers of Europe were less than amused. In their eyes Gregory's was an attempt to revive the antiquated arguments of St Augustine that the state has no moral sanction and derives any authority it possesses wholly from its position as a servant of the Church. Gregory was not merely imposing Augustine's policies but imposing them in a most intransigent form in a European world where such ideals had become largely passé. Under the leadership of the Hohenstaufen Emperor Henry IV, imperial troops were sent into Rome in March 1084. The local population was in no mood to protect a pope who, in its eyes, had pushed papal authority to unacceptable limits. Gregory therefore fled Rome to the protection of the Normans controlling southern Italy, and he died at Salerno in the spring of 1085.[11] A succession of somewhat weak and ineffectual popes then tried vainly to implement the Gregorian reforms in the hope of enforcing their claims as the central power-brokers in European government. The Hohenstaufens, however, increasingly threatened the independence of the papacy, aided by a chaotic political situation in Italy and by a growing popular mood of anti-clericalism against popes who were continuing to behave more like petty Italian despots.

In the meantime a particular abbey run by Benedictines at Cluny, a short distance from Mâcon, began to claim the limelight. Founded in 910 by William, Duke of Aquitaine, Cluny was unusual in that its patron had not insisted that his family exert rights over its future. The abbey was dedicated to St Peter and in 1024 was placed under the direct control of the papacy in Rome. Cluny, however, soon became sufficiently powerful and affluent that it was able to acquire a number of other monastic centres and thus almost threatened to eclipse the papacy. The abbey's monks became known as Cluniacs, and it took it upon itself to spearhead the process of reform that had been inaugurated by Pope Leo IX. So far, so good, one might think. But the reformed Cluniac system progressively abandoned much of its earlier balance of work and private prayer, instead placing a strong focus on recitation of evermore elaborate services in the churches. The Cluniac monks also began to enjoy their material affluence and live in what their founding father, St Benedict of Nursia, would have regarded as unashamed luxury. Once more the lay public became increasingly disillusioned with its spiritual mentors, many of whom had been keen to adopt the Cluniac approach. Priests were now generally regarded as lazy, greedy, immoral and intellectually backward by much of the community. They were better fed and better shod than most people, ingratiated themselves with the aristocracy and did little to earn their keep beyond delivering sacraments. They sermonised in Latin and were therefore incomprehensible and utterly boring to most people. The Cluniacs, it was clear even to some of their own, had betrayed the ideals of their founder. Quality of leadership declined along with self-discipline until some of the Benedictine monks abandoned Cluny under the leadership of Bernard of Clairvaux and in 1098 set up a more austere and rigorous order of Cistercians at Citeaux, which lies some 12 miles south of Dijon in the Côte d'Or region of Burgundy. Less than twenty years later, in 1115, Bernard was founding his own monastery, the so-called third daughter of Citeaux, at Clairvaux on the banks of the Aube river in the Champagne region.

During Gregory's rise to power, one of his most trusted allies was Cardinal Humbert, a former protégé of Pope Leo IX. Humbert had already been at the centre of a messy drama with the Byzantine Church in 1054, when he excommunicated the Eastern Patriarch for closing down Latin churches in Constantinople. As another puritanical radical Humbert was also heavily critical of priestly excesses in the Latin sphere of influence, in particular those of the Cluniac monks, and demanded far higher standards of discipline and modesty. However, his proposals took on a distinctly shocking tone when his speeches began to imply that if the clergy refused to come to heel then the ordinary people should be permitted to judge them on merit and if necessary refuse to take the sacrament from them. Here was Donatism firmly back on the menu but being dished up by a brilliant Christian theorist and respected member of the establishment! It was the stuff of revolution, from which heretical ideas and movements could all too easily arise. Humbert had clearly overstepped the mark with a serious doctrinal faux pas, but to the dismay of Gregory VII, who had once been greatly influenced by him, the lay public loudly applauded Humbert's views.

It was not surprising, with Humbert's recommendations to street-level jurists being widely circulated and given the failure of the establishment clergy to improve its image, that people began to look elsewhere for spiritual inspiration. They were to find it in a new and growing breed of itinerant holy men who emulated the Christian Donatist zealots of centuries earlier in North Africa. Each carried few possessions other than the tatty garb on his back, and each broadcast an unorthodox but seductive brand of evangelism, delivered not in tedious Latin but in local dialects that his listeners could understand. These preachers quickly became the popular choice of religious following. At the same time numbers of informed and highly moralistic laymen, recognising the danger of an unorthodox slide into popular dualism, were also making increasingly hostile noises about the official priesthood and demanding that it adopt better standards.

When it was clear that internal improvements would not be forthcoming the more radically minded critics began to broadcast inflammatory statements that were now even more blatantly dualist and Donatist in tone and so struck at the very foundations of Roman Catholicism. These angry spokesmen claimed there was no longer any distinction between the laity and the priesthood and that, if St Augustine's popular analogy between the Church and the City of God was to be taken seriously, only the utterly pure should qualify to staff his so-called Church of the Saints. It was an elitist image that fell foul of a basic tenet of Roman Catholicism which is that the Church is catholic in nature and serves to bring grace to all of humanity.

A veritable bevy of heretical opinions now began to foment, in one way or another traceable to the Donatist heresy, all set upon a perilous collision course with the authority and unity of the Church of Rome. In the fourth century Constantine had tried and failed to make peace between the Donatists and the orthodox Catholic establishment. Eight centuries later, their renewed presence now brought insomnia to Innocent III. Here was a man staunchly committed to achieving his personal vision of a pan-European Christian republic yet witnessing an assault on the soft underbelly of Christendom that was potentially far more deadly than anything the Moors could throw his way.[12]

Innocent had already seized the opportunity to press home the political side of Gregorian reforms during a temporary period of

Hohenstaufen weakness. A decade before his accession the German dynasty was ruling the empire confidently under the leadership of Frederick I Barbarossa, but, when civil war erupted in Germany after the death of Barbarossa's son Henry VI, Innocent took his chance to quash the dynasty's power under the legal authority of *Dictatus papae*. In May 1199, when Otto of Brunswick and Philip of Swabia had emerged as rival claimants for the imperial crown and had been throwing brickbats at each other for some months, Innocent circulated a blatantly threatening letter to all the ecclesiastical and lay authorities in Germany.

While all realms in which the name of Christ is worshipped regard the Roman Church as their mother, yet the Roman Empire ought to embrace her particularly closely and devotedly, so that she may be succoured by the Empire's defence and may herself contribute to the needs of the Empire. But he who is envious of peace and quiet has now divided the Roman Empire just as formerly he divided the Roman Church and has sown such discord among you that you have presumed to nominate two persons as your kings . . . this division in no small degree emboldens the enemies of the Christian faith against the faithful . . . because you have so far been negligent and idle we, who according to the words of the prophet [Jeremiah] are set by God over nations and kingdoms to root out and to destroy, to build and to plant, anxious to fulfil the duties of our office, fervently admonish you all and exhort you in the Lord, ordering by this apostolic letter that you have fear of God before your eyes and zeal for the honour of the Empire, lest its liberty perish or its authority be annihilated . . . otherwise since longer delay is producing great danger, we shall arrange what we shall find to be expedient and shall take care to give apostolic favour to him whom we shall consider to be supported by the greater zeal of his electors and his own superior merits.[13]

In truth Innocent knew precisely what he was about to arrange 'on the grounds of expediency'. He was going to depose Otto of Brunswick rather than Philip of Swabia. The Pope was able to exercise formidable power over princes and would-be emperors because the ultimate sanction of excommunication was still a terrifying weapon at his disposal in a medieval world full of superstition, but in terms of improving the image of the priesthood he was proving far less successful. By the dawn of the twelfth century Christendom had changed radically from St Augustine's day. Its congregation was better educated than before and had acquired a degree of sophistication. Social betterment among the lay population was, however, in striking contrast with the majority of the Catholic priesthood that had not kept up with trends. So unstable had matters become that the Church was resorting to the unseemly spectacle of evermore vitriolic self-criticism. Monks condemned the cathedral clergy as corrupt and materialistic, while prelates and more modest orders of priests retorted that the monks were useless and selfish. Meanwhile, competing religious orders fired off derogatory remarks about each other at every opportunity.[14]

The chief protagonists of anti-Church of Rome sentiment – saintly leaders willing to divorce themselves from mainstream Roman Catholicism and let the world know it – now stood at the forefront of a clearly recognisable religious movement. This evolved into various sects, including two lookalikes that can be readily confused. The Cathars or 'pure ones', a name derived from the Greek *katharoi* implying catharsis or purification, held to the dualist doctrine of matter being evil, and from this premise they argued that Christ never had an actual physical body, so was really neither born in the flesh nor died on the Cross. Their beliefs were very largely identifiable with those of the Gnostics. They persisted with the claim that the creator of the material world was not the supreme creator because, on the one hand, working on the assumption that God is absolute and good, he cannot be the initiator of evil; on the other, since he is eternally unchangeable, he cannot be responsible for that which is ephemeral. In other words, the world and its matter is the responsibility of an evil master. By observing a largely ascetic code of conduct they believed that they could liberate themselves from the control of the body. Because all matter was assumed to be corrupt they shunned marriage when it involved procreation, but sexual indulgence was given the nod so long as it did not result in childbirth. Not all followers of Catharism were expected to tread an ultra-ascetic path, but those who did pursue the extremes of material denial became known as *perfecti* or perfects, men and women who were believed to have received the Holy Spirit as saints. Aside from these more dramatic distinctions, Catharism was content to make use of orthodox Christian scriptures and the Christian creeds as and when these suited the purpose. The immediate riposte of the Catholic establishment for the ears of the wavering faithful was that Catharism was not a reform movement but a heresy that denied the fundamental doctrine of Christianity.[15]

We actually know very little of Cathar belief and practice with any degree of certainty, because dissident writings were systematically destroyed during the Inquisition, and thus we can only rely on questionable information provided by orthodox heretic-denouncers. The Cathars are believed to have arisen somewhere in south-eastern Europe during the eleventh or twelfth century as an offshoot of another dualist-style heresy, that of the Bogomils, which surfaced in tenth-century Bulgaria during the reign of Peter (927–69). As late as 1147 the Patriarch of Constantinople was deposed for having Bogomil sympathies. The founder of Bogomilism is unknown beyond the legendary account that he was a priest who lived and died in the Balkans and that the sect inherited his name.[16] By the eleventh century Catharism is believed to have been active throughout the region and, according to a letter written in 1050 by an obscure monk named Euthymius, had spread extensively into Anatolia (Turkey). The first concrete evidence of the existence of Cathars comes from a trial at Cologne in 1143 when one of their bishops was prosecuted, but their chief strength would soon lie in Italy. Although the evidence suggests that for some time the Catharist focus lay in promoting an evangelical life, its devotees turned more and more toward an interest in pure dualism.

The Cathars have been frequently lumped together with the Albigenses, with whom their views were practically identical but who are said to have been a distinct sect that first appeared in the

175

town of Albi near Toulouse, from which they earned their name. The Albigensian religion, like that of the Cathars, also became dubbed medieval Manichaeism. This refers to yet another quasi-Christian sectarian belief that first arose in the fourth century under the leadership of a sage named Mani and which may or may not have been fairly identified as the stimulus for the later medieval sects. There existed a body of intellectual opinion during the Middle Ages that heretics such as the Cathars and Albigenses had actually shuffled together a whole ream of ancient heresies to form a new general abomination. Their teachings were thus seen as a reflection of those of the Manichaeans, Gnostics, Muslims, Nestorians, Monophysites and Apollinarists.[17]

The Third Lateran Council, held in 1179, outlawed the Cathars and Albigenses together with the Waldensians, a sect advocating similar ideals and founded just three years earlier than the council by a wealthy Lyonnais merchant, Peter Waldo. But in the eyes of Innocent III, and probably with some justification, no one threatened his vision of a Christian republic more than the Albigenses. By the end of the twelfth century the Church of Rome found itself in the precarious position of losing congregations wholesale to the dissident preachers in an area that reached from the Italian Alps in the east to the upper reaches of the River Garonne in the west, with the Mediterranean and the Pyrenees forming its southern boundary. The region became known loosely as Languedoc, an affluent part of south-western Europe that was among the more culturally sophisticated areas of the Continent. Languedoc was also a region that for a long time had enjoyed neither strong government nor a respectable level of Church life.[18] Its priesthood was lax, liberal and carefree, and its barons were constantly scrapping with one another when not enjoying a hedonistic lifestyle that for many included an energetic perennial round of sexual dalliance. The Albigenses had nevertheless managed to attract a sizeable proportion of the nobility around Toulouse and Provence, most prominently the Count of Toulouse, Raymond VI, whose lands occupying about half of Languedoc were home to many of the sect's rank-and-file members. The spiritual leaders, some of whom were women, led a self-sacrificing, abstemious way of life and promoted their brand of Christianity in language that people could understand. It is undoubtedly true that one of the factors that led to the spread of heretical beliefs in the medieval period was the insistence of the papacy and its missionaries on conducting public worship in Latin. Their opposition to the use of national languages, or at least those that ordinary and generally illiterate people could understand, simply bred resentment and made orthodox evangelism extremely difficult. This practice, coupled with the growing persecution of people who clung to local modes of worship, helped to generate a high degree of exasperation and a widespread mood of hostility to Rome and its rather stagnant teachings.[19]

The stories of redemption that the sectarian evangelists told in local language and dialect were exciting, and the abstinence from sex and all things sexually derived (including eggs and meat) provided an interesting diversion from the half-hearted rhetoric trotted out by parish priests and the scandalous behaviour of the nobility. In the eyes of most orthodox members of the Church, however, the Albigenses represented a disagreeable rabble that threatened to split the Christian world if left unchecked. From the viewpoint of that committed Christian republican and visionary Innocent III, theirs was treachery of the worst kind, an intolerable and growing threat that had to be excised in one way or another for the greater good of Christendom.

As if the latest rise of sectarianism was not enough, Donatism took on a decidedly apocalyptic tone in the twelfth century through the teachings of a radical abbot from southern Italy, Joachim de Fiore, who died in about 1201. Little is known of his life, although he is alleged to have become abbot of the Cistercian monastery of Corace in Calabria before building a new monastery of his own near Cozenza, the regime of which was said to have been exceptionally severe. He delivered a fire-and-brimstone message through two influential works, the *Liber de Concordia Novi*[20] and his *Expositiones*[21]; both suggested that the world had entered an age of the Antichrist, the Second Coming was therefore imminent, and everyone had better watch out. There was nothing particularly new or remarkable about this, since prophets of doom had been trumpeting their warnings on and off for centuries. What made Joachim's pronouncements undeniably shocking and at the same time hugely popular among the masses was his barely veiled suggestion that the papacy was identifiable with the Antichrist. With the popularity of the leaders of the Church of Rome at an all-time low ebb, this was splendid ammunition for anyone with half a grudge against the priesthood and was just the sort of added tonic that the puritans needed. With the promise of Judgement Day fast approaching, which for the pure in spirit meant a safe passage to paradise, the devotees of Joachim were more than willing to withstand any counter-attack that the Church might launch.

Innocent III, like every other influential pope from the mid-twelfth to the beginning of the fourteenth century, was a trained and competent lawyer. He had covered the option for an internal European Crusade through a legal decree of March 1199, *Vergentis in senium*, which lumped heresy under the heading of the crime of *lèse-majesté* enshrined in old Roman law, and made way for penalties that included confiscation of goods owned by the perpetrator. At first, however, he was reluctant to use force, prepared instead to try an assortment of devices to lure the Languedoc populace back into the fold. He felt unwilling to entrust such a sensitive task to the local prelates, whom he rightly assessed to be too bound up in their own temporal businesses and held in too low a regard by their local congregations to be of much use. So he resorted to appointing a band of Cistercian monks, as far as possible natives of the south, arming them with sweeping powers of reform and giving each the title of papal legate. However, if the intention was to send them out as effective missionaries, the Cistercians failed in their task. They managed little beyond surrounding themselves with the trappings of pomp and authority on the mistaken assumption that this would impress the lay population. In fact it did no more than raise the volume of accusations of corruption. In some respects the Cistercians failed because, in succeeding as an Order, they had adopted the habits of the establishment and were quickly seen as unsympathetic to the aspirations of those in revolt against orthodoxy.[22]

By 1204, resigned to the certainty that the Cistercians would not prove effective in combating heresy, Innocent III was desperately seeking alternative solutions. He believed he had found one when, two years later, he picked out another breed of envoy, this time a zealous Castilian ascetic named Dominic de Guzman, the Canon of Osma, who was packed off with instructions to preach true Roman Catholicism among the Albigenses a little more competently. Guzman, however, achieved no more success, although he went on to found the Dominican Order of friar-preachers, mendicant monks whose specific task in the future would be the conversion of heretics through the machinery of the Inquisition. Historically, the Albigenses and Cathars had avoided resorting to violence in defence of their sectarian views, largely out of recognition that there was little possibility of defying the Church of Rome with impunity beyond a certain measure of resistance. On 15 January 1208, however, matters were to enter a new and more dangerous phase with the assassination of one of the most oppressive of the papal legates, Pierre de Castelnau, who had been sufficiently high-handed as to threaten excommunication for the Count of Toulouse himself. During a decade of increasing schism, de Castelnau had witnessed southern bishops fraternising with the region's nobility at the expense of their less well-heeled congregations and becoming increasingly indifferent to pastoral duties in matters of faith. The prelates of the Church were, in short, doing little or nothing to encourage dissidents back to orthodox Catholicism. Nor was the nobility itself of much assistance. The Count of Toulouse, Raymond VI, promised much by way of mending fences and then did precisely nothing to discourage the heretics, to the extent that the exasperated Pope once resorted to firing off a highly critical letter to him in person. Nothing worked. The secular authorities tacitly supported the Albigenses, whose activities did not bother them unduly; the efforts of various Rome-appointed preachers achieved little more than a heightening of the anti-establishment mood, and Raymond VI continued with his double-crossing tactics against

Rome. But the murder of Pierre de Castelnau was the last straw for a frustrated and angry Pope. Innocent III decided that the time had come to resort to coercion and forcible means of suppression. He therefore promoted the imminent prospect of a military Crusade, not against pagans but against fellow Christians who had chosen to deviate from the orthodox doctrine of Rome and who were now threatening the very fabric of Christendom.

Jacques Madaule makes the useful point that in the modern world we are struck by the incongruity and even obscenity of Christians waging religious war against their fellows, but at the time of the Crusades this essential distinction would not have registered in people's minds in the same way. It was acceptable for the Church to call on secular forces and secular authority in order to rid itself of a perceived threat in a region where the local temporal authority refused to take responsibility. Nonetheless, the preaching of such a Crusade would require strong powers of oratory and persuasion, and for this Innocent III turned to the services of Arnaud-Amalric, the Abbot General of the monastery of Citeaux. Arnaud, a particularly violent and self-gratifying religious fanatic from the south, had not been Innocent's first choice of ambassador for a military campaign. Innocent would ideally have selected one of the local barons, but he was unable to approach any of the southern nobility for support because neither Raymond VI, Count of Toulouse, nor the other possible recruit in the area, Raymond-Roger Trencavel, the Viscount of Béziers and Carcassonne, were free from suspicion of aiding and abetting the heretics. Neither man had actually been accused or convicted of heresy, but both were seen to have demonstrated ill will towards the pontiff and his cause and had thus broken a time-honoured, unspoken agreement between the temporal and spiritual powers.[23] Innocent therefore turned for his second option to the higher secular authority, the French King Philip-Augustus. The latter, however, proved reluctant to become involved in a military operation well beyond his strategic southern frontier, at that time defined by the Massif Central. Philip-Augustus also lodged a principled objection with the Pope about the legality of allowing the Church to disrupt one of his crown lands without consent. On the other hand he knew that he had no authority to prevent the Pope preaching a crusade in his lands or from recruiting participants from among his noble barons.

Innocent III thus sent his third choice of a personal appointee, Arnaud-Amalric, to drum up support for the Crusade, and Arnaud proved a remarkably effective rabble-rouser. By the spring of 1209 he had managed to put together a formidable force of some 20,000 armed men at Lyons under the command of himself and four of the most powerful barons from the north: the Duke of Burgundy, the Count of Nevers, the Count of Saint-Pol and, notably, Simon de Montfort from the Île-de-France. These warlords probably had in mind the prospect of a quick and lucrative campaign, lasting a month or six weeks at the most against inferior but attractively well-heeled opposition. At its conclusion they would gather their booty and ride off homeward, richer by far. None may have harboured any fervent dislike of the Albigenses, or envisaged that they would be taking part in the most outrageous and brutal of all slaughters of Christians by fellow Christians in the name of the faith. But then none, at that juncture, may have heard of the town of Béziers.

Béziers, once a provincial Roman garrison, is situated on the side of a hill overlooking the Valley of the Orb some 50 miles south-west of Montpellier on the Canal du Midi. By the start of the twelfth century it had become the effective hub of Albigensian activity in the South of France, and for this reason Arnaud-Amalric singled out Béziers for a vicious object lesson. He would make an example of the town in order to spread fear among other fortified urban centres and quell the possibility of armed resistance. On 22 July 1209 Arnaud's crusading force, the so-called army of the faith, found itself massed beneath Béziers' strongly fortified walls and an order went out to the inhabitants to hand over the 'good men', the saintly leaders of the sect. When this demand was refused, Arnaud issued a fateful instruction to take the town by force. Whether he actually uttered the much-vaunted cry, 'Kill them all for God will know his own', is open to conjecture, but there is no doubt that Arnaud-Amalric was personally responsible for the atrocity that unfolded, since power lay with him to stop it. The Crusaders proceeded to massacre the entire population of Béziers, estimated at some 20,000 people. They then headed towards Carcassonne and, with a quickly acquired reputation preceding them, met with little resistance en route. From this moment on Innocent III was effectively unable to maintain control over the progress of the Albigensian Crusade or to ensure that it was conducted under canonical law.

Now the Albigenses turned to the one authority in which they believed they might find support, Peter II, King of Aragon. He was already not a little alarmed about the appearance of such a large invasion force of northern French in a fiefdom to which he had as much entitlement as did France. But he was also highly critical of Raymond-Roger Trencavel – now holed up in the massively fortified town of Carcassonne and determined to resist – for having recklessly endangered himself on behalf of 'a crazy people and their crazy beliefs'.[24] Arnaud-Amalric proved as inflexible in the demands he placed upon Carcassonne as he had been with Béziers, insisting that the 'good men' were handed over. Through the offices of Peter II, Trencavel was given permission to leave the city freely with twelve chosen knights if the other inhabitants surrendered unconditionally. But Trencavel refused and eventually gave himself up as a hostage, thus allowing the Carcassonne population to escape. On 15 August 1209 the Crusaders moved in, having agreed not to massacre or pillage, only to find themselves in a town deserted by its inhabitants for whom the message from Béziers had proved too strong to ignore.

By the winter of 1209 two of the main centres of Albigensian activity had been taken, and the lands of Raymond-Roger Trencavel had been forfeited to the papal legate under a legal entitlement known as 'exposure as prey'. Trencavel himself died within a few weeks in the tower of Carcassonne where he had been imprisoned. Officially, the cause of death on 10 November was dysentery, but it was widely rumoured that there were suspicious circumstances attached. The instinctive recourse of Arnaud-Amalric was to offer the conquered territory to the northern barons. They, however, were less than enthusiastic about the prospect of administering potentially hostile provinces far away from their own centres of operation, and three of them promptly declined. At this point Arnaud concentrated his entreaties on the man whose name has been most closely associated with the Albigensian Crusade, Simon de Montfort the Elder, Lord of Yvelines and Earl of Leicester. This proved a canny choice. De Montfort, the father of the more famous Anglo-French baron of the same name who defeated Henry III at Lewes in 1258, was an experienced military man who had served in the Fourth Crusade but abandoned the cause when the armies were poised to attack the Christian city of Zara, one of the most important Venetian vassal centres in Dalmatia. He had only recently returned to France when the Albigensian Crusade was first advocated, and by repute he decided to participate after having opened his Bible at random and read a verse of the Psalms, 'for he shall give his angels charge over thee, to keep thee in all thy ways'.[25] De Montfort's response initially was the same as that of the Duke of Burgundy and his compatriots in arms – to decline the offer. But on shrewd reflection he believed that he could negotiate terms, and, on the understanding that the northern barons would pledge an oath to come to his aid if it were needed, he obtained agreement from Peter II that he should be invested as Viscount of Béziers and Carcassonne. The southern barons, more outraged at the bloodbaths that had taken place than from any strong sympathy for the Cathars and Albigenses, ranged themselves against de Montfort. Peter of Aragon, no heretic, was torn between loyalty to the Church on the one hand, and acceptance on the other of a northern French neighbour on his doorstep through whom the French King might well find it easier to extend his control over the lands to the south of the Massif Central. With some reluctance he opted to go to the aid of Raymond VI of Toulouse, whose personal suzerainty was now at serious risk.[26]

Simon de Montfort's position, however, was by no means secure. He was obliged to watch the bulk of the Crusaders heading back to the north, and found himself alone in enemy territory with only a handful of troops and a single properly fortified citadel, that of Carcassonne. To the south and north the fortified hill towns of

Minerve, Cabaret, Termes and Saissac remained solidly in local hands, and de Montfort was only in effective control of the low-lying areas. He had taken the diplomatic precaution of burying Raymond-Roger Trencavel with considerable pomp and circumstance, having displayed his body to the people so that they might mourn a great man; but he was hardly popular and his only accountable support in the well-nigh impossible task of winning over the populace was that of Arnaud-Amalric and the Church. Meanwhile, the southern French inhabitants, having smartly recovered from the shock of Béziers, were not slow to recognise his vulnerability.

De Montfort, however, was not one to be intimidated and took the strategic view that the best means of defence was attack. Accordingly, he sent a request to his wife waiting in the north, Alix de Montmorency, to concentrate on mustering fresh troops, and at the same time he dispatched a dependable ally, Robert Mauvoisin, to seek more tangible military backing from the Pope. Reinforcements duly arrived in the spring of 1210, so that the whole of the south was now threatened by northern invasion. Exploiting a chronic dislike on the part of the people of Narbonne for their neighbours in Minerve, de Montfort captured the citadel at Minerve in late summer. That which had begun as a religious war in the name of the Church of Rome was fast assuming the colours of a nationalist campaign in which religious considerations were scarcely relevant and the purge of Albigenses was little more than a convenient excuse for slaughter and territorial gain. De Montfort saw advantage in adopting terror tactics less as a means of eliminating heresy than of consolidating his own position. In what would become a familiar routine, he selected eighty notable Albigenses at Minerve and burned them in the town square. Later in the autumn, after the fortress at Termes had been overrun following a three-month siege, Cabaret surrendered meekly and de Montfort laid up for the winter. In the spring of 1211 he turned his army on Lavaur, broke down its defences and executed 400 'good men' along with 80 pro-Albigensian knights who met their deaths by hanging. The Lady of Lavaur was tossed alive into a well, the entrance to which was then sealed. In the same summer he captured the fortress of Cassès at Lauraguais and incinerated another sixty Albigenses.

Observing the deteriorating situation, Raymond VI, the Count of Toulouse and unquestionably the most powerful of local barons, reached the conclusion that he must act to prevent what was rapidly becoming a northern French takeover coupled with local anarchy as the price for his tacit support of the Albigenses. In Toulouse, against Raymond's wishes his own metropolitan bishop had formed a so-called White Brotherhood against the heretics, and some of its members had even supported the northern Crusaders in the siege of Lavaur. Matters reached a critical point rather sooner than Raymond might have expected because de Montfort, probably anticipating the possibility of the southern forces taking the offensive, opted to besiege Toulouse. De Montfort, however, found himself at a disadvantage for the first time and was forced to retreat to a scarcely viable defensive position in the fortress of Castelnaudary, where he was promptly surrounded by a substantially larger force. In spite of the weakness of Castelnaudary's defences Raymond's army was unable to take the citadel and had to withdraw. The situation had amounted to nothing more than a temporary setback for de Montfort, and in 1212 he went on to take much of the area north of Toulouse after the arrival of further reinforcements. Although the city itself held out he was able to overrun most of the key fortresses in the region, including most notably Penne d'Agenais, Moissac and Marmande.

Meanwhile, the Church was responding in its own way to the rise of sectarianism. The main objective of the Fourth Lateran Council that took place in 1215 was to raise the quality of the spiritual life of the ordinary Christian in the face of mounting schism, and Innocent III, with the weight of the orthodox Catholic hierarchy barking at his heels, lost no time in roundly condemning the doctrinal views of such radicals as Joachim de Fiore along with the Cathars, Albigenses and Waldensians. Innocent gave his official weight of approval to the Dominicans during the course of the council, but its members were destined to fail in their preaching to the wayward southern congregations, and when this became clear the Dominican friars had few qualms about resorting to more forcible means of their own, including interrogation, torture and burning, and in so doing they brought lasting disgrace on themselves and their Order.

According to the inquisitor Rainerius Sacchoni, by about 1250 the number of Cathar churches 'totally destroyed' in the areas around Albi, Toulouse and Cacassonne exceeded 200. By this time another more devious but no less brutal apparatus was in full swing in the name of God. The Inquisition, under the auspices of Pope Innocent IV (1243–54), eventually emulated the tactics of the Crusaders and approved the use of torture and death to 'promote the work of the faith more truly'.

NINE

Inquisition

The popular history of the Inquisition is based probably almost as much on mythology as hard fact. The spectre of a vicious medieval instrument designed to crush human spirit and bones alike has been romanticised and overlarded with a degree of consistency in the two centuries since the machinery of the *inquisitio* was largely, though not entirely, abolished in the modern world. The mythology has served to further the political purposes of a number of modern regimes much as it served the Protestant reformers of earlier times in their denigration of the Church of Rome.[1]

The medieval Inquisition, or some process like it, was inevitable. The strife that erupted during the eleventh century between the Holy Roman Empire and the priesthood, the extravagance and greed of the monasteries, the abuse of their temporal power by so many bishops, was sooner or later bound to offend the lay population and make them willing to seek alternatives to the extent that, as the writer Voltaire put it, 'there arose a secret independence in their minds'.[2] That covert desire for self-regulation of their beliefs and rituals would trigger an ecclesiastical backlash. Yet the response was so severe that the Inquisition stands as one of the most ghastly Christian chapters of violence carried out in the name of God. Its medieval executors relied not least on ideas put forward by St Augustine in the *City of God* as justification for their attacks on heretics, Jews and anyone else who appeared not to conform willingly to their precise ideas of good orthodoxy. It was, in Voltaire's view, 'the ultimate degree of an absurd and brutal barbarity to support by informers and executioners the religion of a God who himself perished at the hands of executioners'.

When dispensing with the myths of Inquisition it is worth noting that its machinery was not an innovation of the Middle Ages. The origins can be traced back to the final years of the Roman Empire, when the term *inquisitio* described a particular aspect of legal enforcement included under a general heading of *Corpus Juris Civilis*. This, the so-called Justinian Code, an immense legal accomplishment of the Byzantine Emperor Justinian I (527–65), brought together in a single set of volumes all the disparate legislature of the empire that had built up over many centuries but hitherto had never been codified. Under the Justinian Code the Roman magistrate was free to instigate inquisitorial proceedings without relying on an accuser coming forward to testify and, if he thought such means constructive to the ends in mind, he could resort to the use of torture to extract information. He was entitled simply to pick up casual innuendo and conduct a criminal trial on the strength of tittle-tattle, employing jurists who needed only to be experts in evaluating the perceived criminal activity rather than the law.[3]

During the fourth century the Christianised emperors of Rome leaned towards applying the process of *inquisitio* more specifically against heretics, and in 385 the first real test case arose. It had a chilling outcome, for through it the townspeople of Trier in southern France witnessed the execution of Priscillian of Avila, a devout Spanish bishop, put to death by some of his fellow peers only on account of his belief in a particular brand of Christianity to which they did not subscribe. Priscillianism amounted to a strongly ascetic splinter movement but could hardly have been called radical, focusing as it did on repression of sexuality and a demand for celibacy among all dedicated Christians. Yet Priscillian was branded a dangerous heretic and stood accused of promoting sorcery, lechery and a myriad of iniquity against God and humanity. When examined more closely, his 'crimes' appear to lie in allegedly subscribing to Manichaeism, the ideology of an outlawed sect founded in 242 by the Persian philosopher Mani. Not only was Priscillian put to death along with six of his disciples but his followers were generally persecuted, his writings collected up and

destroyed wherever they were discovered, and his name dis-
honoured, obliterated from as many Church records as possible.[4]

Priscillian's execution stands as more than a travesty of justice in
the name of God; it resulted from a hideous landmark ruling, the
first instance of judicial capital punishment for heresy, and with it
the Church took a first critical step in its long-term pledge to
suppress dissenting voices at whatever cost. From that date forward,
a succession of edicts emanated from the Church authorities, so that
from the reign of Theodosius the Great (379–95) the imperial
statutes of the newly Christianised empire dictated that persistence
in heresy was punishable by death.[5] At this juncture, however, the
Christian congregation was hardly ready for such extremes.
Priscillian's sentencing had met with a flood of righteous public
indignation, and the two bishops who had conducted his trial faced
considerable opprobrium. One, Ithacius, was expelled from the
episcopate and the other, Hydatius, resigned. Both were excommunicated and exiled.[6] Nonetheless, an apparently unstoppable
progression had begun towards automatic punishment by death for
persistent deviation from the orthodox brand of Christianity, and
influential voices added impetus to the movement. St Jerome
(342–420), the Italian biblical scholar and author of the first
translation of the Bible from Hebrew to Latin, is on record as
having levelled fierce and passionate criticism at the bishop of a
dissident monk named Vigilantius, crying that he had fallen short of
'destroying the heretic in the flesh'. Vigilantius' 'crime' had been
nothing more profound than to level criticism in the direction of
some of Jerome's most cherished teachings. Jerome responded
indignantly that piety and zeal for God could not amount to cruelty
and that rigorous punishment was the most sincere form of mercy
since temporal punishment was the only certain way to avoid
eternal perdition.[7]

In spite of various Church decretals pointing in the direction of
capital punishment the death of Priscillian and his followers did
not, however, spark off an immediate blood purge. The 500 years
from the fifth to the tenth centuries actually saw fairly limited
amounts of violence committed by Christians on fellow Christians

burdened with the label of heresy, and as the millennium approached Christendom was cloaked with a level of apathy towards dissidence. The stupor of the tenth and early eleventh centuries was certainly too profound for heresy to be a significant worry on the consciences of orthodox ecclesiastics. Men of God thus laid aside their weapons of persecution and tended to forget how to use them, so that when Buchard of Worms compiled his famous collection of canon law in 1018 he virtually omitted any mention of heresy or its punishment.[8]

Notwithstanding occasional spates of persecution, as in the case of Priscillian, it was not until about the turn of the twelfth century that the Church of Rome awoke from its complacent slumbers and chose to revive fully the practices of the Roman imperial courts so that papal justice would apply everywhere that the papal courts functioned. Soon afterwards, and perhaps predictably in view of these changes, the spectre of capital punishment for heresy reappeared. The detractors of a Dutch critic of the Roman Catholic Church, Tranchelmus, chose to hound him on similar grounds to those levelled against Priscillian, for allegedly preaching a doctrine of free love when in reality he had denied the authority of the Pope. Tranchelmus was imprisoned by the Archbishop of Cologne, escaped and was executed after being recaptured in 1115. But even though heresy and persecution of heretics was hardly a new phenomenon in Christendom, the case of Tranchelmus was a rarity and formal punishment was not, as yet, conducted with any degree of orchestration or frequency.

The new protocol, which appeared to put more legal powers back into the hands of the Church, was, however, viewed with irritation by some secular authorities, and at once there arose a tussle for the upper hand between Rome and the temporal sovereigns of Europe. When civil law underwent something of a similar renaissance at much the same time, the newly emergent Holy Roman Empire was not slow in establishing secular courts in which absolute power was handed to the German Emperor's representatives. Lesser kings and princes of Europe willingly fell in with this innovation rather than finding themselves under the legislative thumb of an ecclesiastical authority whose conduct was itself coming more and more under critical scrutiny.

Meanwhile the Church, not to be outdone, promptly pressed its own demands for greater temporal control, and did so by exploiting the terrors of hell and damnation. It can never be underestimated how effectively this form of religious arm-twisting with the threat of fire and brimstone struck mortal dread into the hearts of kings and commoners alike during the Middle Ages and beyond. It was a fear that would be given another massive boost when Dante Alighieri composed his *Divine Comedy*, begun in about 1307 as an allegorical narrative, an imaginary journey by the poet through hell, purgatory and heaven.

Throughout the span of the medieval centuries, religious infidelity was regarded, no matter whether founded on ignorance or education, whether hereditary or acquired, heretical or pagan, as a sin to be punished by public incineration in this world and eternal suffering in the next. This doctrine, monstrous as it may seem to us in the twenty-first century, was the creed of the Church of Rome. It amounted to the basis of the Inquisition and those other forms of religious persecution which have stained the history, at some time or another, of nearly every part of Christendom.[9]

Facing the prospect of instant fiery toasting forks if they strayed from orthodoxy, or even expressed sympathy with dissenters, loyal Catholics living in the early part of the twelfth century were beginning to view their errant brethren with rather more anxiety than they had felt hitherto. Other than the heretics themselves, who were confident that they had found their own salvation, this alarm involved most populations outside troublesome regions like Languedoc and it added a powerful impetus to the prospect of an Inquisition that would earn popular support. The term 'Inquisition' is in some regards misleading because it implies a single centralised adjudicating apparatus, whereas in practice there were several medieval inquisitions, each of different shape and focus from the next, and bound only by a loose authority in the form of guidelines from the papacy, not by direct top-down authority. For a long time the Church of Rome was reluctant to get its hand noticeably dirtied with the apparatus of terror.

The first recognisable charter for an anti-heretical inquisition process was established on 4 November 1184 through a papal decree known as *ad Abolendam*, which translates as 'for the doing away with'. The charter was hatched between a singularly flabby pope, Lucius III, and the somewhat more robust Holy Roman Emperor, Frederick I Barbarossa.[10] Lucius was anxious to arrive at an amicable settlement on various matters dividing Church and empire, among them how to share out responsibility for repressing heretics, in particular those involved in one of his keenest worries, the rampaging Albigensian heresy in southern France. Mainly with this in mind, the first experimental round of anti-heresy tribunals staged under *ad Abolendam* was set to operate under the magistracy of French bishops whose sees were situated in or near the Languedoc region, for which reason they were known as episcopal courts. In principle heretics were to be tried and, if found guilty, excommunicated by the Church before being handed over to the secular authority for punishment. These early tribunals proved largely ineffectual, however, because the senior ecclesiastics appointed to oversee them were more often than not absent from their sees and tended to be unconcerned about local problems unfolding hundreds of miles away from where they were enjoying easy lives of pampered indulgence.

But when Innocent III ascended the papal throne on 11 January 1198, on the day of his predecessor Celestine III's death, he did so as a far more aggressive and determined incumbent than Lucius III. Here was a man born to rule, and heresy was a matter that he did not intend to tolerate for very long. Innocent therefore proposed a new and innovative method of administering justice against religious dissenters. He dispatched two trained and highly determined monks to Languedoc to begin passing more effective judgement on those accused of heresy. Voltaire describes how Innocent also applied undisguised leverage to the secular authorities with the command 'to the Princes, to the Counts, and to all Lords of your lands, to aid them against the heretics, by the authority that they have been given to punish the evil-doers, so that when Brother Rainier [one of the pair of ambassadorial monks] has excommunicated them, the Lords should seize their property, banish them from their lands, and punish severely those who dare to resist'.[11] This would prove to be a more effective salvo from the Church against its dissenting voices, and in March 1199 Innocent pressed home the message in deliberately inflammatory language, declaring that heresy was 'high treason against God'. Recognising the ineffectiveness of the existing episcopal courts, he was ready to put in place a new and more powerful apparatus to deal with such treasonable behaviour.

So, at the beginning of the thirteenth century, the papacy of Innocent III was preparing to set up a special ad-hoc court of its own, operating on the same lines as the civil courts although with the specific brief of prosecuting heretics through the machinery of *inquisitio*. In 1204 the new apparatus of Papal Inquisition was formally announced to replace the old episcopal tribunals. In theory the *raison d'être* had been in place for some time and it had been reinforced from the eleventh century onwards, when ecclesiastical reformers proclaimed Christian society to have a fundamentally religious purpose in which the separation of life into secular and non-secular spheres was untenable. Legitimate society could only be Christian in their eyes, which meant that there was no salvation beyond the Church. Furthermore, deviation from orthodoxy risked bringing down God's anger upon the guilty and innocent together. The fear that had been planted in the mind of the Christian Catholic flock about religious dissent, and which had occasionally resulted in coercion and even executions, as had been the case with Priscillian and his followers, was now to be the driving force for the Papal Inquisition. Nevertheless Church and State alike throughout Europe dithered about the most appropriate punishment for heresy. It was not a case of torture or death sentences becoming de rigueur overnight. At the Council of Tours in 1163, when Pope Alexander III took steps to halt the march of Albigensian influence in Languedoc, he stopped short of insisting on the death penalty and only demanded of the secular authorities that they imprison heretics and confiscate property.[12]

From the outset the procedure of the tribunal in the Latin Church was supposed to follow a strict official formula. Certainly, the object of Innocent III in confronting heresy – and this has often been misunderstood – was not primarily to punish but to protect and conserve the orthodox Catholic faith of the community. Others, however, did not see things in quite the same way and in some countries sentences had already become excessive. The German Church had regularly been more brutal in its dealings with offenders. Rarely allowed to testify on their own behalf in court, those found guilty of heresy could generally expect to suffer the severest physical punishments dealt out on an ad-hoc local basis, often including mutilation. By 1157, for example, the Church in Reims was advocating the application of hot irons to mark heretics with a lasting and public brand of shame, even if they agreed to recant. Elsewhere in Europe for some while the approach was more one of pastoral persuasion, with inquisitors content to arrest and prosecute while steering clear of any undue recourse to violence. Nevertheless, over the span of the twelfth century it is possible to detect trends to indicate that procedures across Europe were becoming increasingly severe.

While the evolution of the Papal Inquisition was gathering momentum, matters were also moving swiftly on the battlefront, and the changing fortunes of war in southern France influenced the speed with which the Inquisition was put in place. From 1216 onwards Raymond VI, Count of Toulouse, and his son began a fightback against Simon de Montfort and everything French. The conflict had turned from a strictly religious crusade into a secular war aiming for southern liberation. But although de Montfort was slain on 25 June 1218 during the siege of Toulouse, which might have presaged victory for the south, final defeat for the southern way of life would prove unstoppable. In the following year the French King sent a new army to the south under the command of Prince Louis and the holocaust continued. Louis oversaw the massacre of some 5,000 civilian inhabitants of the town of Marmande. There were limited successes for the south during the ensuing decade, but the French barons steadily strengthened their grip on the Languedoc region until they completed their conquest of the south in 1229 and Toulouse was obliged to sign up to a surrender document under the Treaty of Medaux.[13] Its people were now bitterly resentful of interference in their affairs by northerners who had forcibly stripped away their lawful sovereignty under the pretence of ridding the land of heretics, and moreover had imposed foreign values in place of the traditions of centuries. For a few of the southerners, patriotism and a reluctant willingness to demonstrate that they were good Catholics swept away allegiances towards Cathars and Albigenses, but the majority still firmly blamed the Roman Church and the French rather than the heretics for piling woes upon them.

Although the years of the Albigensian Crusade had brought their share of notable military atrocities, by and large legal measures against the heretics seem not to have been implemented very effectively, and the dissidents had also learned some useful tactical lessons. At the various times when they had sought refuge en masse in fortresses the result, more often than not, had been to lay themselves open to slaughter. So strategies changed and the leaders of the Albigenses came out into the open, at least for a while. They conducted pastoral rounds and held their religious ceremonies under public gaze to the extent that they progressively won even more followers. Many priests and nuns in the Catholic congregation were starting to show solidarity with the heretics in whose beliefs and practices they could find little to criticise. People of the south were fast coming to regard the Catharist churches as their national focus, and much to the irritation of the implanted French bishops, the new Count of Toulouse, Raymond VII, continued to give the dissenting 'good men' and 'good women' his secular blessing and protection.

The Languedoc revolt against orthodoxy infuriated Innocent III. In effect, much of what he had first set out to achieve through the blunt and bloody instrument of having the Crusaders march to slay heresy with the sword had come to nought. Simon de Montfort, through extremes of brutality and single-minded repression, had passed on a bitter legacy, which now posed an even greater threat to the unity of the Roman Church. When the war took on its distinctly nationalist flavour in the final decades of southern struggle to remain independent, the secular authorities in the north hardly needed reminding that the Albigenses stood as the main rabble-rousers of resistance, and so the need for inquisitorial success took on a new sense of urgency. For its part the pontificate issued a new series of bulls during the 1230s, which served to strengthen the 1204 decree that had launched the Papal Inquisition. The tribunals, no longer staffed by lax bishops often residing far from the seat of conflict and with their minds on other things, were manned by monks now trained professionally for the job. In the wake of Innocent III's death in July 1216, the new ecclesiastical administration of Honorius III was ready to agree that Innocent had hit upon the right idea in turning to monastic henchmen. The solution to dealing with heresy lay in hiring more specialist investigators answerable directly to the papacy. Such men would be immune to local pressures and their task would be to uncover the hiding places of dissidents and hunt them down. The immediate problem, however, was that the papacy did not have enough ground staff to carry out the task on a regular basis, and so Honorius turned to the option of employing more sizeable troops of mendicant monks. The papal office cast its eye over a new Order founded in 1220 by Dominic Guzman, known as the Order of Preachers or the Dominicans, because at face value they possessed the right credentials. The members of the Order were committed to a life of poverty, placed much emphasis on theological training and had demonstrable abilities to preach the message of the Catholic Church. They could, it was felt, exercise an effective 'stick and carrot' approach. So it was that on 8 January 1221 Honorius dispatched a letter that earmarked the Order for the task of suppressing heresy.[14]

In France under the secular authority of Louis IX, keen as ever to toady up to Rome, the Papal Inquisition was formally adopted from 1229 onwards under a new statute known as *Cupientes*. Louis had reached the timely conclusion that, if he and his court were to exercise any kind of realistic sovereignty over the south and maintain valuable standing in the eyes of the papacy, the heretics must be dealt with. Since the necessary cleansing could not apparently be achieved by force of arms, some other strategy had to be employed. After greasing the legal wheels Louis chose the occasion of the start of Holy Week 1229 to gather a crowd in the public space before the Cathedral of Notre-Dame in Paris and deliver a proclamation. When speaking of the duties of the secular authorities controlling the south, and with the backing of the recently appointed Pope Gregory IX, Louis declared, 'We decide and we command that the aforesaid barons and officers should diligently and loyally strive to seek out and expose heretics.'[15]

It is arguably from this pronouncement rather than the 1204 papal decree that the real rise of the Roman and Spanish Inquisitions stemmed, because with it the old *inquisitio* style first adopted in the Justinian Code was brought out of the cupboard and dusted off by a state authority. Hitherto the criminal procedure against heretics had required accusations to be made, frequently encouraged by generous cash rewards to the informers, before any legal course could be followed. Now, however, the method changed to one of positive action. No longer did the authorities have to rely on the tedious process of waiting for one citizen voluntarily to sneak on another. Pressure could be applied to 'persuade' informants to divulge details about the activities of their neighbours, and, when the Roman inquisitorial methods were exploited to their full extent, this would include torture if and when it was deemed necessary.

Sentencing of those convicted of heresy, however, continued to be an uncertain affair in both religious and secular courtrooms. Even when the Holy Roman Emperor, Frederick II, made persecution of religious freedom an integral part of European law, his statute of 22 November 1220 demanded little more than that which had been included in Pope Alexander's 1163 decretal. It only approved confiscation of property and the outlawing of the crime. After another four years of hesitation Frederick was prepared to endorse death by fire or, by way of a lesser punishment, removal of the tongue as appropriate sentences, but then only at the discretion of the presiding judge. Neither Louis IX of France nor, on the other hand, Raymond VI of Toulouse was willing to advocate the death penalty under the terms of the settlement they reached in 1229 at Medaux. Not until Frederick II endorsed the 1231 Melfitan

Constitutions consolidating the Sicilian monarchy, claimed by some authorities to be his outstanding legislative achievement, did the Emperor take the opportunity to incorporate an automatic death sentence by incineration for those found guilty of heresy. Even though such punishment had actually been in accepted use on an ad-hoc basis for many years, it was not until 1270, in the final year of his life, that Louis IX issued a set of decrees known as *Les Établissements*, through which he added his signature to the formal sanction of being burned alive for heresy.[16]

Heresy had meanwhile been afforded a clear definition that effectively barred any form of religious dissent or liberal thinking about God and his ways. Robert Grosseteste, a formidable theorist and the Bishop of Lincoln, born in 1170, identified it as 'an opinion chosen by human faculties, contrary to Holy Scripture, openly taught, and pertinaciously defended'. Such rebellious opinions were now seen by the ecclesiastical establishment to be an assault not just on its own authority but also on the very norms by which medieval society and culture functioned.[17]

Within a year of Louis IX's proclamation of 1229 at Notre-Dame the severity of laws against heretics in various parts of Western Europe had hardened to the extent that ordinary citizens across the region witnessed something of a legal revolution, and the ominous feeling grew that persuasive tactics through pastoral care and Church reform were about to be replaced wholesale by coercion and violent punishment. It was time once more for Cathars, Albigenses and Waldensians to guard their backs against attack from more quarters than just the Crusaders. The Church was gunning for them directly. The heretics returned to underground activities, hiding their identities, and in order to deal with this concealment the Church was obliged to rethink some of its strategy. The new Dominican specialists were called upon to play an ever-stronger role. They acted as a kind of thuggish medieval FBI, able to travel across frontiers, indifferent to the political influences that could so readily bedevil local bishops and deacons. They could also cleanse heretic-hunting of the spectre of individual fanatics striking down the unholy out of personal spite. The official line of the

Church of Rome remained, however grotesquely, that the activity should be conducted 'not from a zeal for righteous vengeance but out of love of correcting an errant brother'.[18]

Unfortunately, the ideal of 'correcting errant brothers' was already well tarnished. A number of freelance heretic hunters had made their presence felt, especially in Germany. Among the more notable, or perhaps notorious, was Konrad of Marburg, one-time confessor of Elizabeth of Thuringia. Contemporary chroniclers describe him as a man of much ability, large theological learning, great eloquence, ardent zeal in defence of the purity of Catholic faith, and a severe ascetic. It is probably a fair description. The first trial in which he took part, in 1222, was directed against Heinrich Minnike, the Provost of Goslar. After proceedings that lasted for two years, Minnike was declared guilty of heresy and delivered to the secular authorities, in whose hands he perished at the stake. By 1231 such was Konrad's proven ability to extract confessions that Pope Honorius' successor, Gregory IX, appointed him Papal Inquisitor, the first such officer in Germany to achieve this revered status. Gregory prudently released Konrad from any obligation he might have felt to follow normal canonical procedure through a bull entitled *Te a cognitionibus causarum habere volumus excusatum*. This amounted to a dispensation giving Konrad carte blanche to tackle the problem of heresy as he thought best, although always with due observance of the papal decrees on the matter. In order to carry out the job effectively, Konrad employed as his henchmen two virtual illiterates, Konrad Dorso and John the One-Eyed, who did little more than raise local resentment and excite varying degrees of terror. On 30 July 1233, after a brief but vicious reign, Konrad of Marburg met a violent end at the hands of an assassin while journeying home with a companion, the Franciscan friar Gerhard Lutzelkolb, who was also murdered.[19]

Almost four years after Louis IX's temporal edict, Gregory IX decided to announce more formal ecclesiastical backing and to do so delivered an encyclical letter to the Dominicans in Languedoc, dated 20 April 1233. The correspondence instructed the senior priors of the province that they should conduct a general inquisition, without further delay, in the areas of Bordeaux, Bourges, Narbonne and Auch, heartlands of the Albigensian dissidents. It marked another stage in the consolidation of the Papal Inquisition. The prior to whom responsibility was given was an affluent member of the Toulouse middle class, Pierre Cella. To his name must be added that of Guillaume Arnaud de Plaigne, Lord of the Chateau de St Ferriol. These two jointly came to represent the power of the Church and the French secular authority. As travelling inquisitors, going from town to town and administering judgement, they would set in motion a reign of terror which by the middle of the century was in full swing.[20]

How did it work in practice? When the inquisition arrived in town, the local inhabitants would be given the opportunity to congregate in the square. This was supposed to be a voluntary exercise, but those who did not comply came under immediate suspicion. Names were named and confessions encouraged. A person arraigned thus on grounds of allegedly subscribing to heresy, either through self-incrimination or accused by a third party, was given a period of grace by the ecclesiastical court, usually about a week. This leeway allowed them time to confess and recant, if they so desired, in spite of the fact that they were not informed of the specific charges against them. Nor were they allowed to confront their accusers. The defendant would be allowed a lawyer, but if that defendant was convicted the legal representative could be penalised and even his ability to practise disallowed, for which reason few lawyers were willing to take on clients accused of heresy. By making a confession the defendant was promised a margin of indulgence, in other words they had the prospect of getting off lightly, especially if their desire to turn over a new spiritual leaf was demonstrated by pointing the finger at someone else. This was hugely advantageous to the inquisitors since it was immediately effective in providing their courts with a constant supply of human fodder as well as a mountain of secret information. The frightened individuals brought before inquisition courts were generally keen to incriminate themselves in order to get off with a lighter sentence and then implicate friends and neighbours, which sometimes freed them from prosecution altogether. Since informants were never publicly identified everyone in a community soon started to view everyone else with considerable suspicion and normal social life fell apart.

Those charged by the courts fell into three categories according to the particular nature of their crime. The least reprehensible form of heresy, and 'least' is merely a comparative term, was that of an ordinary member of the Catharist, Albigensian or Waldensian congregation who stood accused of taking part in dissident ceremonies. Interrogation, including the threat of torture, was usually enough to obtain a confession and a list of names. If the list included information about 'good men' and 'good women' and their hideouts, so much the better. The accused was then offered the opportunity to embrace the Catholic faith once more, and if he or she did so willingly the worst they could generally expect was a short term of imprisonment coupled with forms of penance, although these penances often involved quite severe physical deprivation. If torture was applied to extract a confession, then the confession had to be given freely and without the use of torture on the following day in order to remain valid. The torture methods most commonly included the strappado, a particularly vicious method of applying pain during which the victim's hands were tied behind the back and then attached to a rope by which he or she was hauled up to the rafters before being dropped to just short of the ground. The effect was to dislocate the shoulder and arm joints, and the degree of suffering could be enhanced by tying weights to the legs.[21]

The second category of offender, known as *vestiti*, meaning 'clothed', were the members, men and women, of the dissident clergy. They were offered little alternative once arrested. Either they recanted and agreed to convert back to orthodoxy or the stake beckoned without chance of reprieve. Most refused to deny their brand of faith and died, sometimes by hanging but more often by burning. The third category, in some ways dealt with the most harshly, included those who assisted heretics to escape the law. The inquisitors soon realised that dealing with these abettors in an exemplary manner was vital if dissidents were to be effectively rooted out of their places of concealment, and they employed specially trained investigators known as *exploratores* for the purpose. Those accused were not infrequently tortured to extract as much information as possible and then either given lengthy prison terms or handed over to the secular authorities for the passing and administration of the death sentence.[22]

The ecclesiastical courts were not empowered to mete out the sentence of capital punishment to those they found guilty. The condemned had to be handed over to the secular courts for what was known as *animadversio debita*, carried out under rules governing local criminal law. It had long been forbidden for any ecclesiastic to become directly involved in death or mutilation. In many instances clerics had been barred from the torture chamber so as to avoid the criticism that God's ministers had their hands soiled by such matters. This state of affairs had been first declared during the Third Lateran Council of 1179, which delivered the thoroughly sanctimonious assertion that the Church 'does not seek blood but is helped by the secular laws, for men will seek the salutary remedy to escape bodily punishment'. As thousands of dissidents were being slaughtered in Languedoc at the height of the Albigensian Crusade, the Lateran Council of 1215 had kept up the charade, expressly prohibiting priests, monks and friars from 'uttering judgement on blood' or being present during an execution. Four decades later the Council of Bordeaux in 1255 went so far as to ban clerics from dictating or writing letters connected with judgements that involved capital punishment. In 1279 the Church authorities added another bizarre clause preventing the practice 'of any surgery requiring burning or cutting' by members of the Church.[23]

In spirit, however, the hands of the medieval Church were well and truly bloodied from the outset, and most of the professed reluctance about getting involved in practice amounted to nothing short of cant. The degree of duplicity became clearer by 1184, when Pope Lucius III issued a decretal at the so-called Council of Verona that all kings, princes and other authorities should take an oath of obedience in front of their bishops.[24] This pledge guaranteed that they would enforce the ecclesiastical and secular laws against heresy 'fully and efficaciously', without mercy or expediency, in the knowledge that the Church would respond to any refusal or neglect with the threat of excommunication. Enforcement under the disguise of 'guidance' was a top-down policy. The ceremony of coronation for the Holy Roman Emperor included his admission to the lower orders of the priesthood, through which he was obliged to carry out the wishes of the Church by whatever means. When accepting the ring of office from the Pope, the crowned Emperor was informed that this was a symbol of his sacred duty to destroy heresy. By similar token he was decked with the ceremonial sword of office in order to strike down the enemies of the Church. The Church thus opted to coerce European secular leaders into carrying out its dirty work with the most terrifying weapon at its disposal, the threat of being cut off from Holy Communion and thus facing the prospect of eternal damnation unless readmitted. Lower down the pecking order, matters were scarcely different. In 1229 delegates to the Council of Toulouse insisted that any minor official should forfeit his property and be rendered ineligible for public office if he was not sufficiently robust in persecuting heretics. In 1244 the Council of Narbonne went so far as to adjudge that anyone involved in the administration of secular justice who delayed the sentencing of heretics was effectively tarred with the same brush and could be subjected to the penalties associated with being a heretic. From the Emperor to the meanest peasant the duty of persecution was enforced with all the sanctions, spiritual and temporal, that the Church could command. These principles were tacitly or explicitly received into the public law of Europe. Time after time successive popes demanded that they should be incorporated into the laws of all states over which the papacy had any degree of influence, and the inquisitors acting on behalf of the papacy were left in no doubt that these were canons they were expected rigidly to enforce.[25]

The Holy Roman Emperor, Frederick II, took the anti-heresy decretals very seriously and was happy to embellish them by introducing some of the most barbaric methods of torture that an inventive medieval mind could come up with. Furthermore, his imperial decrees on the matter became an obligatory area of study in one of the most influential European law schools, at Bologna. Yet apologists for the Church were never slow to deny its involvement in capital punishment. The legislator Compte Joseph de Maistre was arduous in his insistence that 'It is an error to suppose, and much more to assert, that Catholic priests can in any manner be instrumental in compassing the death of a fellow creature.'[26] It was not until as late as February 1418 at the Council of Constance that the Church came clean about policies it had been discreetly endorsing for 250 years. When considering the heresy of the Hussites and others, it was decreed that all who defended the teachings of Huss or Jerome of Prague, and even those who regarded them tacitly as holy men, should be subjected to *puniantur ad ignem*, or death by fire.

Some of the most brutal among the inquisitors were, perhaps predictably, poachers turned gamekeepers. For a time the name Robert le Bougre, a former leather-worker and Catharist minister who had become a reformed Dominican, instilled particular dread in the hearts of the innocent and the guilty alike. Popular historians of the Inquisition have been tempted to translate his name as Robert the Bugger, since the Roman Catholic propaganda machine was keen to spread the malicious rumour that dissidents practised sodomy (and they did become widely known in more credulous Roman Catholic circles as buggers). More accurately, however, 'bougre' is a corruption of 'bulgar' – as in the Bulgar sect to which Robert had previously belonged – because it was recognised by more informed commentators that the sect had stemmed from the Balkans and particularly from Bulgaria. Nonetheless, over time the word 'bougre' came to be associated with sodomy, hence our modern words *bougre* (French) and bugger (English).[27]

So fanatical did the purge against heretics become that not even the dead were free from retribution. If a deceased person was subsequently denounced for dissident conduct, he or she could be exhumed and their remains publicly burnt. It was an outrageous desecration that would provoke riots on more than one occasion, most notably in Albi and Toulouse.[28] Nor were the inquisitors themselves entirely free from danger, with Pierre de Castelnau not the only interrogator to fall foul of sectarian vigilantes. In 1235 Guillaume Arnaud, the Chief Inquisitor, was destined to suffer a similar bloody fate along with ten other inquisitors and their assistants. According to the record of the incident, Arnaud was living at the time in the comparative security of the castle at Carcassonne, from where he issued his sentences. Objects of his attention included the castle of Montsegur, a well-nigh impenetrable mountain-top fortress looming above the town of Avignonet. Montsegur was also the family home of Esclarmonde, the aristocratic sister of the Compte de Foix. She had been singled out by the inquisitors as one of the most influential *vestiti* of the region, who had effectively turned the castle into a heretics' refuge.

Raymond VII, the incumbent Count of Toulouse, had given tacit support to his nephew, Raimon d'Alfar, to go ahead with a plot to assassinate Arnaud. The circuit inquisition courts under Arnaud had become increasingly harsh to the point where certain members of the local nobility decided to take matters into their own hands and were merely looking for the right opportunity to dispose of him. It arose when he and his assistants, including a Franciscan colleague named Etienne de St Thibery, were journeying from the town of Prouille back towards Carcassonne. The party of eleven travellers made the ill-fated decision to rest overnight at Avignonet. When they arrived, weary and hungry, on the eve of Ascension Day, it is reported that Raimon d'Alfar greeted their party with utmost courtesy. He served them with an excellent meal and packed them off to bed in a small house positioned close to the castle ramparts and belonging to Count Raymond. When all was still and under cover of darkness, a small group of local knights and their retainers arrived at the gates of the city armed with axes. Having been discreetly admitted by residents they entered the guesthouse and proceeded to massacre the entire inquisitorial party, hacking them to death as they sang *Salve Regina*.[29]

In spite of such mayhem going on under the noses of the papal authorities, it was not until 1252 that Pope Innocent IV (1243–54) officially sanctioned the use of torture by the ecclesiastical court through a decretal entitled *ad extirpanda*, in order 'to promote the work of the faith more truly', in other words to ramp up the rate of conviction. The medieval judiciary across Europe commonly employed torture, but this was the first time that such a facility had been extended to Church courts.[30]

The tribunals of the Inquisition were not held everywhere in medieval Europe. The institution spread north after the thirteenth century but never gained a foothold in northern France, nor did it penetrate across the Channel to England; and it had only a lacklustre history in Scandinavia. The tribunals took place chiefly in southern France, Germany, Italy, and especially in Spain, where the Inquisition started somewhat later than in France but was destined to make up for lost time in spectacular fashion. At first it operated much like the legal persecution of the Albigenses, but in 1478 it was reorganised and directed more effectively against the peninsula's Moorish immigrants, whose control was now much eroded, and against the substantial Jewish community, the largest in Europe at that time, some of whose members were allegedly plotting to overthrow the government. Under the joint rule of Ferdinand II of Aragon and Isabella of Castile, Spain was in the process of reunification after the expulsion of the Moors from large parts of the peninsula, although the region still amounted not so much to a single state as it did to a confederation of autonomous kingdoms. It was Ferdinand rather than Isabella who savoured the exploitation of religious passions to control his people, envisaging the Inquisition, above all, as a convenient means of eliminating the cultures of Judaism and Islam from Iberia. Here was a prime case of what amounted largely to a secular campaign in which religion was used as a means of stoking up hatred. There is even some suggestion that Ferdinand employed the purge of Jews and Muslims to weaken the influence of political rivals and to cancel debts that his father, John II, had run up with Jewish financiers in his efforts to cement a marital alliance with the Castilian crown. Certainly, the right to appoint inquisitors and direct the machinery of the tribunal was reserved for the Spanish Crown from 1479 onwards despite objections from Pope Sixtus IV. With this in mind Catholic historians are generally happy to disclaim any and all ecclesiastical responsibility for the actions of the Spanish Inquisition, despite unmistakable evidence that the Spanish Church was prepared to tolerate the conduct of the tribunal even in its most outrageous forms.[31]

The Spanish inquisitors were also members of the clergy, among whom the most notorious was Tomás de Torquemada. Born in 1420 he became a member of the Dominican Order and in 1479 was subsequently appointed confessor to Ferdinand and Isabella. Four years later, at the age of 63, Torquemada took on the job of Inquisitor General of Castile and Aragon, with the specific responsibility of coordinating the machinery of the Inquisition tribunal throughout Spain. From the close of the fourteenth century the Jewish communities in Spain had been targets of Christian oppression, and massacres had taken place in 1391. Torquemada, however, was primarily responsible for the major programme of ethnic cleansing begun in 1492 and which became known as *limpieza de sangre* or *sangre limpia*, meaning 'pure blood'. In order to create Spanish *limpieza de sangre* – in theory at any rate since there was probably very little pure blood in Spain – large numbers of Jews were to be expelled under an edict of expulsion issued by the Spanish monarchy. The decretal instructed that 'The aforesaid Jews, men and women, are commanded forthwith to leave our kingdoms and never to return.' The Jewish population was informed of the terms of the edict on 31 March 1492 and was given until 1 July to comply or risk immediate execution if found within the borders of Spain. Needless to say, under these circumstances the machinery of the Inquisition became an easy tool for those seeking revenge on rivals or wishing to gain the favour of the Crown.[32]

It is difficult to establish precisely how many were executed or died under atrocious conditions of captivity during the years of the Spanish Inquisition. Certainly, as with the Papal Inquisition, figures have been inflated as and when necessary to serve political ends. The Inquisition authorities in Spain kept reasonable records, and recent research suggests that during the eighteen-year reign of terror implemented by Torquemada some 8,000 to 9,000 people may have been slaughtered after being handed over to the secular authorities.[33]

Hernando de Pulgar, one of Queen Isabella's secretaries, cites 2,000 having been burnt to death before 1490. But of 49,000 trial records analysed for a later period between 1540 and 1700, for example, only 776 executions resulted.[34] The justification for such extreme measures had been trumped up through the careful orchestration of a show trial that opened in the winter of 1490. Despite total lack of material evidence, eight people were accused of performing a diabolic ritual on the previous Good Friday at the climax of which they crucified a Christian child. Jews had long been the objects of suspicion in Christian Europe and occasionally, probably grossly unfairly, they stood accused of Christian infanticide in what became dubbed around European capitals as 'the blood libel'. Attention was particularly focused on Jews in Spain and Portugal, where they made up the largest ethnic population in medieval Europe. After the 1391 massacres some had converted willingly to Christianity, but others became known as Marranos, people making an outward show of devotion to Christianity while still practising Judaism. It is not obvious how the term 'Marranos' came to be popular, but some authorities consider it to be a derogatory corruption of the Spanish word for swine. The 1490 tribunal, known as the LaGuardia trial, stands as one of the most infamous proceedings of the Spanish Inquisition. Like many similar trials it bore the hallmarks of an irregular kangaroo court, but as a measure of extreme injustice it stands out above others. Tomás de Torquemada clearly savoured it as a show trial, an exercise in preparing public opinion for the subsequent expulsion of Jews. Rumour had it that a Catholic child had gone missing in the town of LaGuardia and the Jewish community was promptly held responsible. So fired up with religious fervour did the local populace become that, despite the lack of evidence that anyone had actually disappeared, the phantom absentee became known as the Holy Child of LaGuardia. The tribunal was to have taken place in Segovia but was eventually moved to Ávila, where it opened on 17 December 1490. The accused, two Jews and six *conversos* from the towns of LaGuardia, Trembleque and Zamora, stood condemned despite the fact that no victim was identified and no body had ever been recovered.

Eventually, each one confessed under extremes of physical torture and the trial concluded on 14 November 1491. All were burnt at the stake. Known as the auto-da-fé or 'act of faith', this was the most severe form of punishment adopted by the Spanish Inquisition although even this had its grotesque variations. If a victim fully recanted before death he or she could be garrotted as an act of mercy prior to immolation. Alternatively, the fire could be set with seasoned and therefore quick-burning wood. For those who elected not to recant, the unwholesome prospect was a prolonged and more agonising death in the smoke and flames of slower-burning green faggots. In reality most probably choked to death before the flames actually reached them, but that made the practice no less reprehensible.[35]

Tomás de Torquemada himself was a religious fanatic of the worst kind and, perhaps because of a sense of vulnerability that his own grandmother had been a converted Jew, he frequently singled out *conversos* rather than Jews for punishment. During his reign of terror many Spanish and Portuguese Jews fled to countries with regimes that had become less repressive about foreign religions. Initially, this migration was to Muslim lands such as Morocco, but eventually many of the émigrés turned up in England, which had an on-off relationship with Roman Catholicism from the time of Henry VIII onwards. A Jewish settlement was also founded in Hamburg in Germany and, after the Union of Utrecht in 1579, others found comparative safety in the new Protestant state of the Netherlands.

It will come as a surprise to many people that the Spanish Inquisition continued, with interruptions, until as late as 1834. Its last victim was a schoolmaster named Cayetano Ripoli, garrotted in Valencia on 26 July 1826, having been convicted of allegedly promoting Deist principles.[36] Nor has the situation changed entirely in the wider world of modern Roman Catholicism, although more extreme sanctions have been dropped. The Church is still prepared to go to extraordinary lengths to preserve and enhance its orthodox brand of ideology. In 1988 the French Archbishop Marcel Lefebvre was excommunicated for supporting the movement in favour of the ordination of women to the Catholic clergy.[37] Nor can the Anglican

Communion claim to be free from ideological division, especially when it comes to the deep controversy over the ordination of women priests, homosexuality and other sensitive issues. The distinction perhaps is that Rome has the more effective means of enforcing orthodoxy!

The institution of the Spanish Inquisition gave rise to similar machinery in the Americas, and it formed the model for overseas ecclesiastical courts among which the inquisitions of Mexico and Lima are the best recorded. In some respects the Inquisition was at its most effective in the Hispanic American colonies, since its primary purpose was to pursue those who had escaped the judgement of the tribunals in the home country. They had done so with the assistance of miscellanies of explorers, adventurers, mercenaries and reprobates. It is to the saga of the sixteenth-century Spanish Conquistadors and their violent rape of an entire culture in the name of God that the story now turns.

TEN

The Spanish Crusade

Military conquest frequently involves a political dimension that requires the destruction of heritage. This has to be obliterated, or so the logic goes, because it may otherwise provide a focus of resistance; and in past centuries cultural heritage has been inextricably linked with religion. In some parts of the world today little has changed. In 2001 the Taliban destroyed huge age-old statues of the Buddha carved into sandstone cliffs at Bamiyan in Afghanistan precisely because they represented a religious culture alien to that demanded by Islamic fundamentalism.

The Conquistadors of the fifteenth century left Spain for the Americas not merely in search of new lands over which to fly the Spanish flag. They went in search of prodigious quantities of mineral wealth reported to be available in the shape of gold, silver and emeralds along with other baubles, all sought after by a Spanish Crown desperate to fill its depleted coffers. And, of course, they also went as ambassadors for Christendom. Together with Portugal, Spain was destined to lead the world into a new Christian age of exploration and discovery under the watchful and acquisitive eye of the Catholic Church. Yet Christian values of love and charity were not foremost among the Church's motives. Some of the intention was to obliterate any cultural heritage that did not conform to Christian ideals.

The Iberian adventure was given official Roman Catholic blessing in 1455, though not even-handedly. The incumbent of the papacy, Callistus III, an austere and rigidly pious man, issued a papal bull heavily weighted in favour of Portugal, offering the country a virtual blank cheque to 'reduce to servitude all infidel peoples' whom its explorers came across on their voyages of discovery. Clearly,

Callistus savoured the prospect of forcibly imposing Christian ideology in places beyond Europe and Western Asia. His abiding preoccupation had been waging holy war against the Turks, but in issuing his latest decretal he turned a covetous eye elsewhere. Although he gave Portugal the initial advantage, it was a situation over which her larger Spanish neighbour was not slow to raise objection. Matters were then left in the hands of one of Callistus' successors, Alexander VI, who was prompted to issue another bull in 1493 delivering a more equitable settlement. Under the terms of this arrangement a line was drawn down the map, north to south, 100 leagues west of the Azores. Spain was now at liberty to explore to the west of the line and Portugal to the east, although later amendments under the Treaty of Tordesillas signed in 1494 also permitted Portugal to colonise Brazil. In terms of the history of what transpired in Central and South America, shortly to become known as New Spain, it is significant that Alexander's bull contained a similar mandatory and moral obligation to that of Callistus, to Christianise any and all conquered territories.[1]

Spanish exploration teams armed with papal endorsement wasted little time in heading out across the Atlantic to the Americas, where they anticipated a first-come, first-served advantage. Their brief was ostensibly to subdue any local opposition and send back the rumoured wealth of New Spain to fill the coffers of the kingdom, then colonise, subjugate the native people and deliver Jesus to whomever they happened upon. Christopher Columbus had already provided much information about lucrative future prospects in the New World after his second transatlantic homecoming to Lisbon in 1497, when he also disembarked onto the quayside 300 surviving Amerindian slaves from a somewhat larger original consignment; the remainder had perished en route. These unfortunates were promptly packed off to the newly built slave market in Seville. At some stage, Columbus also probably brought back with him syphilis, which his crew passed willingly if unwittingly to various dockside communities. The Conquistadors who sailed west in Columbus' wake gifted the South American Indian population by way of reward an assortment of infectious European ailments including typhus, smallpox and pleurisy in what became quaintly dubbed the 'Columbian Exchange'.[2]

But it is also clear from the surviving correspondence of such notables as Hernando Cortés and Francisco Pizarro that the exploration leaders saw themselves as personal Crusaders in the name of Christ without necessarily placing Christian values high on their list of priorities. Hernando Cortés was born at Medellín in the Extremadura region of Spain in 1485. His father, Martin Cortés de Monroy, served as an officer in the Spanish army and educated his son with a military career in mind. In 1504, the year of Queen Isabella's death, Hernando joined up with a convoy of five ships under the command of Alonso Quintero, destined for the island of Hispaniola. Anticipating a future as a soldier of fortune and messenger for Christ in the new Spanish colonies, Cortés carried with him letters of commendation addressed to a family relative, Don Nicholas de Obando, who at the time occupied the position of governor. Cortés remained in Hispaniola for seven years making friends and enemies. This was a comparatively uneventful period of his life, aside from the fact that he contracted syphilis and subsequently recovered, both probably attributable to contact with the native population. Next he became heavily enmeshed in the conquest of Cuba in 1511 under the authority of Diego Velázquez, a campaign from which he emerged with both considerable wealth and military distinction. By 1517, at the age of 32, he was one of the leading lights of the island, employed as a magistrate, owning a large ranch and enjoying the comforts of a mistress of questionable health and morals named Catalina Juarez.[3]

The following year Velázquez, by now elevated to the governorship of Cuba, reluctantly commissioned Cortés to undertake what was called in diplomatic language 'an exploration' of the mainland coast of Mexico, but which in reality was intended to be an overture to invasion and conquest. From the outset Velázquez had been wary of Cortés' ambitions, viewing him as a sufficient threat to have twice resorted to arresting and imprisoning him on trumped-up charges. During the spring of 1518 the two appeared to have become reconciled, but Cortés can have harboured few illusions about his vulnerability at the hands of Velázquez and now believed that the only safe future lay in achieving an independent command and seeking to conquer unsettled lands elsewhere. The Central American mainland beckoned.

Several expeditionary voyages had already been undertaken along the coastline of the Yucatán peninsula from 1508 onwards, and the most recent, under the command of Juan de Grijalva, had not yet returned when Cortés and Velázquez signed their agreement. Previous expeditions had set a precedent of violence against the native inhabitants. In February 1517 an expeditionary force under the command of Hernández de Córdoba had discovered that the Indian tribes of Yucatán not only built on a grand scale using hewn stone but were also skilled goldsmiths. The prospect of apparently unlimited supplies of precious metal was undoubtedly the strongest lure for the Conquistadors, with crusading in the name of Christendom coming a strong second. The remarkable and sophisticated culture of the Indians did not feature among their interests.

Just over a year later, in May 1518, Velázquez fitted out Grijalva's expedition with four ships. Grijalva captained one, while the others were commanded by Alonso de Ávila, Francisco de Montejo and Pedro de Alvarado. This fleet first made landfall at Champotón on the Gulf of Campeche and then proceeded down the coast towards the settlement of Pontonchan where, after various brutal maulings at the hands of the Spanish, the Indians agreed on peace, albeit at a cost of some 20,000 pesos-worth of gold collected from them over a subsequent six-month period and shipped back to Spain by Grijalva. During preliminary skirmishes the diminutive strength of the opposing local forces had rapidly become apparent, the Indians being equipped with weapons including a part-sword, part-club made of wood, with grooves in which were set razor-sharp slivers of obsidian; spears also set with obsidian blades; and a dart-thrower called the *atlatl*. Bows and arrows were, incidentally, a late innovation and in some areas had not been adopted at all. Potent as these weapons were, they scarcely proved a match for those of the Spaniards, who were equipped with muskets, crossbows and small cannon, and were well protected with padded armour that provided effective defence against blows by obsidian.[4]

Cortés privately regarded the commission from Velázquez as an opportunity to negotiate a deal with the Indians of the Yucatán peninsula. The Indians would provide gold in substantial quantities and he, Cortés, would provide them with the Christian God to replace the barbarous pantheon revered locally. That there was a messianic, perhaps fanatical quality to Cortés' spiritual ambitions was soon to become manifest when he arranged for two banners to be manufactured for the excursion. Each was worked in gold and adorned on both sides with an image of the Cross paired with the Spanish royal coat of arms. Alongside these emblems of Cortés' mission the inscription read, 'Brothers and comrades, let us follow the sign of the Holy Cross in true faith, for under this sign we shall conquer.' There was in this symbolism a tenacious echo from the distant past of 'my god against your god'.

Hernando Cortés was probably not untypical of many Spanish men pursuing military careers in the early part of the sixteenth century. The European Crusades had petered out and, in the absence of action, there was a hankering for combat coupled with a passionate and deep-rooted desire among at least some Spaniards to extend the realms of Christendom and purge the world of 'infidels'. Yet these were often brutal and cavalier men used to a life of marching armies and racial intolerance. Many were ex-crusading knights with time on their hands, equipped with varying degrees of religious fervour and experiencing a generalised surfeit of boredom. As the twentieth-century Jesuit commentator Mariano de Cuevas put it succinctly, the make-up of the army included adventurers inspired at least partly by a greed for gold, unscrupulous in their methods of getting it and exceedingly vicious. We should remember that by modern standards the Christian conduct of sixteenth-century Spain was extremely immoral and charges of corruption and licentiousness could have been pinned with justification not only on the military but on much of the clergy as well. To read the social history of the Iberian peninsula during the period of the medieval Crusades is to discover a world of occupational inebriates, treachery, rape and casual plunder. The same history book records the pious exhortations of Cortés and his all-night prayer vigils before decimating virtually defenceless Indian tribes who had caused no harm to Spain or her people. Hypocrisy was a fact of life.

Writing at the turn of the twentieth century, when Christian Catholic evangelism was still very much in vogue, the historian Francis MacNutt made some pithy observations about prevailing Spanish attitudes 400 years earlier. He described a race of sixteenth-century Christian warriors whose piety, born of an intense realisation of love for a militant Christ, was of a martial complexion, beholding in the symbol of salvation, the Cross, the standard of Christendom around which the faithful must rally, and for whose protection and exaltation swords must be drawn and blood spilled if need be. The discovery of a new world peopled by barbarians opened up a new field to Spanish missionary zeal, in which the kingdom of God could be extended and countless souls rescued from the obscene idolatries and debasing cannibalism which enslaved them. This was the white man's burden, which in that century lay squarely on the Spaniard's shoulders. So enamoured was MacNutt of Cortés' religious devotion that he went so far as to claim that, had the influence of Cortés' faith on his morals been proportionate to its strength, he would have merited canonisation.[5]

MacNutt was in fact echoing the sugared sentiments of one of Cortés' near contemporaries, the Spanish Church historian Gerónimo de Mendieta. Writing in the latter part of the sixteenth century, Mendieta asserted that Cortés was a divinely chosen instrument for effecting God's purpose of winning Indians to Christianity; everywhere he went he destroyed idols, forbade human sacrifices and preached the faith in the one true God and His only begotten Son, our Lord Jesus Christ. A truly objective observer might have noticed that Cortés' sense of morality did not extend to compassion for the Indian and that most of the Conquistadors felt their Crusaders' task ended with the political conquest rather than extending to the promulgation of Christianity among the people they overran. Indeed, Mendieta was to concede elsewhere in his writings that any religious zeal displayed by the troops was probably mainly down to Cortés himself, whose religious efforts largely inspired indifference among his followers.[6]

Putting to one side the hagiographic biographies and examining Hernando Cortés rather more soberly, he was, or rather appears to have become, religiously obsessive, matching in fervour anyone that Islamic fundamentalism produces today, though with considerably fewer scruples. Cortés once wrote, 'It is notable that the greater part of those that come out [to Spanish America] are of the baser sort and extremely vicious.'[7] Yet this uncompromising label could equally have been applied to Cortés himself.[8] He evolved into a callous butcher who believed that purging the world of idolatry was worth any price in loss of life. If the purging could be conducted in the name of Jesus Christ it would tend to free the activity of the more inconvenient moral considerations. Matters were destined to unfold along these questionable lines in Spanish America. Cortés, pushing westwards with his army into Central America, and his compatriot Francisco Pizarro carving out Spanish colonies in the hinterland to the south, were both equally determined to replace any and all native religion and ritual they came across with that of the Catholic Church. Each was offended, not without reason, by the human sacrifice that characterised Maya, Aztec and Inca ceremonies but thought nothing of mass slaughter, which in numerical terms probably far outstripped the periodical bloodletting at the altar carried out by Indian priests in order to assuage and cool the passions of their fiery tutelary deities.

With God and gold in mind, Cortés set sail towards the Yucatán coast on 10 February 1519 in command of eleven small vessels, the largest weighing no more than 100 tonnes. These ships were equipped with just over 500 soldiers, 100 sailors, 200 forcibly enlisted Cubans, 16 horses and a number of brood mares. But Cortés had scarcely arrived en route at the port of Trinidad when Velázquez, sitting in his governor's residence back in Cuba, decided to tear up their agreement. Cortés' response, on receiving this unwelcome news, was to ignore any messages of restraint arriving from Velázquez and to sail on around the horn of the Yucatán peninsula to the island of Cozumel. Having dropped anchor Cortés discovered to his annoyance that Pedro de Alvarado had sidestepped instructions, gone on ahead and ransacked at least one village. Placing de Alvarado under arrest for his temerity, Cortés made his first contact with the local Indians.

Cortés' interpretation of Christian evangelism thus found itself being put into practice, albeit initially on a restrained scale, since it was on Cozumel that he discovered the reality of native rites and ceremonies and came to stand before the carved stone visages of foreign deities. Cortés' response was to assemble the local Indian chiefs and convey to them – presumably through sign language since at this stage of the enterprise he had no obvious recourse to interpreters – that if they wished to become brethren of the visiting Spaniards they must give up sacrificing to such grotesque idols. These, he conveyed, were not gods but evil beings by which the Indians were led into error and their souls sent into hell.[9] The chiefs, not surprisingly, were reluctant to acquiesce to Cortés' demands, which effectively asked them to discard centuries of tradition and the beliefs of their ancestors at the behest of total strangers. When they indicated their resistance Cortés' response was to order the demolition of religious statues and the erection of a Christian altar on which, in future, was to repose an image of the Virgin Mary. Predictably, it was incomprehensible to the Indians of Cozumel that they should replace one set of idols with another.

Cortés' fleet weighed anchor on 4 March and a week later was off the mouth of the newly named Grijalva river which runs roughly from north to south over the Isthmus of Tehuantepec, dividing the Yucatán and Guatemala from the main part of Mexico. On the morning of 14 March, having absolved his troops of possible moral stain by celebrating Mass, he sent a detachment of one hundred to launch an unprovoked attack on the small town of Pontonchan, later to be renamed Tabasco. Reports of Alvarado's plundering activities on Cozumel had by now spread, and Tabascan defenders were seen ranged along the shoreline gesturing defensively with their weapons. Allegedly, up to 12,000 Indians assembled in Pontonchan, ready to confront the invaders. At this juncture Cortés made a showy pretence of negotiations with the local leaders for the launch of peaceful trading, but in the meantime he lined up his shipboard artillery, disembarked the remainder of his troops and cavalry, and instructed them to kit themselves out in full steel armour. Reminding them that they were about to fight a new crusade as soldiers of Christ with God firmly on their side, he sent them to wreak havoc among a defence force whose simple weapons were immediately outclassed. At the end of the Tabasco incident the Spaniards held a thanksgiving service, claiming to have slaughtered 800 in the name of Christendom. For their part the Indian chiefs presented Cortés with an assortment of gold trinkets plus twenty females, among whom was a girl that Cortés named Doña Marina, took as his mistress and subsequently converted to Christianity; she was destined to become one of his best interpreters of the local Nahuatl language.

According to Bernal Díaz del Castillo, the soldier diarist who accompanied Cortés during the expedition, 'the Indians now showed more readiness to comply with the wishes of Cortés that they should do away with their idols and human sacrifice after he had preached to them with some idea of our holy faith and how we adore God'. Bernal Díaz identifies that the twenty women were more or less the first to be baptised and that Doña Marina shortly afterwards became pregnant with Cortés' son, Martin. The representatives of the Catholic Church who accompanied Cortés and his troops seem generally to have accepted or cast a blind eye over the lax sexual relationships entered into by the Conquistadors.[10]

The confrontation at Tabasco marked the first significant massacre of native Indians by the Spaniards, but it would not be the last. Cortés, having received the full support of his own troops in defiance of Velázquez, proceeded to found the Spanish coastal colony of Vera Cruz, which neighbours Tabasco on a line of latitude slightly to the south of modern Mexico City. Meanwhile, word of the invasion was spreading. While it was still in its initial phase, Moctezuma, the Emperor of the dominant Aztec civilisation occupying the central southern valley of Mexico and residing several days' march away across the highlands in his capital city of Tenochtitlan, received a bizarre report from a courier. The man, who had witnessed the formidable sight of a Spanish vessel for the first time, claimed that 'a great mountain' had been seen on the waters of the Gulf Coast, 'moving from one part to the other without touching the rocks'. Further inquiry brought reports of strange beings with white faces and long beards having left Grijalva's ship and now advancing inland from the coast. Some of the information that he received subsequently persuaded Moctezuma that these were no mortal men but incarnations of the tutelary gods of the Aztecs: Quetzalcoatl, Tezcatlipoca, Huitzilpochtli and their supernatural entourage.

Moctezuma, or Motecuhzoma Xocoyotzin to give him his correct Nahuatl title, sent two of his senior representatives, Cuitlalpitoc and Teudilli, to investigate the newcomers, and, when they met up with the advancing Spanish column at San Juan de Ulloa, the story goes that Cortés presented them with a Spanish infantry helmet. According to Bernal Díaz' diary this symbol of militarism was given with purpose in the gift since Cortés, the polished strategist, had already assessed that he could only effectively control the vast Mexican interior either by importing a much expanded army or with the tacit cooperation of Moctezuma. He would therefore need to play a war of wits, and in fact he had managed to aid his own cause through this particular gesture, albeit unwittingly. The Aztec ambassadors were not slow in noting a resemblance between this and the headwear that was associated with their semi-mythical forebears of the classic period of their history. These included the immediate predecessors of the Aztecs in central and southern Mexico, the Toltecs, and the people of the more ancient urban civilisation of Teotihuacan. Something remarkably similar to the Spanish gift now adorned the heads of the statues of the Aztec creator deities, including Huitzilpochtli.

On their return to the Aztec capital, Mexico-Tenochtitlan, having been instructed by Cortés to convey suitably intimidating information about the massive superiority of Spanish weaponry wielded under the supervision of the Spanish Catholic God, the ambassadors handed over the helmet. On examining this, the superstitious Moctezuma seems to have reached a similar conclusion to that of his emissaries that the Spaniards were themselves gods, descendants of the ancestral rulers whom his forefathers had prophesied would one day come and dominate the country.[11] According to contemporary reports Cortés received the helmet back seven days later crammed with freshly mined gold and accompanied by a plethora of gifts lugged through the mountains by one hundred Indians. Observing the sheer volume of offerings Cortés anticipated that Moctezuma was afraid of him. The reactions of Cuitlalpitoc and Teudilli to the helmet gift had also not passed unnoticed, and after their departure Cortés is reported to have commented, 'Methinks, gentlemen, we already pass here for great heroes; indeed after what has happened these people must look upon us as gods or as a species of beings like their idols. Now I am of the opinion that we ought to strengthen them in this notion, so in order that they may think that one single man of us is sufficient to dislodge the Aztecs.'[12]

The Aztec power base was not, however, Cortés' most immediate quarry. His more urgent objective was to subdue the Tlascalans, the nation dominating a large part of the Yucatán peninsula, who, to Cortés' immense advantage as the campaign progressed, declared themselves the sworn enemies of the neighbouring Aztecs. Initially, the Tlascalans were faced with the daunting prospect of a similar level of attrition to that already experienced by the Tabascans and were clearly intimidated by the military superiority of the Spanish invaders; some 6,000 capitulated and agreed to fight under Cortés' banner. Accordingly, they marched inland with him, north-west towards the Aztec capital. At a particular stage of the advance, however, in the town of Cholula less than 100 miles to the south and east of Mexico City, Cortés detected treachery, and this heralded one of the worst atrocities of his campaign.

According to reports partly gleaned from letters from Cortés to the Holy Roman Emperor, Charles V, and partly from other written accounts by contemporary observers, Cortés decided to deliver exemplary punishment to the Cholulans. The majority of their warriors were herded into the town square after Cortés, unknown to most of them, had accused the leadership of conspiracy, a charge against which they were given no redress. At a prearranged signal the full firepower of the Spanish troops surrounding the square was levelled at the unfortunate Cholulans as they stood crowded together, it was said by observers, 'like a herd of deer' in the centre. Inadequately armed, they were taken unawares and could offer little resistance to the Spaniards, who followed up the initial fusillade with hand-to-hand combat. Spanish swords decimated the half-naked and virtually defenceless crowd, so went the report, with as much ease as the reaper mows the ripe corn in harvest time. Some frantically tried to scale the city walls, but in doing so only afforded an easier target for musketeers. Others tried to get away through the town gates but found themselves impaled on pikes. Among the few that escaped on that day were those who hid themselves beneath the bodies of the slain. Almost the entire 6,000 died in the space of two or three hours, and according to one contemporary witness, Bartolomé las Casas, later to become the Bishop of Chiapa, Cortés ordered more than one hundred of the leaders to be impaled or roasted at the stake as an exemplary punishment. Cortés undoubtedly believed that he and his troops were threatened, but there can be little question that his response exceeded any reasonable bounds. A brutish policy of 'total anathema' was unfolding, which was to become a trademark both of Cortés and Francisco Pizarro. It bears striking resemblance to the policies of overkill adopted by Simon de Montfort and, if one looks further back in time, those of the ancient Israelities. In each case fighting in the name of God appears to have cancelled out any norms of decency or moderation and absolved the perpetrators of moral responsibility for their actions. In effect each military leader was adopting a position that it was not his free will that directed the course of events but rather that of a superior force over which he possessed no control. It permitted men to use God as an excuse for venting the worst of aggressive human instincts.

By now Cortés and his troops were viewed by many of the Indians as divinities of particularly violent temperament, and the slaughter at Cholula indeed served as a salutary warning of their invincibility. It effectively encouraged the rest of the Tlascalan forces to fight more enthusiastically on Cortés' side, and this combined column approached the final route to the Mexican capital virtually unopposed. On 8 November 1519 Cortés arrived on the shores of the vast lake in the centre of which Tenochtitlan had been built. Moctezuma adopted delaying tactics from the outset and was clearly reluctant over a face-to-face encounter with Cortés, but eventually he was obliged to concede defeat and accepted the position of a vassal king to the Spanish. Part of the price was to hand over gold estimated at a value of 100,000 ducats, but he refused consistently to embrace Christianity.

After some six months of the occupation, and recognising a degree of dissatisfaction among Cortés' troops, Moctezuma urged him to abandon Mexico and return to the comforts of home. It is improbable that Cortés would have acceded to this request, but in any event the situation changed abruptly when a new expeditionary force arrived at Vera Cruz under the leadership of Pamphilo de Narvaez, who had come with instruction from Diego Velázquez to crush Cortés. The Conquistador's response was to take his troops out of Tenochtitlan, leaving the Mexican capital in the hands of his compatriot, Alvarado. Cortés caught the substantially larger invasion force by surprise and routed them in a night attack, taking Narvaez prisoner. In his absence, however, the Indians at Tenochtitlan rebelled against the much-reduced Spanish garrison, and on the night of 1 July 1520 the garrison was obliged to retreat from the city once again, this time making its own escape under the cover of darkness. Six days later, however, Cortés, supported by Tlascalan troops, massively defeated the Aztec forces at a battleground named Otumba. At some time during this stage of the conflict Moctezuma died where he was being held effectively as a captive in the Spanish quarters. The manner in which he met his death is unclear, but the reign of his replacement, Cuitlahuac, lasted barely four months. Cuitlahuac was then succeeded by the last great warrior emperor of the Aztecs, Cuauhtemoc, a man labouring under few of Moctezuma's illusions that the invaders were gods. They were, Cuauhtemoc appreciated, killers bent on total destruction of his people, and he responded with all the resistance he had available.[13]

The ending of the so-called final siege of Mexico took place a year later on 13 August 1521 after seventy-five days of fighting in and around the city of Tenochtitlan, and only when the defenders had suffered the most appalling level of attrition. An eyewitness description provided by Bernal Díaz makes grim reading.

> Hundreds of famished wretches died every day from extremity of suffering. Some dragged themselves into the houses and drew their last breath alone and in silence. Others sank down in the public streets. Wherever they died there were they left. There was no one to bury or to remove them. Familiarity with the spectacle made men indifferent to it. They looked on in dumb despair, waiting for their own turn. There was no complaint, no lamentation, but deep, unutterable woe. In other quarters of the town the corpses might be seen scattered over the streets; here they were gathered in heaps. They lay so thick that one could not tread except among the bodies. Cortés himself added that a man could not set his foot down unless on the corpse of an Indian. They were piled one upon another, the living mingled with the dead. They stretched themselves on the bodies of their friends, and lay down to sleep there. Death was everywhere. The city was a vast charnel house, in which all was hastening to decay and decomposition. A poisonous steam arose from the mass of putrefaction, under the action of alternate rain and heat, which so tainted the whole atmosphere that the Spaniards including the general himself in their brief visits to the quarter were made ill by it and it bred a pestilence that swept off even greater numbers than the famine.[14]

Through this horrific climax the Aztec Empire collapsed, replaced in a welter of blood by the Christian colony of New Spain.

In 1523, some might have felt rather late in the day, the Spanish King, Philip II, addressed a letter to Cortés in which he gave an instruction that 'prohibits the Christians from making war upon the Indians and doing them any harm, or taking anything from them without paying for it, for fear that they rise up in rebellion. Rather you shall punish severely those who treat them ill or do them harm without your express order. In this way the Indians will come into more contact with the Christians which is the best way to bring them to the knowledge of our holy faith', H. Cortés, *The History of the Conquest of Mexico* (London, 1759). In reality contact between Christians and natives came to be considered one of the chief hindrances to winning them over.

Set beside the conduct of Cortés and his troops during the military part of the conquest, that of the immigrant Spanish settlers and armies of Catholic priests who stepped ashore following the surrender of Mexico was probably as reprehensible as anything that has ever been committed in the name of Christendom. Cuevas describes how in only a quarter of a century thousands of teocallis, the Mayan and Aztec temples or, as he put it, bulwarks of Satan, and the most barbarous in the world, were reduced to dust. In a quarter of a century, with enviable zeal and method, 8 million Indians were brought to profess, understand and love the laws of government and truth condensed in the doctrine of the Catholic Church.[15] Even Cortés himself expressed reservations about such wanton destruction, maintaining that at least some temples should be preserved as relics. However, from his point of view as a soldier the action was justifiable since it delivered a stark message to the Indians, made them deeply fearful and stifled the likelihood of militant revolt. The Catholic priesthood and lay clergy saw the buildings as the visible reminders to the Indians of their own religion. Cortés had made an absolute ban on human sacrifice, but the Aztec and Mayan priests regularly ignored the edict and continued openly to practise their time-honoured faith. It is clear that they would have settled for a compromise, incorporating the key elements of Christianity into their rites, but the demands of the Church of Rome that they should recognise Christianity alone merely aroused their resentment and resistance. As time went by the view of the missionaries was that they were largely wasting their time so long as the temples and cult statues remained in place. The conclusion was that all native places of worship had to go, and it was agreed that a systematic destruction of temples and their images should begin in various sections of the country, to continue until every one had been dismantled. The demolition process was begun in 1525 by Catholic priests with the help of converts to Christianity in the city of Tezcuco, probably singled out because it contained some particularly magnificent temples. Later the temples in Mexico-Tenochtitlan, Tlaxcala and Guaxocingo received the same treatment, and gradually this process of wanton destruction extended throughout the country.

Flattening of the temples amounted to the near-obliteration of a great and complex culture (about which the Spanish Christians understood little and cared even less), because these sacred buildings also served as the repositories of priceless ancient writings and works of art, the sum of pre-Hispanic religious tradition in Central America. The chief architect of destruction was the first Archbishop of Mexico, Juan Zumárraga, who took up his post some seven years after the coming of the first missionaries. Zumárraga refused to permit the preservation of any of the Aztec literary treasure on the argument that its very existence would prove an obstacle to Christianisation, and in this he was clearly emulating the line taken by Cardinal Ximines a generation earlier when he had sanctioned destruction of the literary heritage of the Moors in Spain. Countless thousands of codices were thus consigned to the flames.[16] Not surprisingly, the Aztec priests did all they could to oppose the obliteration of their cult. They frequently encouraged children to report on the activities of their parents if these involved collaboration with the Christian authorities, and many of the same children were slain by their fathers for abandoning the native religion and destroying the family's sacred images.

Within a short space of time after Cortés had completed the military conquest of Yucatán and Mexico, he issued a number of directives about the machinery of Christian conversion. Ostensibly, his *Requerimiento* did not oblige the Indians to accept Christianity, but they were powerless to prevent the new religion being preached and taught. The message was clear. 'The Roman Catholic Church is superior in the world and the Pope is superior in matters spiritual.' Ironically, the Spanish military and other settlers came to regard the conduct of the priesthood, and especially the Franciscan friars, with a degree of disgust. The *religios* were frequently accused of unwarranted severity in their treatment of potential converts, whose induction into Christendom was regularly encouraged through physical punishment.

A small insight into this form of persuasion is contained in the *Codice Franciscano*: 'At daybreak the Indians are gathered into the patio of the Church . . . they are counted and those who are recalcitrant about coming when they are obliged to are given half a dozen lashes over their clothing, since they are in the Church – outside they are given lashes on the bare back when they make any mistake or do their common tasks wrongly. This is the punishment they have always known even for very light offences. To take this away, in the temporal as well as the spiritual government, would be to take away the only way of controlling them, for they are like children.' Mendieta's comment on the use of the lash and that the Franciscans whipped the Indians as if they were children received an addendum: 'seeing that we do it in love and for their good, they not only endure it patiently but thank us for it'.[17]

Eventually, the tide of criticism about the cruel treatment of Indians meted out by the friars led to improvements of a kind. A Church Council of 1539, noting shrewdly that the criticisms had been brought by Spaniards 'with no thought for the welfare of Indians but desire only to trouble the priests', passed an order that 'in the evangelisation of Indians they must not be put in stocks, nor beaten, particularly grown men'. According to Mendieta, popular claims that the King might have had a hand in the legislation towards more human treatment were spurious. In a letter to the Commissary General of the Jesuits in 1562 he poured scorn on the notion that the King could have made such a declaration, when to take away the power of the priests would be to undermine the force of their preaching and the doctrine of Jesus Christ. 'These people are so low and so miserable that if one has not all authority with them he has none.'[18]

The enforcement of Christian values on the Indians of Mexico and Yucatán proved little short of a cultural and social disaster, and by and large the Indians took all possible measures to distance themselves from the Spanish immigrants. Writing in the latter part of the century, Mendieta described a memorial through which the chiefs and natives of the newly named Mexico City sought redress at the hands of the King: 'On account of the different conditions and treatments which the Indians and the Spaniards enjoy, the frequency of ill treatment of the slaves and servants on the part of the Spaniards, and especially on account of the vices and offences against God our Lord which the Spaniards, negroes, *mestizos* and other Indians reared by the Spaniards invent every day, we pray you that the natives and Spaniards be not allowed to live together in the same sections.'[19]

One of the most piquant condemnations of Spanish policy, however, is contained in a document written in about 1574 by Alonso de Zurita, one of the official *visitadores* of the King. He refers, indirectly via a third-party priest, to an agreement on the part of the Indians of Oaxaca 'either to have no access to their wives or other women, or to seek some means of avoiding conception or of causing miscarriage in the case of those already pregnant; because, they said, they could not pay the tribute exacted of them. They did not wish to have children, lest their offspring suffer in the same way as they themselves had suffered.'[20]

If Hernando Cortés has been remembered as the 'hero' of the Mexican conquest, Francisco Pizarro has obtained a similar, if less widely known, reputation as the conqueror of Peru. He was born at Trujillo in Extremadura, Spain in either 1475 or 1478, the illegitimate son of an infantry colonel, Gonzalo Pizarro, who had engaged in an illicit liaison with a servant girl, Francisca González. After a stint of military service in Italy under Gonsalvo di Cordova, the younger Pizarro obtained the consent of the Holy Roman Emperor, Charles V, to conquer Peru, on the understanding that he would be entitled to a major part of the spoils. In 1532 he sailed to America with Diego de Almagro and crossed the Andes to Cajamarca. His experience in dealing with the Inca inhabitants of Peru amounts to another catalogue of mindless and thoroughly unjustified butchery. Initially, the Inca Emperor, Atahualpa, received the Spanish expeditionary force cordially and, instead of attacking them as invaders, plied them with gold and other gifts much as Moctezuma had done in Mexico.

Pizarro's response was to send his brother Gonzalo and Hernando de Soto to Atahualpa, armed with a friendly greeting from the Pope, with an invitation to visit the Spanish camp. It was a deliberate piece of treachery that remains one of the most infamous chapters in the annals of Spanish military history. When Atahualpa arrived his army was massacred and he himself taken prisoner. The following year Pizarro and Almagro ransacked the ancient Inca capital of Cuzco, and over a nine-year period Pizarro consolidated the Spanish conquest of the Inca Empire, founding the city of Lima in 1535. Almagro then went on separately to conquer Chile with much the same disregard for the native population, but on his return to Peru he discovered that Cuzco had come under siege from the Indians. He relieved the Spanish garrison there, but strife subsequently erupted between the two Spanish overlords and Almagro became embroiled in a civil war with Pizarro. Almagro was defeated and executed in 1538, but his supporters took their revenge three years later when they assassinated Pizarro in Lima.[21]

A telling indictment of the Spanish Crusade is to be found in a passing observation made by Mendieta some eighty years after the conquest. He describes having been present when the alarm was raised about the imminent arrival of Europeans in a village belonging to the Chichemecs. These were primitive nomadic hunters rather than agriculturalists, reliant on bows and arrows; they ranged over the inner plateau of northern Mexico, a vast rocky desert bounded by the Sierra Madre mountains. In truth they had earned the name 'Chichemeca' from the more sophisticated Aztecs as a derogatory title translating roughly as 'lineage of the dog'.[22] Nonetheless, by and large these were peaceful people, and when warned that 'the Christians' were coming the population fled into the mountains in a state of great agitation. The Spaniards left many lasting legacies, among the most damning of which was to permit the word 'Christian' to be discredited, since it was used for a long time as a derogatory term for the white European dominating and oppressing the native Indian.

The rape of Mexican culture was, however, the greatest and most lasting tragedy of the Spanish Crusade. In 1521 the German artist

Albrecht Dürer was staying in Brussels and had the opportunity to examine some of the hoard of treasures sent by Cortés to the Emperor Charles V. 'All the days of my life I have seen nothing that rejoiced my heart so much as these things, for I have seen among them beautiful works of art, and I marvelled at the subtle intellects of men in foreign places', G. de Mendieta, *Historia Ecclesiastica Indiana*, ed. J.G. Icazbalceta (Mexico, 1876). These things reflected complex modes of thought. There was massive destruction of codices, sculpture and other native art works, but more profound was the loss of indigenous customs and beliefs through death, disease, slavery and mass conversion. That which the Conquistadors had not already destroyed by the sword and the cannon was finished off, courtesy of European-bred diseases and the enslavement of Indians in the lethally inhuman conditions of the gold and silver mines. Much of the culture only survives in the mythological beliefs and speech of the living descendants of the Aztecs, Maya and other native peoples.[23]

The catastrophe of Spanish America's rape at the hands of the Conquistadors remains one of the most potent and pungent examples in the entire history of human conquest of the wanton destruction of one culture by another in the name of religion. In 1524, three years after the conquest of Tenochtitlan, the friar chronicler Bernardino de Sahagún recorded a telling conversation between the newly arrived Franciscans and a group of Aztec scholars. The latter protested along these lines: 'You said that we know not the Lord of the Close Vicinity to whom the heavens and earth belong. You said that our gods are not true gods. New words are these that you speak; because of them we are disturbed, because of them we are troubled. For our ancestors before us, who lived upon the earth, were unaccustomed to speak thus. From them we have inherited our pattern of life, which in truth they did hold; in reverence they held, they honoured our gods.'[24]

ELEVEN

Loving Them to Death

On 26 August 1936, the Spanish right-wing newspaper *Heraldo de Aragón* printed an account of the triumphal entry to a shrine dedicated to the honour of the Virgin Mary at Zaragoza by a Falangist general at the head of his troops. With cries of 'Long Live Death! Long live the Virgin of the Pillar' ringing in his ears, he offered his cap to her statue in salute. Some three years later in his victory speech, also delivered at Zaragoza, the Falangist chief Generalissimo Franco conceded that if the Virgin of the Pillar 'had not given us all energy, bravery, the spirit of sacrifice, living conscience of the past and blind faith in our future, our armed guards would have kept vigil in vain'. Similar traditions continued. During the Second World War, Spanish troops of the 'Blue Division' carried Mary's militaristic colours into battle on the Russian Front, committed to her defence against communism. Each man was armed with a rifle and a photograph of the Virgin of Zaragoza.[1]

Zaragoza, on the River Ebro in Aragon in north-east Spain, obtained its reputation and association with the mother of Jesus in her capacity as Nuestra Señora del Pilar, who according to legend had sought refuge in Aragon 'in the flesh' and had planted a stone pillar to mark her safe arrival. The Virgin of Zaragoza subsequently became allied to the army both at home and in the Latin American colonies, and in images the blue sash of a captain-general frequently found its way to her waist. That visionaries had reported Mary to be wearing a sash coloured blue was always going to be politically expedient since it implied that politically she stood on the right of centre, against socialism and communism and solidly behind monarchies.

Spain had long been captivated by the belief that Mary was their champion in matters of conflict. Military honours were constantly showered upon her, often to the accompaniment of martial music and artillery salutes.[2] During the seventeenth century, when Spanish imperial power was beginning to wane, morale was boosted when Philip IV proclaimed Mary to be Our Lady of Victories, Patroness of the Royal Arms, and instructed that there should be strict celebration of her feast days throughout the Spanish dominions.[3] But Spain was not alone in this curiously jarring linkage between the imagery of the gentle mother of Jesus Christ and a militant warrior queen.

It may seem incongruous that a figure of mercy and compassion, of motherhood and fertility, should also preside over war, yet this has been a familiar paradoxical feature of more than one mother goddess throughout history, and Mary, the mother of Jesus, has been no exception. Several of the Roman Emperors in Byzantium set an early precedent by erasing the images of their pagan war goddesses from seals and replacing these with images of Madonna and child. This, however, was just a foretaste of what was to come. In the Thirty Years War (1618–48) between the Catholic armies of Archduke Ferdinand of Austria and the Protestant reformers, an icon of Mary was considered instrumental in securing a crucial victory near Prague in 1620. Shortly afterwards this merited the renaming of a church in Rome, already strongly associated with Marian visions, as S. Maria della Vittoria. All over the Catholic dominions she gained the following of troops through her miraculous appearances, and as late as the Crimean War nurses are known to have surreptitiously inserted talismanic medals bearing the image of the Madonna between the bandages of the wounded as a healing aid.

In later times the Catholic Action movement introduced the so-called 'Marian Oath', and with it continues to recruit millions of converts. Initiates swear a defence of the Immaculata 'to the death'.[4] In Poland, national security was entrusted to Mary from the seventeenth century onwards, when she was proclaimed Queen of the Polish Crown.[5] This became especially relevant when Poland came into conflict with Soviet Russia in August 1920. The so-called 'Miracle of the Vistula', attributed to the direct intervention of Mary, enabled inferior Polish forces to rout the Russians and take a sizeable bite of Russian territory. Worldwide she became associated with a plethora of quasi-militant, often secretive Marianist clubs. In the 1920s and 1930s in Poland the Militia Immaculatae thrived, claiming nearly a million subscribers by the outbreak of the Second World War. Ireland saw the foundation of the Legion of Mary and the Knights of St Columbanus. Australian devotees launched the Knights of the Southern Cross. North America saw the rise of the Knights of Columbus.

During the 1950s and 1960s, when the McCarthyite witch-hunts against 'reds under the beds' were in full swing in the United States, Marianism was said to underpin much of the anti-communist obsession of the Un-American Activities Committee.[6] In fact, nowhere was militant Marianism taken more seriously than in the United States, the scene of a remarkable fundamentalist Catholic awakening. In this climate of fear and patriotism the Blue Army of Mary was founded with the precise brief of crushing the Soviet Red Army under Mary's heel through the militant power of the rosary. Taking up the now widely accepted colour code, members of the Blue Army recognised each other by wearing a discreet blue ribbon or string. Indeed, one of the most potentially catastrophic outcomes of the association between Mary, war and victory might well have come during the Reagan era. Some of the hawkish posturing of Republicans towards the Soviet Union is said to have stemmed from an implicit belief among born-again Christian fundamentalists that détente had been a waste of time because Mary alone controlled the options. Here once more was the spectre that human free will and moral choice was an irrelevance because destiny was controlled on a higher plane. In November 1984 the *National Catholic Reporter* went so far as to print the extraordinary allegation that during his term of office Ronald Reagan subscribed to the view that at the moment of Armageddon, in the seconds before the unleashing of thermonuclear conflict, Mary's righteous millions would be lifted into the air and saved.[7] Whether this story can be substantiated or not, it is well recorded that during his term of office Reagan expressed close spiritual links with Pope John Paul II and was in sympathy with many Christian fundamentalist views.

Why is Mary the mother of Jesus so closely associated with war? Is it because she is also intimately associated with death? In an excellent study of Marianism the Catholic writer Marina Warner went so far as to identify Mary as having represented the Queen of Hell.[8] Until 1900 in the Forum at the foot of the Palatine Hill in Rome there existed a church known as S. Maria Liberatrice, though this was a comparatively recent name. In earlier times the place was known as S. Maria de Inferno, recalling a legend that it marked the entrance to the underworld and that Mary was stationed there as an intercessor. Herein lies some of the strength of the rosary, and it is no coincidence that the Hail Mary, one of the oldest and most oft-recited prayers of Catholics worldwide, ends with the cry, 'Pray for us sinners, now and at the hour of our death.' In the medieval Catholic world temporal violence was matched by the brutality of the afterlife, and some of this notion still persists. Throughout Christian history the faithful have frequently possessed an unremitting terror of hell with its flames and its predatory shop stewards equipped with red eyes, curly tails and toasting forks. But the road to this ultimate sanction has an escape lane, the very medieval concept of purgatory.[9] In the eyes of many a Catholic the somewhat intimidating figure of Jesus is set to judge the quick and the dead in a questionable mood of attrition, and the fate of many a soul lies in the clemency of Mary and her ability to tip the scales in their favour. This same perceived capacity is, I believe, responsible for the visionary warnings of disaster that have regularly been attributed to Mary.

At one time during the 1930s apparitions of the Madonna were seen to be foretelling the dangers inherent in the rise of Nazi Germany. After Hiroshima and Nagasaki and during the Cold War period some of her spectral messages were interpreted as premonitions of an atomic holocaust, and this was taken especially seriously in the United States among fundamentalist born-again Christians.

The dual role of the mother goddess, the Queen of Heaven, is time-honoured. If we trace history back to the ancient Near East and the cultures revealed in the first chapter, we find similar characters. Like so many of her later counterparts Inana, the first lady of the Sumerian pantheon, took on the conflicting roles of goddess of love, fertility and war. She was, as one of the surviving cuneiform texts reads,

> Arrayed in battle,
> beautiful . . . who handles the *utug* weapon,
> who washes the tools in the blood of battle.
> She opens the door of battle.
> The wise one of heaven, Inana.[10]

An inscription found at the site of her temple at Zabalam reveals a similar mood. By this time she was known by her Akkadian name of Istar, the star of the heavens.

> The great dragon who speaks inimical words to the evil,
> who makes everything as clean as the whitest of things,
> who goes against the enemies' land.
> Through her the firmament is made beautiful in the evening.

One of the most beautifully executed cylinder seals from the period, the great seal of the scribe Adda, encapsulates her public image: imperious on the summit of a mountain, commanding, armoured, wings spread. Just as Mary is for today's Christian believer, Inana revealed a paradoxical character, capable of profound concern and compassion yet also willing to be petulant and vengeful. Imitations of the Sumerian Inana gestated throughout the ancient Near East. In biblical Canaan, Anat, the sister of the national god Baal, emerged with a similar complex personality. On the one hand Anat exhibits the persona of a mother goddess, a diva concerned with fertility, love and life. She plays the virgin bride taken by Baal as his fervent, incestuous mistress.

> He is passionate and he takes hold of her vagina,
> She is passionate and takes hold of his testicles,
> Baal makes love by the thousand with the virgin Anat.[11]

Yet Anat is no mere oversexed mistress. When Baal is slain and dragged off to the underworld by the demonic Mot, she exacts terrible retribution.

> Much she fights and looks, battles and views.
> Anat gluts her liver with laughter,
> her heart is filled with joy.
> Anat's liver exults,
> her knees she plunges in the blood of soldiery,
> thighs in the gore of troops.

The world over we envisage a stark correlation between death and rebirth, decay and genesis, destruction and creation. 'Grand design' has to be a euphemism, because it would be naive to expect identical spiritual activities and experiences. But there have been and will continue to be remarkable similarities. In the Late Neolithic period of Western Europe, most notably France, one can discover mother-goddess images in tombs, and on the walls of caves association with inhumation, as the paramount diva, as yet perhaps unnamed, became identified not only with fertility but also with war and death. In Celtic times the goddess went with and was inseparable from the parcel of land to which she gave fertility and life in peace but also protected with great ferocity in war. There evolved three bonded and inseparable images of the goddess in the form of the Deae Matres. In Irish literature these three aspects became known as the Morrigne, whose separate components included Medb or Maeve, the aspect of fertility, Morrigan, the ruler of the underworld and 'Queen of Demons', and Badb Catha, the arbiter of battle and destruction.

Similar traditions arose in Scandinavia. Like Inana of old the goddess Freyja was a diva of war and death to whom went half of all victims of battle; she was also the patroness of plenty. In keeping with the character of her more ancient counterpart she is portrayed as a highly sexed lady in the intimate company of her brother Freyr, the god of fertility. In literature and art she is symbolised by an assortment of animals, none especially known for their sexual restraint. Cats frequently drew her chariot, and by night she seduces her lovers in the form of a goat.

In order to make sense of these seemingly paradoxical associations, we might do worse than consider a fundamental plank in a religion we have otherwise only touched on in passing – Hinduism. Here there is an implicit understanding that the universe is finite, so that nothing can be added to it and nothing taken away. The logic follows that if something is to be created then something else must first be destroyed to provide the raw material of that creation. Genesis is not possible without dissolution and each is dependent on the other. Hence we find a trinity, three aspects of the one celestial power, Vishnu, Shiva and Brahma. Vishnu represents all that is positive and constructive in the universe and Shiva is his antithesis, representing the negative and destructive forces around us, while Brahma maintains an even-handed cosmic balance. Vishnu, the creator, is not possible without Shiva and Shiva cannot exist without Vishnu. This idea seems to be embedded in the psyche of humankind in many other cultures and it probably accounts for the dual roles of the mother goddess. Often she is required to destroy, or at least to witness destruction, before she can put on her mantle of fertility and bring regeneration to the world. In the ancient religion of Egypt this pattern became deeply engrained more than 5,000 years ago. Osiris, the fertility god and incestuous brother of Isis, suffered dismemberment by Seth and his parts were scattered across Egypt before Isis collected them together and breathed new life into them. This cosmic activity is symbolic of the threshing and winnowing of grain before it can be scattered in the ground to germinate into a new season of plenty. Isis did not kill Osiris, but she watched over his death and restored him to life. The essential need to scatter seed on the land was perhaps at the heart of the mythological smashing and scattering of Osiris' body. According to some Egyptian traditions, human sacrifice encouraged the germination of the corn. Victims were slaughtered and cremated in a field close to one of the legendary graves of Osiris.[12] The ashes were strewn with winnowing fans in a ritual enactment of the scattering of the pieces of the god. In Canaanite mythology Anat, the sister of Baal, played a violent role with similar elements after the demonic Mot dragged Baal off to the underworld.

> She seized divine Mot,
> with a blade she split him,
> with a sieve she winnowed him,
> with fire she burnt him,
> with mill stones she ground him,
> in a field she scattered him.[13]

Always in these mythic sagas we are witnessing a confrontation between good and evil, chaos and order, death and resurrection, and the imagery of this tussle became a universal explanation of origins. The violence of the symbolic death in the celestial world reflects the violence witnessed in nature as the seasons take their course. Without the winter storms to rip apart the old, the gentle germination of spring cannot occur, and the mother goddess stands in command of both. She is life and she is death, war and peace, motherhood and slaughter, the morning and evening of our lives. As Hermann Hesse put it so succinctly, 'Without a mother we cannot die.'

TWELVE

Infinite Wrath

Ｎone of the areas of history that I have covered in this book
thus far explains why violence in the name of God has
consistently encouraged us into the most extreme forms of cruelty
and brutality. Yet history indeed reveals that religious wars tend to
result in levels of atrocity and inhumanity rarely if ever experienced
in purely secular conflicts. I believe that the explanation lies in a
shared understanding among the three faiths – Judaism, Christianity
and Islam – firstly that God has a capacity for infinite wrath and
secondly that his measure of justice is to repay everyone as he or she
deserves. When this justice is administered on a larger collective
scale it translates into holy war. God applies his anger to re-establish
justice in history and preserve a sense of order in human existence
despite its suffering. God's chosen people – and whether they are
Israelite, Christian or Muslim matters little – believe that they have
been specifically delegated to punish those who are unfaithful to
divine law and to restore God's correct rule on Earth. The
unfaithful, the infidels, become the sinful and unjust, and holy war
thus becomes an act of correction against injustice and is therefore
always fought between extremes of good and evil. The punishment
of the unjust by the just demands comparable extremes. Divine
punishment, however, is rarely employed to stop further injustice.
It is a form of retribution, cancelling out a debt allegedly incurred
against God, and the ferocity of violence in holy war only reflects
the enormity of the crime. The debt of the perpetrator is infinite,
his sin immeasurable, so in principle no limit is placed upon
the violence inflicted on him by way of retribution.[1] This
uncompromising totality is spelled out in stark language in the Old
Testament Book of Ezekiel: 'Now will I shortly pour out my fury

upon thee, and accomplish mine anger upon thee: and I will judge thee according to thy ways, and I will recompense thee for all thine abominations. And mine eye shall not spare, neither will I have pity: I will recompense thee according to thy ways and thine abominations that are in the midst of thee; and ye shall know that I am the Lord that smiteth. Behold the day, behold it is come: the morning is gone forth; the rod hath blossomed, pride hath budded. Violence is risen up into a rod of wickedness: none of them shall remain, nor of their multitude, nor shall any of theirs.'[2]

Reading such vituperative stuff it is not hard to see why, if the faithful are conditioned to believe they have a sacred duty to implement the wrath of their god, the exact manner in which they carry this out is unimportant so long as it is done with sufficient ferocity to effectively communicate the magnitude of God's wrath.[3] The extent of the slaughter and the degree of inhumanity in its implementation become secondary considerations. Warfare becomes a tool in the hands of a transcendent God, to be applied without hesitation or limit if it can be shown to serve his will – and, since the will of God is inscrutable, who is to say that it is ever wrong! Whichever method of force best realises God's purpose on Earth is not just permitted, it is commanded. 'Good brother, we must bend unto all means that give furtherance to the Holy cause.'[4]

Throughout this survey of violence in the name of God I have focused largely on the trio of monotheistic faiths. This is not to suggest that these are the only examples of religious entities that condone violence, but they do stand as the most consistently belligerent. Part of the reason for this lies in the perceived nature and personality of God. In Judaism, Christianity and Islam the transcendent power is male, and he builds the world by command rather than through a process of gestation that might be the case if the deity were female. In some senses God becomes alienated from the product of his own creation because humanity by nature is fallen, not holy, and is produced from base matter. Mainstream Christians have outlawed the ideology of dualism, the language of the Gnostics, the notion that the ambiguities of mortal existence can be explained through two independent powers, one imperfect and

240

the other perfect. In the eyes of the Christian heretic the Old Testament God of Israel was palpably flawed and had brought into being a world filled with disease, pain, violence and suffering. He was therefore incompatible with a god proclaimed by Jesus Christ to be one of love and redemption. In many respects Islamic logic supports the same ambiguity. Allah is merciful but Allah also declares war on unbelievers. The dualist principle may have been condemned as a heresy in orthodox circles but it has proved remarkably tenacious. We are flawed and we know it!

In Christendom the medieval Crusades and the inquisitive tribunals that followed stand as pithy examples of the unpalatable truth, as Sigmund Freud put it, that uncivilised behaviour lies just beneath the surface inside every human being and needs only a small impetus to push it from one side of the divide to the other. Religion has provided that impetus perhaps more than any other recognisable engine, stimulating war and other forms of violence too frequently during history for us to be able to avoid that conclusion. But, conversely, we should recognise that violence also empowers religion. One of the realities that emerge from this book is that, when holy wars and violence in the name of God erupt, there is a corresponding strengthening of religious devotion, and with it comes religious fanaticism.

The Christian world turns to the pages of the Old Testament to find justification for enterprises such as the Crusades. It prefers, by way of contrast, to attribute to its founding inspiration, Jesus Christ, an abhorrence of violence by man towards his fellow man. Yet we should not forget that in an incident cited by Matthew he declared to his twelve disciples that he had come to set the man at variance with his father and the daughter against her mother. This instruction came to be relied on, in part, as justification for the aggressive inquiry within the Christian medieval world during which horrific wrongs were inflicted upon Christendom's own recalcitrant but otherwise innocent members.

When seeking answers to the question of why religion and violence are such constant bedfellows, we are constantly reminded that a common denominator binds the two – death. Religion

241

generally involves belief in a spiritual afterlife beyond our mortal span; religious violence generally expects death of the adversary to be the end product. This is not, however, the recognisable and often gentle passing away of old age but the sudden and brutal curtailing of our normal existence. The purpose, when assailing the religious adversary, is to remove a form of spiritual pollution from this world and to consign it to eternal damnation in the next. Yet the victim may face death in a quite different frame of mind.

Jesus Christ met a violent physical end in defence of his convictions and as a form of global atonement for humanity's sins. If biblical accounts are to be trusted he met his end willingly in the belief that union with God in paradise beckoned. Death as an act of faith has been sought in Christianity and Islam as a passport to paradise. The Christian martyrs of ancient Rome listening to hysterical crowds baying for their blood in the arena faced the wild animals that were to tear them to pieces with, it is said, extraordinary courage and even joy. They believed genuinely that after a few terrible moments of agony they would be transported to heaven in glory. Similar irrational conviction today drives Islamic warriors to commit no less terrible atrocities not merely upon themselves but also upon others. These men and women, the twenty-first-century martyrs for Muhammad, are conditioned to the implacable belief that the more unbelievers they 'take out' as they blow themselves to bits, the greater the reward due to them in paradise.

Arguably, it is the impulse towards martyrdom that occasionally drives members of religious cults to perform acts which most rational people would consider bizarre and even horrific. Religious cults offer an escape route to salvation, a special 'nod from God'. In their eyes, the initiates who receive these divine blessings are the sane and chosen ones destined for heavenly salvation, while the rest of us are the lunatics bound for annihilation.

Jehovah's Witnesses have relied consistently on predictions of the date of Judgement Day as a persuasive tool with which to recruit members, and they demonstrate an absolute belief in their exclusive destiny to the extent that one of their early leaders, Joseph Franklin Rutherford, had deeds drawn up holding his property in trust for

Noah and other Old Testament elders who would make use of it in the new, post-doomsday world order. In 1929 a disaffected Bulgarian immigrant to the United States, Victor Houteff, launched the Branch Davidian sect as an offshoot of the Seventh Day Adventists. He claimed to be a 'prophet from the east' who had been chosen to oversee the selection of 144,000 Servants of God who would first be guided to Israel, there to await the Day of Judgement followed by the establishment of a new heaven and earth.[5] These chosen servants would, predictably, staff the awaited Utopia. Various subsequent prophets of doom came and went until 1986, when a self-proclaimed final messenger, who had renamed himself David Koresh, gained control of the sect's commune at Waco in Texas. In common with others suffering delusions of religious grandeur, Koresh announced himself as the bearer of the key to the Seventh Seal of the Book of Revelation by which the faithful would be marked and saved from doom. He also preached polygamy and violent resistance to outside authority. On 28 February 1993, the federal authorities decided that enough was enough and, after a fifty-one-day stand-off, they stormed the compound, resulting in a well-publicised final conflagration and the incineration of seventy-four cult members. Allegedly, during this time the commune members remained steadfast in their belief that they were God's chosen people.[6]

One of the most horrific incidents of religious self-destruction took place on 18 November 1978 deep in the jungles of Guyana. The members of the People's Temple cult, an obscure quasi-Christian sect with a little over 1,200 members living in a commune under the rule of the self-styled Reverend Jim Jones, died in an infamous massacre. Some committed mass suicide by cyanide poisoning, others were executed with firearms, and less than 200 escaped. The survivors reported poison being ladled out by the commune doctor and nurse while loudspeaker announcements delivered promises about the beauty of death and resurrection.[7]

In September 1994 a similar though less spectacular event took place at various locations in Switzerland. At the Alpine village of Cheiry, twenty-three members of the Temple du Soleil sect were found dead wearing red, gold and black cloaks and having laid themselves out like the radial points of a star. They had apparently drunk champagne laced with a lethal cocktail of drugs prior to an attempt to incinerate themselves by detonating a delayed-action petrol bomb that failed to go off. Another twenty-five members of the same sect succeeded in their attempt at incineration at another village, Granges-sur-Salvan. In both cases one of the cult members, Patrick Vuarnet, had posted a 'Last Testament' to the Swiss and French authorities indicating that the cult was preparing for a final purification ritual by fire before journeying to a new spiritual life on a planet orbiting the star Sirius.[8]

None of the people involved in these bizarre events could be labelled as a terrorist intent on slaying bystanders, although it is not clear how many of them died voluntarily and how many perished at the hands of their fanatical cult leaders. The greater significance lies in that all those involved presumably, at some time or other, had been rational human beings. Each, however, was clearly susceptible to irrational influences and became conditioned as a religious 'junkie'. It is not hard to make the intellectual leap between these deranged individuals and others who take on board similar levels of religious brainwashing, but with one added dimension, the destruction of the innocent. By killing others who are not of their persuasion they believe that they serve to cleanse their distorted world of impurities and in doing so are promised that they will earn the highest rewards, whether in heaven or an outer planet of the solar system.

We should not be lulled into thinking that in modern times the Islamic countries have been alone in producing fundamentalists prepared to commit lethal violence against others. In the USA in the mid-1990s with the millennium fast approaching, an ex-navy serviceman named William Cooper set up an armed militia group at St Johns in Arizona. He published a journal called *Veritas* and also wrote a handbook called *Behold a Pale Horse* (a clear reference to an apocalyptic warning in the biblical Book of Revelation), both of which contained alarming predictions of American dissolution at the hands of a vague amalgam of Catholics and Jews. With Pope John

Paul II and George Bush high in its rankings, the group would shortly be attempting to set up a new world order. This Catholic–Semitic conspiracy was, according to Cooper, planning a war against the principles of freedom and, more specifically, against uniformed American gun clubs. He claimed, however, that with the dawn of the year 2000 the secret chambers of the Pyramid of Giza would be opened and that Satan would ride out with only the American militia blasting away to stop him. In May 1995 one militiaman, Timothy McVeigh, took the message to heart that the American administration represented this rumbling anti-Christ and that, as Cooper exhorted his members, 'You must prepare to fight and if necessary die to preserve your God-given right to freedom'. McVeigh planted a bomb that exploded and reduced the Federal Building in Oklahoma City to rubble. It was detonated on the second anniversary of the Waco massacre. In the last decade the nature of the conspiracy has changed in the eyes of most Americans. Catholics and Jews tend to be the good guys and catastrophic events including the destruction of New York's twin towers ensure that the militant sights are aimed elsewhere. Some may feel that the resurgence of right-wing Christian fundamentalism in the USA now represents a loaded gun, potentially as dangerous as anything we have yet seen among Muslim diehards. A theoretical scenario presents itself in which a third global conflagration erupts between two diametrically opposed ideologies, each convinced that it is acting in the name and on behalf of God.

Notes

Chapter One

1. Genesis 10:11.
2. H.C. Rawlinson, *The Cuneiform Inscriptions of Western Asia* (London, 1861).
3. G. Waterfield, *Layard of Nineveh* (London, 1963), p. 178ff.
4. M. Jordan, *Gods of the Earth* (London, 1992), p. 97.
5. A.H. Brodrick, *Lascaux: a Commentary* (London and Paris, 1949), p. 81, pl. 140.
6. W. Jochelson and W. Bogoras, *Koryak, Jesup North Pacific Expedition* (MAMNH 10, 1905).
7. Jordan, *Gods of the Earth*, p. 330.
8. M. Jordan, *Witches* (London, 1996), p. 135.
9. T.G.E. Powell, *The Celts* (London, 1958), p. 130.
10. M. Green, *The Gods of the Celts* (London, 1986), p. 104.
11. Powell, *The Celts*, p. 121.
12. B. Rying, *Denmark: Prehistory* (Copenhagen, n.d.), vol. 1, p. 62.
13. J.N. Postgate, *Early Mesopotamia: Society and Economy at the Dawn of History* (London and New York, 1992), p. 245.
14. Waterfield, *Layard*, pp. 121, 122.
15. S.N. Kramer, *Sumerian Mythology* (Philadelphia, 1944), p. 35ff.
16. S. Dalley, *Myths from Mesopotamia* (Oxford, 1989), p. 203.
17. J.A. Montgomery and Z.S. Harris, *The Ras Shamra Mythological Texts* (Philadelphia, 1935).
18. G. Dossin, 'Une Lettre de Iarim-Lim, roi d'Alep, à Iasub Iahad, roi de Dir', *Syria*, 33 (Paris, 1956), 63–9, in Postgate, *Early Mesopotamia*.
19. Julius Caesar, *De Bello Gallico*, vi.14.
20. Daniel 12:2.
21. Green, *Gods of the Celts*, p. 72.
22. D. Walters, *Chinese Mythology* (London, 1992), p. 123.
23. R. Champakalakshmi, *Vaisnava Iconography* (New Delhi, 1981), p. 36ff.

Notes

Chapter Two

1. Jeremiah 1:9.
2. Qur'ān, al-Baqarah 2:1.
3. M. Jordan, *Islam* (London, 2002), p. 90ff.
4. Jordan, *Gods of the Earth*, p. 151.
5. A.C. Myers (ed.), *The Eerdmans Bible Dictionary* (Michigan, 1987), p. 280ff.
6. A. Cruden, *Complete Concordance of the Bible* (Cambridge, 1839), p. 144ff.
7. J.A. Aho, *Religious Mythology and the Art of War* (London, 1981), p. 165ff.
8. H.H. Ben-Sasson (ed.), *A History of the Jewish People* (London, 1976), p. 5.
9. R. Firestone, 'Conceptions of Holy War in Biblical and Qur'ānic Tradition', *Journal of Religious Ethics*, 24.1 (Spring 1996).
10. M. Walzer, 'The Idea of Holy War in Ancient Israel', *Journal of Religious Ethics*, 22.2 (Autumn 1992), 215–27.
11. A. Schleifer, 'Understanding Jihad: Definition and Methodology', *Islamic Quarterly*, 27.3 (1983), 118–31.
12. Jordan, *Gods of the Earth*, p. 110ff.
13. Exodus 20:5.
14. Numbers 21:14.
15. J.A. Brundage, 'Holy War and the Medieval Lawyers' in T.P. Murphy (ed.), *The Holy War* (Ohio, 1976), p. 116.
16. Deuteronomy 32:16ff.
17. Genesis 6:7.
18. Genesis 14:20.
19. Genesis 18:20–1.
20. Deuteronomy 32:32ff.
21. Exodus 23:27ff.
22. Joshua 1:2ff.
23. Joshua 3:10.
24. Joshua 11:20.
25. Deuteronomy 20:15ff.
26. Joshua 7:11.
27. 2 Kings 24:3.
28. Jeremiah 21:4–6.
29. J.H. Charlesworth (ed.), *The Old Testament Pseudepigrapha* (2 vols, New York, 1983), 1 Enoch 56:5ff.

30. M. Jürgensmeyer, *Terror in the Mind of God* (Berkeley and Los Angeles, 2000), p. 25ff.
31. Matthew 10:33–4.
32. Luke 12:51.
33. Nag Hammadi Library, *Gospel of Thomas* (Coptic version) 16.
34. Matthew 5:44.
35. Qur'ān, al Ma'idah 5:51.
36. N.J. Dawood (tr.), *The Koran* (London, 1959), introduction, p. 2.
37. Qur'ān, al-Ma'idah 5:31.
38. Qur'ān, al-Baqarah 2:191ff.
39. Qur'ān, al-Hujurāt 49:9.
40. Qur'ān, al-Anbiyā' 21:40ff.
41. Qur'ān, al-Hijr 15:91–7.
42. Qur'ān, al-Hajj 22:43ff.
43. Qur'ān, al-Tawbah 9:4.
44. Firestone, 'Conceptions of Holy War'.
45. E. Easwaran (tr.), *Bhagavadgita* (London, 1986), 2.19ff.
46. K. Klostermaier, *A Survey of Hinduism* (New York, 1994), pp. 103–4.
47. Easwaran (tr.), *Bhagavadgita*, 2.37ff.
48. Exodus 15:3.
49. Jürgensmeyer, *Terror in the Mind of God*, p. 149.
50. www.forteantimes.com/articles/189.
51. www.christianidentity.org.uk.

Chapter Three

1. H. White, 'The Value of Narrativity in the Representation of Reality' in H. White, *The Content of the Form: Narrative Discourse and Historical Representation* (Baltimore, 1987).
2. A. Malamat, 'Conquest and Settlement' in Ben-Sasson (ed.), *History of the Jewish People*, p. 56.
3. A. Malamat, 'Origins' in Ben-Sasson (ed.), *History of the Jewish People*, p. 21ff.; Myers (ed.), *Eerdmans Bible Dictionary*, p. 310.
4. Judges 5:1ff.
5. 1 Samuel 10ff.
6. Myers (ed.), *Eerdmans Bible Dictionary*, p. 828.
7. Malamat, 'Origins', in Ben-Sasson (ed.), *History of the Jewish People*, p. 7.
8. Dio, 52.36, in T.D. Barnes, *From Eusebius to Augustine: Selected Papers 1982–93* (Aldershot, 1994).

9. E.P. Sanders, *Jesus and Judaism* (London, 1985), p. 231.
10. R.L. Fox, *Pagans and Christians* (London, 1986), p. 428.
11. G.E.M. de St Croix, in M.I. Finlay (ed.), *Studies in Ancient Society* (London, 1974).
12. Revelation 17:4ff.
13. R. Fletcher, *The Barbarian Conversion: from Paganism to Christianity* (Los Angeles, 1999), p. 23.
14. J. Ferguson, *The Religions of the Roman Empire* (London, 1970), p. 233.
15. Tacitus, *Annals*, tr. D.R. Dudley (London, 1966), 15.44.
16. St Croix, in Finlay (ed.), *Studies in Ancient Society*.
17. Fox, *Pagans and Christians*, p. 433.
18. *Ibid.*, pp. 419, 437.
19. Pliny, *Letters*, 10.96.2, in Barnes, *From Eusebius to Augustine*.
20. Clement I, *Apologies of Justin Martyr*, I, 4 and II, 2, tr. Revd Temple (London, 1851).
21. Barnes, *From Eusebius to Augustine*, vol. 1, p. 232.
22. *Ibid.*, vol. 1, p. 233.
23. Athenagoras, *Plea*, 3.1.31–2, in Barnes, *From Eusebius to Augustine*.
24. Tertullian, *Apology*, in Barnes, *From Eusebius to Augustine*.
25. J.W.C. Wand, *A History of the Early Church to AD 500* (London, 1937), p. 68.
26. W.H.C. Friend, 'Prelude to the Great Persecution: the Propaganda War', *Journal of Ecclesiastical History*, 38.1 (1987); Wand, *History of the Early Church*, p. 99ff.
27. Eusebius, *The History of the Church from Christ to Constantine*, tr. G.A. Williamson (London, 1965), p. 331.
28. Origen, *Contra Celsum*, iii, 55, tr. H. Chadwick (London, 1980).
29. *Ibid.*, iv, 11.41.
30. C.H.V. Sutherland, 'Flexibility in the reformed coinage of Diocletian', in R.A.G. Carson and C.H.U. Sutherland (eds), *Essays Presented to Harold Mattingly* (London, 1956), p. 179.
31. D.L. Edwards, *Christianity: the First Two Thousand Years* (London, 1997), p. 31.
32. Eusebius, *Ecclesiastical History*, 5.1.7ff.; H.A. Musurillo (tr.), *The Acts of the Christian Martyrs* (Oxford, 1972).
33. H.A. Musurillo (tr.), *Acts of the Christian Martyrs*, p. 12.
34. *Ibid.*, p. 25.
35. Psalms 116:15.
36. 'Letters of Cyprian of Carthage' in J. Quasten, W.J. Burghardt and T.C. Lawler (eds), *Ancient Christian Writers* (New York, 1984).

37. Genesis 3:19.
38. Aho, *Religious Mythology*, p. 165ff.
39. *Ibid.*, p. 145ff.

Chapter Four

1. M. Khadduri, *The Law of War and Peace in Islam* (London, 1940).
2. Genesis 45:7.
3. Judges 3:9.
4. Deuteronomy 20:3–4.
5. Numbers 21:3.
6. Joshua 10:40.
7. Myers (ed.), *Eerdmans Bible Dictionary*, p. 600.
8. Joshua 4:9.
9. Exodus 17:8–13.
10. Deuteronomy 25:17ff.
11. 1 Samuel 15:2ff.
12. J. Wellhausen, *Prolegomena to the History of Israel*, tr. J. Sutherland Black and A. Menzies (Edinburgh, 1885).
13. C. Ryder Smith, 'Theocracy', in J. Hastings (ed.), *Encyclopaedia of Religion and Ethics* (Edinburgh, 1908–26), vol. 12, pp. 287–9.
14. 1 Samuel 15:18.
15. 1 Chronicles 4:42–3.
16. 1 Kings 11:16.
17. Judges 20:5ff.
18. 1 Kings 14:10–11.
19. 1 Kings 18:19ff.
20. 2 Chronicles 28:20ff.
21. 2 Kings 16:10.
22. Jeremiah 16:13.
23. M. Jordan, *Mary – the Unauthorised Biography* (London, 2001), p. 55.
24. 2 Kings 19:10–11.
25. 2 Kings 21:3–4.
26. Charlesworth (ed.), *Pseudepigrapha*, 1 Enoch 89:42ff.
27. G. Vermes, *The Complete Dead Sea Scrolls in English*, IQSbv (London, 1962), 20–9.
28. Vermes, *Dead Sea Scrolls*, IQSa, 11, 20.
29. Daniel 11:40–5.
30. Numbers 24:24; Daniel 11:30.

31. Vermes, *Dead Sea Scrolls*, 1QM1.
32. J.A. Goldstein, *The Old Testament Apocrypha in English* (New York, 1977), 1 Maccabees 1:41ff.
33. Deuteronomy 20:16.
34. R. Firestone, 'Conceptions of Holy War'.
35. Exodus 32:27.
36. 1 Samuel 18:27.
37. A. Malamat, 'The Period of the Judges', in Ben-Sasson (ed.), *History of the Jewish People*, p. 69.
38. *Ibid.*, p. 73.
39. H. Tadmor, 'The United Monarchy' in Ben-Sasson (ed.), *History of the Jewish People*, p. 97.

Chapter Five

1. St Jerome, 'Against John of Jerusalem' in *Dogmatic and Polemical Works*, tr. J.N. Hritzu (Washington, 1965), 8PL23.377.
2. R.P. McBrien, *Lives of the Popes* (San Francisco, 1997), p. 63.
3. H. Chadwick, *The Early Church* (London, 1967), p. 167.
4. H.E. Rufinus, *Ecclesiastical History*, tr. and ed. C. Torben (Copenhagen, 1989), 11.33; St Augustine, *City of God*, 5.26.22ff.
5. Chadwick, *The Early Church*, p. 168.
6. Buchard of Worms, *Decretum*, xix, 5, in J.P. Migne, *Patrologiae cursus completus*, Series Latina 140.953 (Paris, 1841–64).
7. J. Madaule, *The Albigensian Crusade*, tr. B. Wall (London, 1967), p. 61.
8. J. Flori, 'Chevalerie et liturgie' (109a) in P. Contamine, *War in the Middle Ages*, tr. M. Jones (Oxford, 1984).
9. Luke 14:23.
10. H.G. Voigt, *Brun von Querfurt* (Stuttgart, 1907).
11. Myers (ed.), *Eerdmans Bible Dictionary*, p. 12.
12. C. Erdmann, *The Origin of the Idea of the Crusade*, tr. M.W. Baldwin and W. Goffart (New York, 1977).
13. Jeremiah 1:10.
14. R.W. Southern, *Western Society and the Church in the Middle Ages* (London, 1970), p. 100ff.
15. McBrien, *Lives of the Popes*, p. 186.
16. *Ibid.*, p. 190.
17. *Ibid.*, p. 191.
18. N. Davies, *Europe: a History* (London, 1996), p. 358.
19. Edwards, *Christianity*, p. 124.

20. Davies, *Europe*, p. 358.
21. A. Maalouf, *The Crusades through Arab Eyes*, tr. J. Rothschild (London, 1984), p. 5.
22. *Ibid.*, p. 19.
23. *Ibid.*, p. 17.
24. E. Gibbon, *The Decline and Fall of the Roman Empire* (abridged) (New York, 1952), ch. 48; Jacques le Goff, *La Civilisation Medievale de l'Occident* (Paris, 1965), p. 98.
25. J.C.S. Runciman, *A History of the Crusades* (3 vols, Cambridge, 1954), vol. 1.
26. C.G. Addison, *The History of the Knights Templars* (London, 1842).
27. Runciman, *History of the Crusades*, vol. 1, p. 463ff.
28. J.N.D. Kelly, *Dictionary of the Popes* (Oxford, 1986), p. 186.
29. E. Bradford, *The Great Betrayal: Constantinople 1204* (London, 1967).
30. Edwards, *Christianity*, p. 125.
31. Davies, *Europe*, p. 360.
32. Runciman, *History of the Crusades*, vol. 1, p. 139ff.

Chapter Six

1. Jordan, *Islam*, p. 10ff.
2. Qur'ān, al-Isra 17:1.
3. Ibn Hisham, *As Strah*, ed. Wustenfeld (Göttingen, 1858).
4. P.M. Holt, A.K. Lambton and B. Lewis (eds), *The Cambridge History of Islam* (2 vols, Cambridge, 1970), vol. 1, p. 40.
5. Khadduri, *Law of War and Peace in Islam*, p. 23.
6. Qur'ān 61:11ff.
7. Al-Baladhuri, *Kitab Futuh ul-Buldan*, ed. M.J. de Goeje (Leiden, 1866).
8. Al-Tabari, *Annales*, ed. M.J. de Goeje (Leiden, 1879–1901).
9. Khadduri, *Law of War and Peace in Islam*, p. 35.
10. Ash Shafi'I, *Kitab-ul-Umm* (Cairo, Bulaq, AH 1321), p. 115.
11. Ibn Rush'd, *Al-Muqaddmah* (Cairo, AH 1325), vol. i, p. 286.
12. Khadduri, *Law of War and Peace in Islam*, p. 57.
13. Mark 12:17.
14. Jordan, *Islam*, p. 53.

Chapter Seven

1. Jordan, *Mary*, p. 51ff.
2. Jordan, *Islam*, p. 57.

3. E. van Donzel, W.P. Heinrichs and G. Lecomte, *Encyclopedia of Islam* (10 vols, Leiden, 1997), vol. 1, p. 257.
4. Jordan, *Islam*, p. 57ff.
5. Donzel, Heinrichs and Lecomte, *Encyclopedia of Islam*, vol. 8, p. 853.
6. *Ibid.*, vol. 1, p. 381; vol. 2, p. 293.
7. Jordan, *Islam*, p. 63.
8. Qur'ān, al-Hujurāt 49:9.
9. Donzel, Heinrichs and Lecomte, *Encyclopedia of Islam*, vol. 7, p. 263ff.
10. *Ibid.*, vol. 3, p. 607ff.
11. S.H.M. Jafri, *Origins and Early Development of Shi'a Islam* (Beirut, 1979), p. 292.
12. M.Q. Zaman, *Religion and Politics under the Early 'Abassids – the Emergence of the Proto-Sunni Elite* (Leiden, 1997), p. 63.
13. Holt, Lambton and Lewis (eds), *Cambridge History of Islam*, p. 82ff.
14. Donzel, Heinrichs and Lecomte, *Encyclopedia of Islam*, vol. 5, p. 345ff.
15. *Ibid.*, vol. 6, p. 626.
16. Zaman, *Religion and Politics*, p. 42.
17. Donzel, Heinrichs and Lecomte, *Encyclopedia of Islam*, vol. 3, p. 1035.
18. www.iranian.com/Jan96/Opinion/Secular/Nationalism.html.
19. Sunni League, 'Iran's Fifty Year Plan' (London, September 1998).
20. www.ummah.org.uk.
21. J.O. Haneef, *The Wahhabi Myth*, 2nd edn (Toronto, 2004).

Chapter Eight

1. Kelly, *Dictionary of the Popes*, p. 186.
2. Chadwick, *The Early Church*, p. 219.
3. Wand, *History of the Early Church*, p. 143.
4. J.N.D. Kelly, *Early Christian Creeds* (New York, 1960), p. 263.
5. A.P. de Entrèves, *Aquinas: Selected Political Writings* (Paris, 1948), p. 84.
6. 'The Confrontation with the Donatists' in S. Lancel (ed.), *Gesta Conlationis Carthaginiensis, Anno 411* (Corpus Christianorum, Series Latina, 1974).
7. A.J. Macdonald, *Hildebrand* (London, 1932).
8. Southern, *Western Society*, p. 91.
9. Edwards, *Christianity*, p. 198.

10. Kelly, *Dictionary of the Popes*, p. 154.
11. *Ibid.*, p. 155.
12. N.E. Cantor, *Civilization of the Middle Ages* (New York, 1963), p. 51.
13. C.R. Cheney, *The Letters of Pope Innocent III*, reprinted from the 'Bulletin of the John Rylands Library', vol. 35, no. 1 (September 1952).
14. Cantor, *Civilization*, p. 385.
15. M.D. Lambert, *Medieval Heresy: Popular Movements from Bogomil to Hus* (London, 1977).
16. Cosmas, Presbyter, *Le Traité contre les Bogomiles de Cosmas le prêtre*, tr. André Vaillant (Paris, 1945).
17. J. Pelikan, *The Christian Tradition: a History of the Development of Doctrine*, vol. 3: *The Growth of Medieval Theology (600–1300)* (Chicago, 1978), pp. 238–9.
18. Edwards, *Christianity*, p. 207.
19. E. Holmes, *The Holy Heretics* (London, 1925), p. 30ff.
20. E. Randolph Daniel (ed.), *Liber de Concordia Novi ac Veteris Testamenti* (Philadelphia, 1983).
21. Joachimus de Fiore, *Expositiones – explanation figurate & pulchra in Apochalypsim* (Venetiis, *c.* 1520).
22. Southern, *Western Society*, p. 270.
23. Madaule, *Albigensian Crusade*, p. 67.
24. *Ibid.*, p. 72ff.
25. Psalms 91:11.
26. Madaule, *Albigensian Crusade*, p. 72ff.

Chapter Nine

1. E. Peters, *Inquisition* (New York, 1988), p. 1.
2. Voltaire, *Wars against the Cathars of Languedoc* (Paris, 1756).
3. 'The Enactments of Justinian' in S.P. Scott (tr.), *The Civil Law* (17 vols, Cincinnati, 1932).
4. H. Chadwick, *Priscillian of Avila* (Oxford, 1976), p. 138ff.
5. H.C. Lea, *A History of the Inquisition of the Middle Ages* (3 vols, London, 1906), vol. 1, p. 215.
6. *Ibid.*, p. 148.
7. J.N.D. Kelly, *Jerome – His Life, Writings and Controversies* (London, 1975), p. 286.
8. Lea, *History of the Inquisition*, vol. 1, p. 215ff.

9. W.H. Prescott, *History of the Conquest of Mexico* (2 vols, London, 1957), vol. 1, p. 315.
10. Kelly, *Dictionary of the Popes*, p. 180.
11. Voltaire, *Wars*.
12. Lea, *History of the Inquisition*, vol. 1, p. 136ff.
13. Madaule, *Albigensian Crusade*, p. 96.
14. Kelly, *Dictionary of the Popes*, p. 189.
15. Madaule, *Albigensian Crusade*, p. 96.
16. Lea, *History of the Inquisition*, vol. 1, p. 218ff.
17. Peters, *Inquisition*, p. 41.
18. *Ibid.*, p. 56.
19. A. Hausrath, *Der Ketzermeister Konrad von Marburg* (Heidelberg, 1861).
20. Madaule, *Albigensian Crusade*, p. 99.
21. H.B. Piazza, *True Account of the Inquisition* (London, 1722), p. 96.
22. Madaule, *Albigensian Crusade*, p. 101.
23. Lea, *History of the Inquisition*, vol. 1, p. 534ff.
24. *Ibid.*, vol. 1, p. 401ff.
25. *Ibid.*, vol. 1, p. 225.
26. J.M. de Maistre, *Lettres à un Gentilhomme Russe sur L'Inquisition Espagnole* (Paris, 1864).
27. Voltaire, *Wars*.
28. Madaule, *Albigensian Crusade*, p. 103.
29. *Ibid.*, p. 109.
30. Kelly, *Dictionary of the Popes*, p. 193.
31. P. Schaff, *History of the Christian Church* (Edinburgh, 1883).
32. G. Parker, 'Some Recent Work on the Inquisition in Spain and Italy', *Journal of Modern History* 54 (1982), 3.
33. H.C. Lea, *A History of the Inquisition in Spain* (4 vols, London, 1906), vol. 4, p. 519.
34. *Ibid.*, vol. 4, p. 518.
35. *Ibid.*, vol. 3, p. 209.
36. *Ibid.*, vol. 4, p. 401.
37. T.J. Reese, *Inside the Vatican* (Cambridge, Mass., 1996), p. 248.

Chapter Ten

1. M. Jordan, *The Great Abolition Sham* (Stroud, 2005), p. 17ff.
2. *Ibid.*, p. 21.
3. H. Cortés, *The History of the Conquest of Mexico* (London, 1759).

4. *Ibid.*

5. F.A. MacNutt, *Letters of Hernando Cortés to Charles V* (2 vols, New York, 1908), vol. 1, p. 38.

6. G. de Mendieta, *Historia Eclesiastica Indiana*, ed. J.G. Icazbalceta (4 vols, Mexico, 1876), vol. 1, pp. 311–13.

7. M. de Cuevas, *Historia de la Iglesia en Mexico* (5 vols, El Paso, Texas, 1921–8), vol. 2, p. 22.

8. *Ibid.*

9. B. Diaz del Castillo, *The Conquest of New Spain*, tr. J.M. Cohen (London, 1974), vol. 1, p. 61.

10. *Ibid.*, p. 20.

11. *Ibid.*, p. 5.

12. C.S. Braden, *Religious Aspects of the Conquest of Mexico* (Durham, 1930), p. 91.

13. M.D. Coe, *Mexico* (London, 1984), p. 169.

14. Diaz del Castillo, *Conquest of New Spain*, vol. 1.

15. Cuevas, *Historia*, vol. 1, p. 452.

16. Extract from *Carta de, a su Majestad*, published in part as appendix to MacNutt, *Letters of Hernando Cortés*, vol. 2.

17. S.C. Heyhoe (ed.), *Codice Franciscano . . . cartas de religiosos 1533–69* (Mexico, 1941), pp. 66–8.

18. *Ibid.*, p. 316.

19. G. Icazbalceta, *Nuevos Documentos para la Historia de Mexico* (5 vols, Mexico, 1858–66), vol. 4, p. 186.

20. J.F. Pacheco, *Colección de Documentos Inéditos Relativos al Decubrimiento, Conquista y Colonización de las Posesiones Españoles* (42 vols, Madrid 1864–84), vol. 2, p. 122.

21. A. Helps, *Life of Francisco Pizarro* (London, Bohn's Standard Library Edition, 1869).

22. Coe, *Mexico*, p. 122.

23. K. Taube, *Aztec and Maya Myths* (London, 1993), p. 7.

24. *Ibid.*, p. 31.

Chapter Eleven

1. Jordan, *Gods of the Earth*, p. 396.

2. N. Perry and L. Echeverría, *Under the Heel of Mary* (London and New York, 1988), p. 43ff.

3. *Ibid.*, p. 47.

4. *Ibid.*, p. 221ff.

5. M. Helm-Pirgo, *Virgin Mary, Queen of Poland* (New York, 1957), preface, p. 8.
6. D.F. Crosby, *God, Church and Flag: Senator Joseph R. McCarthy and the Catholic Church 1950–57* (North Carolina, 1978).
7. *National Catholic Reporter*, 2 November 1984.
8. M. Warner, *Alone of all her Sex: the Cult of the Virgin Mary* (London, 1976), p. 315ff.
9. Jordan, *Gods of the Earth*, p. 382.
10. A. Sjøberg and E. Bergmann, *Texts from Cuneiform Sources* (Augustin, Texas, 1969).
11. C.H. Gordon, *Ugaritic Literature* (London, 1949), p. 53.
12. Jordan, *Gods of the Earth*, p. 146.
13. Gordon, *Ugaritic Literature*, p. 18.

Chapter Twelve

1. Aho, *Religious Mythology*, p. 150ff.
2. Ezekiel 7:11.
3. Aho, *Religious Mythology*, p. 150ff.
4. *Ibid.*, p. 150ff.
5. M. Jordan, *Cults* (London, 1996), p. 46.
6. *Ibid.*, p. 60.
7. *Ibid.*, p. 58.
8. *Ibid.*, p. 62.

Bibliography

All references to the Bible are taken from the King James version (1611).

Abbot, St, *Abbonis Abbatis Floriacensis Apologeticus*, n.p., originally published 1781, and reproduced in J.P. Migne, *Patrologiae cursus completus* (Series Latina 140.953), Paris, 1841–64

Addison, C.G., *The History of the Knights Templars*, London, 1842

Aho, J.A., *Religious Mythology and the Art of War*, London, 1981

Barnes, T.D., *From Eusebius to Augustine: Selected Papers 1982–93*, Aldershot, 1994

Baynes, N.H., 'The Great Persecution' and 'Constantine', in *Cambridge Ancient History*, vol. 12, Cambridge, 1923

Ben-Sasson, H.H. (ed.), *A History of the Jewish People*, London, 1976

Bisson, T., *The Medieval Crown of Aragon*, Oxford, 1986

Bosworth, C.E., Donzel, E. van and Lecomte, G. (eds), *The Encyclopaedia of Islam*, 10 vols, Leiden, 1997

Braden C.S., *Religious Aspects of the Conquest of Mexico*, Durham, 1930

Bradford, E., *The Great Betrayal: Constantinople 1204*, London, 1967

Brocklemann, C., *History of the Islamic Peoples*, tr. J. Carmichael and M. Perlmann, London, 1980

Brodrick, A.H., *Lascaux: a Commentary*, London and Paris, 1949

Camus, A., *The Rebel*, tr. A. Bower, New York, 1956

Cantor, N.E., *Civilization of the Middle Ages*, New York, 1963

Chadwick, H., *Priscillian of Avila*, Oxford, 1976

Champakalakshmi, R., *Vaisnava Iconography*, New Delhi, 1981

Charlesworth, J.H. (ed.), *The Old Testament Pseudepigrapha*, 2 vols, New York, 1983

Cheney, C.R., 'The Letters of Pope Innocent III', reprinted from the *Bulletin of the John Rylands Library*, Manchester, 1952

Clavigero, Abbé, *History of Mexico*, tr. W. Cullen, London, 1787

Clendinnen, I., *Ambivalent Conquests: Maya and Spaniard in Yucatán 1517–70*, Cambridge, 1987

Coe, M.D., *Mexico*, London, 1984

Cohen, M.J., *Churchill and the Jews*, Berkeley, Ca., 1985

——, *The Origins and Evolution of the Arab–Zionist Conflict*, Berkeley, Ca., 1987

Cohn, N., *The Pursuit of the Millennium*, Oxford, 1970

Contamine, P., *War in the Middle Ages*, tr. M. Jones, Oxford, 1984

Cortés, H., *The History of the Conquest of Mexico*, London, 1759

Crosby, D.F., *God, Church and Flag: Senator Joseph R. McCarthy and the Catholic Church 1950–57*, North Carolina, 1978

Cruden, A., *Complete Concordance of the Bible*, Cambridge, 1839

Cuevas, M. de, *Historia de la Iglesia en Mexico*, 5 vols, El Paso, Texas, 1921–8

Dalley, S., *Myths from Mesopotamia*, Oxford, 1989

Davies, N., *Europe: a History*, Oxford, 1996

Dawood, N.J. (tr.), *The Koran*, London, 1959

Diaz del Castillo, B., *The Conquest of New Spain*, tr. J.M. Cohen, London, 1974

Dickson, H.R.P., *The Arab of the Desert*, London, 1949

Donzel, E. van, Heinrichs, W.P. and Lecomte, G., *The Encyclopedia of Islam*, 10 vols, Leiden, 1997

Easwaran, E. (tr.), *Bhagavadgita*, London, 1986

Edwards, D.L., *Christianity: the First Two Thousand Years*, London, 1997

Edwards, M. (tr. and ed.), *Optatus: Against the Donatists*, Liverpool, 1997

Eichmann, E., 'Die sog. romische Konigskronungsformel', *Zeitschrift der Savigny-Stiftung für Rechtsgeschichte* (kanon 6), Munich, 1916, p. 527ff.

Entrèves, A.P. de, *Aquinas: Selected Political Writings*, Paris, 1948

Erdmann, C., *The Origin of the Idea of the Crusade*, tr. M.W. Baldwin and W. Goffart, New York, 1977

Eusebius, *The History of the Church from Christ to Constantine*, tr. G.A. Williamson, London, 1965

Fazlur, R., *Islam*, London, 1961

Ferguson, J., *The Religions of the Roman Empire*, London, 1970

Firestone, R., 'Conceptions of Holy War in Biblical and Qur'ānic Tradition', *Journal of Religious Ethics*, 24.1 (Spring 1996)

Fletcher, R., *The Barbarian Conversion: from Paganism to Christianity*, Los Angeles, 1999

Flori, J., *Chevaliers et Chevalerie au Moyen Age*, Paris, 1998

Folsom, G. (ed.), *Dispatches of Cortés*, Boston, 1843

Fox, R.L., *Pagans and Christians*, London, 1986

Friend, W.H.C., 'Prelude to the Great Persecution: the Propaganda War', *Journal of Ecclesiastical History*, vol. 38, no. 1 (1987)

Gager, J., *The Origins of Anti-Semitism*, Oxford, 1983

Gibbon, E., *The Decline and Fall of the Roman Empire* (abridged), New York, 1952

Glubb, J.B., *The Great Arab Conquests*, London, 1963

Goeje, M.J. de (ed.), *Al-Baladhuri: Kitab Futuh ul-Buldan*, Leiden, 1866

Goff, Jacques le, *La Civilisation Medievale de l'Occident*, Paris, 1965

Goldstein, J.A., *The Old Testament Apocrypha in English*, New York, 1977

Gordon, C.H., *Ugaritic Literature*, London, 1949

Green, M., *The Gods of the Celts*, London, 1986

Grunebaum, G.E. von, *Classical Islam: A History 600–1258*, tr. K. Watson, London, 1970

Gurevitch, A., *Medieval Popular Culture: Problems of Belief and Perception*, Cambridge, 1990

Haim, S.G., *Arab Nationalism: an Anthology*, Berkeley and Los Angeles, 1962

Hamilton, B., *Religion in the Medieval West*, London, 1986

Haneef, J.O., *The Wahhabi Myth*, 2nd edn, Toronto, 2004

Haring C.H., *The Spanish Empire in America*, New York, 1963

Hastings, J. (ed.), *Encyclopaedia of Religion and Ethics*, Edinburgh, 1908–26

Hausrath, A., *Der Ketzermeister Konrad von Marburg*, Heidelberg, 1861

Helm-Pirgo, M., *Virgin Mary, Queen of Poland*, New York, 1957

Helps, A., *Life of Francisco Pizarro*, London, 1869

——, *Life of Cortés*, London, 1871

Heyhoe, S.C. (ed.), *Codice Franciscano . . . cartas de religiosos 1533–69*, Mexico, 1941

Hisham, I., *As Strah*, ed. Wustenfeld, Göttingen, 1858

Hodgson, M.G.S., 'How did the early Shi'a become sectarian?', *Journal of African and Oriental Studies*, lxxv (1955), 1–13

Holmes, E., *The Holy Heretics*, London, 1925

Holt, P.M., Lambton A.K. and Lewis, B. (eds), *The Cambridge History of Islam*, 2 vols, Cambridge, 1970

Icazbalceta, G., *Nuevos Documentos para la Historia de Mexico*, 5 vols, Mexico, 1858–66

Innes, H., *The Conquistadors*, London, 1986

Irani, G.E., *The Papacy and the Middle East: the Role of the Holy See in the Arab–Israeli Conflict 1962–84*, Indiana, 1986

Bibliography

Jafri, S.H.M., *Origins and Early Development of Shi'a Islam*, Beirut, 1979

Jerome, St, *Dogmatic and Polemical Works*, tr. J.N. Hritzu, Washington, 1965

Jochelson, W. and Bogoras, W., *Koryak, Jesup North Pacific Expedition*, MAMNH 10, 1905

Jordan, M., *Gods of the Earth*, London, 1992

——, *Witches*, London, 1996

——, *Cults*, London, 1996

——, *Mary – the Unauthorised Biography*, London, 2001

——, *Islam*, London, 2002

——, *The Great Abolition Sham*, Stroud, 2005

Jürgensmeyer, M., *Terror in the Mind of God*, Berkeley and Los Angeles, Ca., 2000

Kelly, J.N.D., *Early Christian Creeds*, New York, 1960

——, *Jerome – His Life, Writings and Controversies*, London, 1975

——, *Dictionary of the Popes*, Oxford, 1986

Khadduri, M., *The Law of War and Peace in Islam*, London, 1940

Klostermaier, K., *A Survey of Hinduism*, New York, 1994

Kramer, S.N., *Sumerian Mythology*, Philadelphia, 1944

Lambert, M.D., *Medieval Heresy: Popular Movements from Bogomil to Hus*, London, 1977

Lea, H.C., *A History of the Inquisition of the Middle Ages*, 3 vols, London, 1906

——, *A History of the Inquisition of Spain*, 4 vols, London, 1906

Leon-Portilla, M., *The Broken Spears: The Aztec Account of the Conquest of Mexico*, London, 1962

Lewis, B., *Islam from the Prophet Muhammad to the Capture of Constantinople*, New York, 1974

Luchaire, A., *Innocent III: Les Croisades des Albigeois*, Paris, 1905

Luther, M., *Selected Political Writings*, ed. J.M. Porter, Philadelphia, 1974

Maalouf, A., *The Crusades through Arab Eyes*, tr. J. Rothschild, London, 1984

McBrien, R.P., *Lives of the Popes*, San Francisco, 1997

Macdonald, A.J., *Hildebrand*, London, 1932

MacNutt, F.A., *Letters of Hernando Cortés to Charles V*, 2 vols, New York, 1908

Madaule, J., *The Albigensian Crusade*, tr. B. Wall, London, 1967

Maistre, J.M. de, *Lettres à un Gentilhomme Russe sur L'Inquisition Espagnole*, Paris, 1864

Means, P.A., 'History of the Spanish Conquest of Yucatán and of the Itzas', *Papers of the Peabody Museum of American Archaeology and Ethnology*, vol. 7 (1917)

Mendieta, G. de, *Historia Eclesiastica Indiana*, ed. J.G. Icazbalceta, 4 vols, Mexico, 1876

Migne, J.P., *Patrologiae cursus completus* (Series Latina 140.953), Paris, 1841–64

Mills, L.H. (tr.), *The Zend Avesta*, Oxford, 1867

Montgomery, J.A. and Harris, Z.S., *The Ras Shamra Mythological Texts*, Philadelphia, 1935

Morgan, K.W. (ed.), *Islam – the Straight Path*, New York, 1958

Musurillo, H. (tr.), *The Acts of the Christian Martyrs*, Oxford, 1972

Meredith, P. and Tailby, J.E. (eds), 'The Staging of Religious Drama in Europe in the Later Middle Ages', in *Early Drama, Art and Music*, Monograph Series 4, Kalamazoo Medieval Institute Publications, 1983

Myers, A.C. (ed.), *The Eerdmans Bible Dictionary*, Michigan, 1987

Olmstead, A.T., *History of Assyria*, Chicago, 1923

Pacheco, J.F., *Colección de Documentos Inéditos Relativos al Decubrimiento, Conquista y Colonización de las Posesiones Españoles*, 42 vols, Madrid, 1864–84

Parkes, H.B., *A History of Mexico*, London, 1962

Pelikan, J., *The Christian Tradition: a History of the Development of Doctrine*, vol. 3, *The Growth of Medieval Theology (600–1300)*, Chicago, Il., 1978

Perry, N. and Echeverría, L., *Under the Heel of Mary*, London and New York, 1988

Peters, E., *Inquisition*, New York, 1988

Piazza, H.B., *True Account of the Inquisition*, London, 1722

Postgate, J.N., *Early Mesopotamia: Society and Economy at the Dawn of History*, London and New York, 1992

Powell, T.G.E., *The Celts*, London, 1958

Prescott, W.H., *History of the Conquest of Mexico*, 2 vols, London, 1957

——, *History of the Conquest of Peru*, London, 1963

Rawlinson, H.C., *The Cuneiform Inscriptions of Western Asia*, London, 1861

Reese, T.J., *Inside the Vatican*, Cambridge, Mass., 1996

Richards, J., *Sex, Dissidence and Damnation: Minority Groups in the Middle Ages*, New York, 1991

Riley-Smith, J., *The Crusades: a Short History*, Yale, 1987

Robinson, I.S., *The Papacy 1073–1198: Continuity and Innovation*, Cambridge, 1990

Robinson, J.M. (ed.), *The Nag Hammadi Library*, Leiden, 1988

Rosenbloom, J.R., *Conversion to Judaism: From the Biblical Period to the Present*, Cincinnati, Ohio, 1978

Rufinus, T., *The Church History of Rufinus of Aquileia*, tr. P.R. Amindon, New York, 1997

Runciman, J.C.S., *A History of the Crusades*, vol. 1, Cambridge, 1954

Rying, B., *Denmark: Prehistory*, Copenhagen, n.d.

Sanders, E.P., *Jesus and Judaism*, London, 1985

Schaff, P., *History of the Christian Church*, Edinburgh, 1883

Schleifer, A., 'Understanding Jihad: Definition and Methodology', *Islamic Quarterly*, 27.3.118–31 (1983)

Schmidt, C.G.A., *Histoire et Doctrine de la secte des Cathares ou Albigeois*, Paris, 1849

Scott, S.P. (tr.), *The Civil Law*, 17 vols, Cincinnati, Oh., 1932

Sejourne, L., *Burning Water: Thought and Religion in Ancient Mexico*, London and New York, 1956

Servita, P., *The History of the Inquisition*, London, 1639

Setton, K.M. (gen. ed.), *A History of the Crusades*, Milwaukee, 1969

Sjøberg, A. and Bergmann, E., *Texts from Cuneiform Sources*, Augustin, Texas, 1969

Sourdel, D. and J., *La Civilisation de l'Islam Classique*, Paris, 1968

Southern, R.W., *Western Society and the Church in the Middle Ages*, London, 1970

Tacitus, *Annals*, tr. D.R. Dudley, London, 1966

Taube, Karl, *Aztec and Maya Myths*, London, 1993

Thompson, J.E., *The Rise and Fall of the Maya Civilisation*, New York, 1956

Vaillant, G.C., *Aztecs of Mexico: Origin, Rise and Fall of the Aztec Nation*, New York, 1962

Vaux, R. de, *Ancient Israel, its Life and Institutions*, tr. J. McHugh, London, 1961

Vermes, G., *The Complete Dead Sea Scrolls in English*, London, 1962

Voigt, H.G., *Brun von Querfurt*, Stuttgart, 1907

Voltaire, *Wars against the Cathars of Languedoc*, Paris, 1756

Walters, D., *Chinese Mythology*, London, 1992

Walzer, M., *The Revolution of the Saints*, Harvard, 1965

——, 'The Idea of Holy War in Ancient Israel', *Journal of Religious Ethics*, 22.2.215–27 (1992)

Wand, J.W.C., *A History of the Early Church to AD 500*, London, 1937

Warner, M., *Alone of all her Sex: the Cult of the Virgin Mary*, London, 1976

Bibliography

Waterfield, G., *Layard of Nineveh*, London, 1963

Watt, J.M., 'Shi'ism under the Umayyads', *Journal of the Royal Asiatic Society* (1960), 158–62

Weber, Max, *Ancient Judaism*, tr. H. Gerth, New York, 1952

——, 'The Sociology of Religion', in S. Whimster (ed.), *Collected Essays*, London, 2004

Wellhausen, J., *Prolegomena to the History of Israel*, tr. J. Sutherland Black and A. Menzies, Edinburgh, 1885

White, H., 'The Value of Narrativity in the Representation of Reality', in H. White, *The Content of the Form: Narrative Discourse and Historical Representation*, Baltimore, 1987

Wills, G., *Saint Augustine*, London, 1999

Zaman, Muhammad Q., *Religion and Politics under the Early 'Abassids – the Emergence of the Proto-Sunni Elite*, Leiden, 1997

Index